CONSCIOUS YOU: BECOME THE HERO OF YOUR OWN STORY

Praise

Very rarely does it happen that you read a book, and discover it's not a story, but a teacher. *Conscious You* is one of those precious books. You will return to it time and again. Nadjeschda's book is a magnificent tapestry, at once a *tour de force* intellectually, a soaring treatise of philosophy, an intimate chat with a dear friend, and a hands-on workbook with practical exercises, all sewn together with deliciously clever drawings by the author herself. Throughout the book, from examples of coaching her clients to citing research, to sharing stories from her own life's journey, Nadjeschda's unique voice shines: wise, funny, clear, and always loving. *Conscious You* will bring you back to your own heart, and from there, help you reconnect with your soul. As I turned the last page, I realized the book had given me so much insight, and was written so beautifully, that the tapestry became poetry. I loved it, and you will, too.

Erica Ariel Fox, author of the New York Times bestseller *Winning From Within: A Breakthrough Method for Leading, Living, and Lasting Change*

The daily demands on our lives are growing more complex, at work and at home. Our response is often to do more: download the latest 'app' or learn about yet another innovative system. Unless we update our own inner operating system first, doing more will only re-emphasise old patterns. Through stories, metaphors, and simple practices, Nadjeschda helps us to reinvent ourselves from within and helps us discover how to navigate our complex world with more lightness, grace, and impact.

Johanne Lavoie, partner, McKinsey&Co, co-author of *Centered Leadership: leading with clarity, purpose and impact*

You have to know that Nadjeschda is the real deal – she's an accomplished executive and team coach. Her book is terrific: well written and easy enough to read; it's arranged in a way that is like reading a story, only the story is yours (in this case, mine). Nadjeschda manages to not be preachy; she is a fellow traveller on the road to peace within one's self. I felt she held my hand as I travelled with her, and I enjoyed the trip. Also, if I could illustrate like Nadjeschda does, I would write more books. She's as brilliant in her visual aids as she is in her writing. It helps keep the adventure light-filled.

Miles Kierson, leadership consultant and coach, author of *Discovering Execution: The Key to High Performance Organization*

Nadjeschda offers a powerful present to all of us. The book provides a true opportunity for a long-lasting transformation and increased consciousness. It is a masterpiece grounded on many years of experience in coaching, psychology, and life experience. To me it is more than a book; it is a piece of art and a door opener for a new life. If you ever seriously want to consciously create your life this is the book to read.

Christa Schöning, CEO Global Coaching Group

Nadjeschda has distilled all the latest findings in psychology and psychotherapy about what makes for a successful and happy life, and presented them in a way that can be used by coaches with their clients, or by individuals on their own. The book is easy to read and helps us all on the journey of discovery, which is the life of each one of us. The illustrations, which have been drawn specially by the author for the book, summarize the themes of each chapter. I recommend this book for anyone who wants to understand why they act as they do at the moment and wants to confirm the good and change the not-so-good parts of their lives.

Mark Forster, author of *Do it Tomorrow*

I find Nadjeschda's book refreshingly unpretentious. She doesn't pretend or promise any quick fixes or solutions, happiness, wealth, peace of mind, loss of weight or a perfect partner. Yet, with the intelligence, gentleness and fastidiousness with which she's distilled her favourite processes, the generosity and simplicity with which she shares them, there's every chance you'll be so lucky! Her texts exhibit a deep understanding of perennial wisdom, expressed in the simplest of modern terms.

Peter Koenig, author of *30 Lies About Money*

Nadjeschda masterfully uses a combination of well-grounded psychological and scientific research, personal stories, tools and self-reflection exercises to guide the reader in a journey of self-discovery and transformation. A journey that challenges one's deeply held beliefs and enables the shift of old and unproductive patterns. A journey that is most necessary for coping with life's complexity and shaping one's future more consciously. This book is a must read when you get stuck, but also when you yearn to live a more creative life.

Giovanna D'Alessio, CEO of Asterys and author of *Personal Mastery: The Path to Transformative Leadership*

This book is a treasure chest if you are looking to create a better life for yourself. In this book you have an opportunity to dive in with Nadjeschda – a world-class coach who creates lasting, deep impact with her clients. Nadjeschda is a highly sought after coach for a reason - now you have a way to experience her impact for yourself. Nadjeschda explains the psychological frameworks behind her coaching, she shares research findings in simple terms and she makes this all very accessible by sharing some very personal stories of her own journey; and that of her clients too. I laughed, I learned and I was moved to tears as I read. The combination of her deep understanding of the principles behind personal transformation, her willingness to be vulnerable and her charming illustrations make this an extraordinary book.

Rich Litvin, Author of *The Prosperous Coach*

. . . .

Reading Nadjeschda's book is somewhat like having a fireside conversation with an old friend; I found space for personal reflection and recollection, time for self-assessment, intimacy, discovery, clarity... To have this type of conversation with Nadjeschda is particularly enriching as, throughout these pages, she openly shares her own history, past and present, joys and sorrows, and synthesis of a life-long personal and professional quest. Not only does Nadjeschda offer an intimate space to revisit personal history and motivations, but she does it with a very high degree of theoretical exigency. This book offers a very intelligent and practical review of a number of essentially useful psychological approaches through the prism of personal history, a number of professional case studies, clearly presented theoretical grids and tools and many other illustrative anecdotes and stories.

Alain Cardon, Author of *Masterful Systemic Coaching*

. . . .

I love books on personal and leadership development that make me feel heard. I love books that make my mind and heart sing 'Hell, yes!' And I love books that share something relevant in an easy to understand and fresh way. *Conscious You: Become The Hero of Your Own Story* is such a book. Nadjeschda shares her personal story beautifully and humbly. It makes me feel close to her and to my own story. Through her book, Nadjeschda takes my hand and stands by my side, while I am on my unstable path of fulfilling one of my deepest longings: to lead my life and to become true to my essence. Nadjeschda's insights and invitations encapsulate a lot of what is known about personal transformation and leadership.

And while avoiding over-simplification and silver bullets, she expresses simple and clear thoughts. Immediately after reading it, I added Nadjeschda's book to my 'Top Three' list of recommendations for my coaching and leadership clients.

Dr Matthias Müller-Lindenberg, Executive Coach

RETHINK PRESS

First published in Great Britain 2018
by Rethink Press (www.rethinkpress.com)

© Copyright Nadjeschda Taranczewski

CHAPTER OVERVIEW

Chapter 11 — Grow Like a Lobster   **315**

Transformation does not merely change our actions,
does not merely give us new options from which to choose.
Transformation uncovers the structure of our being and interpretations
on which we are grounded,
often unaware of our grounding in them.
This is the work of transformation, this revealing of ourselves to ourselves,
which occurs in a profound way and which alters
the possibility of being that we are.
Inescapably. Decisively. Forever.

—*Werner Erhard*

CHAPTER 1

Informed vs. Inflamed

Dear Reader!

Since I obtained my master's degree in psychology in 2001, I have been working internationally as an executive and team coach in the areas of leadership, team development, and culture transformation, as well as being a speaker and author. Whether working with individuals or teams, and independent of their work context and the specific challenges they are facing, I essentially support all of my clients in one core endeavour: to create the life they love by living their full potential.

Most of my clients live lives that are successful by common standards: They have jobs or sometimes even companies, they have relationships, and they have kids. Yet somehow, they are still not fully excited about their life for a number of reasons:

- The same people keep pushing their buttons; they feel as if they are going in circles in relationships with their family or with people at work.

- They are not quite where they thought they should be at their age – or they are where they thought they should be, but that hasn't made them as happy as they expected it would.

- They don't feel as if they are living their full potential but are afraid to change – or are not even quite sure what exactly needs changing.

If any or all of the points above sound familiar, this book is for you.

Becoming conscious to who we are

I believe that in order to create the life we want, we need to become more conscious. Conscious to who we are – and why. Conscious to what we do and the results we create. To be conscious is the foundation to make choices about who we want to become: our new story.

For most people, life isn't an overnight success story. It took me a rather long time to feel confident in my own skin and write my new story. As a teenager and young woman I was outwardly the successful student while struggling with an eating disorder behind closed doors. Because of my talent for drawing, everyone expected I would grow up to be an artist. The pressure I put on myself sucked all the joy out of the artistic process. I dropped out of Art School and wouldn't even go near a pencil or brush for years. Only after finishing my master's degree in Psychology did I slowly begin to make choices that were more aligned with who I am. Because freedom is more important to me than security, I chose to become a self-employed coach instead of accepting the well-paid position in a consultancy. On the personal

2

front, at the age of 29, I found my soulmate. To my surprise, my soulmate turned out to be a woman – even though I had thus far only dated men and considered myself straight. When I discovered I was in fact bisexual, I had to make the decision whether to pursue the traditional family model or to spend my life with the woman I love.

To realise that nobody will hand us a script for how to live a good life can be painful. We have to become the person who consciously writes her or his own story. In order to become this person, we have to challenge our real and imagined confinements and discover who we are beyond social expectations and norms.

All models are wrong

Throughout my time as a coach, I have relentlessly searched for the Holy Grail of self-development: the one process or method that would reliably bring enlightenment to everybody.

Some of the teachers with whom I studied claimed that their particular approach would cure anything from rotten teeth to broken hearts or business failures. Despite their best intentions, I have come to believe that a universal formula for personal growth doesn't exist. An approach that your best friend found life-changing may do absolutely nothing for you. Your process is as unique as you are.

Because of this, this book neither contains a recipe for happiness nor ten steps that will make you successful. Instead this book is a collection of diverse and powerful approaches that I have found to be most impactful in kick-starting consciousness and personal growth.

Many of the models described in this book are hybrids, meaning that I borrowed from the work of great teachers whose ideas inspired me and reinterpreted their ideas in my own words to point towards what seems to me to be a deeper truth. The viewpoints and stories I tell are a *description* of different perspectives I have found to work, *not a prescription* for what you must or should do. As a guiding principle, I love this quote:

> *All models are wrong and some of them are useful*
>
> George. E.P. Box

Ultimately, all models and maps are approximations to help us make sense of our own, often confusing, experience. When we dare to challenge the accuracy of our thinking to date and allow fresh thinking to emerge, we will be amazed what there is to discover. As a result of this 'revealing of ourselves to ourselves', to use the words from the Werner Erhard quote at the beginning of this chapter, we 'alter the possibility of being that we are' – and just might transform our lives.

How to work with this book

In order to make it easier for you to manoeuvre to the sections of most interest to you, most of the chapters follow the same basic structure:

A. a description of the model, theory, or process;
B. a case study describing a session with a client around this topic;[1]
C. an 'in a nutshell' synthesis of the core ideas of the chapter;
D. the most important references from the chapter.

In the reference section of each chapter, you will find links that allow you to download selected illustrations from this chapter. **If you would like to download a free copy of the workbook containing self-reflection exercises for each chapter, please go to: http://book.conscious-u.com**

To make the concepts come alive, I share stories from my own life, as well as stories from my clients, and I make frequent use of metaphors. I find that many people have a more immediate connection to pictures than to concepts or words alone. If you think in pictures as well, you will find a lot of richness in these pages, but if metaphors don't do it for you, feel free to skim over these sections and see if you can distil the core message of the chapter in a way that makes sense to you (the 'Chapter in a nutshell' section should help with that). Naturally, some chapters will resonate for you more than others. There is no way of knowing when a certain word or idea or model may bring you new insights, and I encourage you to read the same chapter a second or even a third time. My wish is that you may connect with whatever touches you and find the contents of this book as transformative in your own life as I have in mine.

To take your learning deeper, you can engage with the content of each chapter and make it your own by working through the exercises in the accompanying workbook. The questions and exercises in the workbook will help you to apply the models and viewpoints in such a way that you will become more conscious of the narrative you created of your life until this point; and begin a new narrative for your life moving forward (and truly become the hero of your own story). And finally, you can also visit **www.conscious-u.com** to discover the online coaching programme we developed for people wanting to create whole system transformation within their team or organisation.

Updating your GPS

If you are anything like many of my clients, you are already the proud owner of a collection of self-help books, all of them holding the promise to happiness, riches, or fame. Some of them you have read and some of them may even have brought you insights and new ideas. Yet for whatever reason, the penny hasn't dropped, and you're left wondering why your life hasn't become any easier overall.

In truth, there is no way to predict when or why our penny drops: that life-changing moment when a new insight emerges clearly enough to challenge our deeply held perspective and powerfully enough to transform our experience. For some, understanding appears instantaneously and with such vigour that they literally hear a choir of angels singing. For many others (myself included), transformation resembles a somewhat more prosaic process of two steps forward, one step back. Perhaps you belong to the lucky ones who easily awaken to the nature of consciousness. If so, you might almost immediately begin to experience a sense of lightness and well-being while reading this book. If not, it is the purpose of this book to guide you in sequential steps towards progressively deeper levels of insight until your own penny drops, and you gain new insight into what's possible for you and your life. It is my intent to provide various perspectives from which to understand the truth behind the mysterious mirage we call reality. If you read this book, fully engaged with heart and mind, it will clarify what you need to know to let go of the shadows of your past and live a self-authored and happy life.

You probably know that bats navigate through their surroundings with ultrasound. A client of mine, who is a biologist, told me that, in familiar territory, bats literally fly blind, relying upon an internal map they have created of each tree, building, or obstacle in their environment. These bats don't seem to update their inner maps without being prompted to do so, and therefore continue to navigate as if an obstacle is still in place until proven otherwise. The bats will continue to fly around a particular tree, even weeks after the tree has been removed. He said that some researchers tested this phenomenon by installing a perforated wall into an exit tunnel that a colony of bats used to leave their cave. After flying into the unexpected barrier once, each bat surveyed the obstacle and determined where it contained fly-through holes and which one they would use. From then on, each bat would always use exactly the same hole to exit the tunnel. Once the researcher removed the barrier, the bats continued to exhibit the exact same flight patterns, targeting the same fly-through hole that they had mapped in the past. In the bats' consciousness, in their internal maps, the barrier still existed.

Now, I don't know if this bat story is true or if it is true for only a subset of bats, but I found this story to be a beautiful metaphor for the human mind. Many of us rely on maps which have remained largely unchanged from those we created as children in the sandpit. This is normal, but not necessarily productive. In a sense, with this book I am proposing that we update our GPS, so that we can notice whether we may have been avoiding imaginary obstacles.

Venturing beyond your comfort zone

Here is what you can expect from reading — or even better — from working through this book:

Firstly, greater **self-awareness**: A deeper understanding of why you have turned into the person you have been until now, what has been driving you unconsciously, and what is truly important to you moving forward.

Secondly, greater **self-acceptance**: Discovering and embracing the hidden gifts in every facet of your personality — even those you don't particularly like.

Thirdly, greater **ownership**: Seeing the story of your life to date and being more creative and pro-active in the simultaneous roles of narrator and hero of your future story.

Because each chapter of the book is designed to take you progressively deeper than the previous one, I recommend that you read the chapters in sequence:

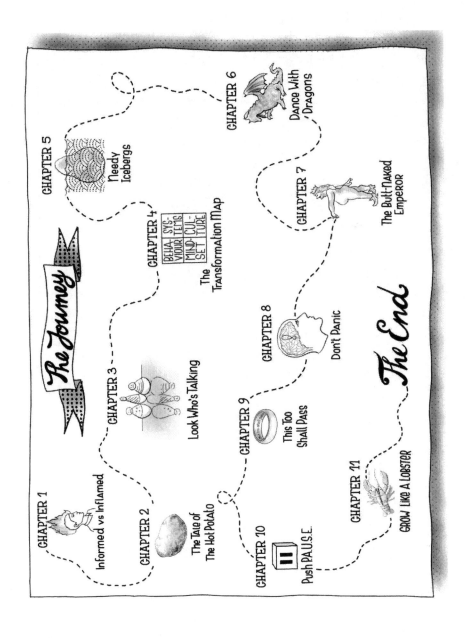

At times you might find yourself feeling puzzled, frustrated, or saddened by something you read. Rather than question or berate yourself for having those feelings, use your reaction as a friendly signpost to direct your further inquiry and exploration. In fact, if you want to get the most out of this book, I dare you to be uncomfortable! As long as we stay within the safe boundaries of our comfort zone – our old ways of thinking and being – we won't learn anything new.

I have found that whatever makes me feel uneasy often indicates an area in which I am still unconscious, or have a blind spot. In facing my discomfort, I challenge myself to leave my comfort zone, and am often rewarded with a thought or insight I haven't had before. Whenever I am confronted with new ideas, I try to notice whether I feel *informed* or *inflamed* by what is being presented to me. When I feel *informed* by something, my consciousness flows freely and I investigate with curiosity how this idea may apply in my own life. I may still disagree with what has been presented to me, but I don't feel enraged by it. When I feel *inflamed* by information or ideas, it is as if the light of my consciousness dims and my thinking becomes rigid and defensive.

If you notice that something in this book *inflames* you, you can certainly choose to throw the book into a corner – but you can also choose to pick it back up and take a fresh look at what exactly triggered you. Mental inflammation is a neon sign directing us towards the forbidden or forgotten doors in our mind. And of course, the forbidden doors are usually the most interesting ones!

Naturally, a book will never replace a conversation with a real person. If you do not happen to be currently working with a coach, I highly recommend that you find a friend who is willing to share with you the journey in this book. Together, you can dive deeper into areas you find interesting or unclear and help each other work through the questions in the workbook. Dialogue with another person about the content presented here will deepen your understanding and speed up your own transformation.

This path isn't easy. It requires courage to see yourself as you are. But when you start using your own script you'll be surprised by how much lighter life feels and how much more acceptable, or even loveable, you'll find yourself and the people in your life.

On a final note: I wrote this book for people like you, people with a curious mind, who are ready to be free (from fear, worry, guilt, doubt, conventions and the past), people who yearn to access their innate wisdom and clarity, and well-being. It is my hope that *Conscious You: Become The Hero of Your Own Story* will serve as a valued companion on your journey. May you discover many new and beautiful vistas along the way!

With love,

Nadjeschda

ENDNOTE

1. To protect my clients' anonymity, I have changed their names and any recognisable details of their stories.

WHERE IS THE PAST?

WHERE DOES THE PAST HAPPEN?
THE PAST APPEARS HERE, WHERE *you are*.

IT ARISES AS MEMORY,
DREAMS, SHADOWS AND FRAGMENTS OF COLOUR AND SOUND,
IMAGE AND FEELING—HERE AND NOW.

THOUGHTS ABOUT THE PAST ARE PRESENT THOUGHTS.

THOUGHTS *ABOUT THE FUTURE ARE PRESENT THOUGHTS.*
THE PAST DIDN'T HAPPEN IN THE PAST—IT HAPPENS NOW.

THE FUTURE DOESN'T *HAPPEN IN THE FUTURE—*
IT HAPPENS *now.*

Beyond all past and future dreams
WHAT YOU ARE IS ALWAYS
deeply at rest.

—JEFF FOSTER

CHAPTER 2

The Tale of The Hot Potato

Since the content of the book is very personal to me, I would like to start out by telling you a bit about my journey – which ultimately is what inspired me to write this book.

I am the daughter of a German mother and a Russian/Polish father, and I will begin the tale of my transformation starting with my father's parents. The paths of my Russian grandfather and my Polish grandmother intersected during the events of World War II. Through the chaos of war, my grandmother and grandfather barely survived German work and concentration camps respectively and, at the end of the war, they were left stranded in enemy territory in the middle of West Germany. Their inability to adequately process what they had experienced during the war continued to affect not only my father's life, but subsequently my life as well. Not surprisingly, my father's upbringing as a Russian in post-war Germany didn't make for a carefree childhood. His disenfranchised parents struggled to make ends meet while desperately trying to obtain reparations from the German government for the atrocities they had endured under the Nazi regime (a request that was later denied). On my mother's side, things were somewhat less dramatic, but naturally, there wasn't a family in Germany unaffected by the loss of life, the overbearing silence of the collective denial, and the sense of guilt and shame that continued to haunt the generations that followed.

By the time I was born, in the 1970s, life in Germany was pretty much back to normal. Germany was wealthy again by any standards, and I had the privilege of growing up in a middle class environment and receiving a decent education. Nevertheless, I grew up a depressed teenager, plagued by feelings of sadness and helplessness that seemed to originate from a place deeper and larger than myself. In an attempt to understand why I felt what I felt, to understand the impact of my parents' divorce, and generally to find the meaning of life, I started therapy and soon afterwards began to study for my master's degree in psychology. Although both therapy and the academic study of psychology provided me with more insights, neither offered a solution for a happier life.

Following the paradigms and theories that were (and are) accepted in the profession of psychology, I discovered how much of my sadness was a direct consequence of how my father had raised me, which in turn was a direct consequence of how my grandparents had raised him – which had a lot to do with their experiences during the war. This seemed like a logical enough explanation, only it didn't bring me any closer to happiness. I was compelled to embark upon a long journey of self-discovery, one which would prove to be more challenging but ultimately also more liberating than I could ever have imagined. During my quest for healing, answers, and personal development, I spent a significant amount of time with teachers, therapists, and various coaches, in numerous workshops, and with my nose frequently buried in books. This period of soul-searching can be summarised by two life-changing insights.

First insight: I had inherited a hot potato

During therapy, I was taught that the unexplainable feelings and mysterious symptoms I experienced could be traced all the way back to the events my grandparents and parents had endured. Since my grandparents had no access to therapy and did not know how to process their experiences, they reverted to the same subconscious solution that most of their generation (and presumably the generations before them) employed: they tried to bury their memories, their fear, and their anger. Unfortunately, pretending not to feel something is not the same thing as not feeling something. Failing to acknowledge their fear and anger led to a phenomenon that one of my early therapists called *passing on the hot potato*. What he meant by this was that a trauma (defined as an event that overwhelms a person's processing capacity), if not resolved, is passed on to the next generation as a blueprint for how to live one's life. If the next generation also fails to deal with the fallout of that experience, the hot potato (the pattern of the trauma) is passed on yet again to the next generation, with the associated symptoms growing increasingly imprecise and generalised. In the case of my family, this encompassed symptoms such as depression, alcohol abuse, physical violence, and eating disorders.

It became clear to me that the numerous unacknowledged patterns that were passed down in my family were the cause of many destructive behaviours and a general sense of suffering. Unfortunately, the more hot potatoes I discovered through therapy, the heavier I felt and the more resentful I became towards my family for having burdened me with a weight that wasn't mine to carry.

After some time juggling hot potatoes from one hand to the other, I reluctantly realised that if I ever wanted to be happy, I would have to figure out a better way to handle my inherited hot potatoes. Regardless of whatever experiences my grandparents and parents might have endured, re-enacting their heartache was in no way bringing me any closer to my own happiness. As clueless as this realisation left me, it also inspired me to stop looking for the source and the solution of my well-being outside of myself, and instead to turn my attention inward. To my great surprise, this search for deeper answers within eventually led me to my second, very different insight.

Second insight: there is no hot potato

As I investigated the connection between trauma and emotional and behavioural patterns, I wanted to learn more about how our experience of reality is actually created. What particularly interested me was understanding how two different people could experience the same event in two different ways. Why can something be traumatising to one person, but not necessarily to another? Why do some people experience post-traumatic growth[1] but others don't? Why was I feeling depressed when a friend of mine with a remarkably similar background seemed unfazed by his family's past and walked through life with a positivity that seemed to mock my misery? The more I understood about the creation of reality, the clearer it became: *There was no hot potato outside of my own head.*

The collected findings from neuroscience, psychology, and philosophy all pointed me in the same direction: the hot potato I thought I was carrying was a creation of my mind – literally a figment of my own imagination. My family's history, which had seemingly been weighing me down and holding me hostage, was in fact no more real in my life today than a shadow on the wall. Now, you may say, 'Wait a minute, but all of that stuff did happen to your grandparents!' So let me try to explain. There is indeed evidence from the field of epigenetics that biochemical reactions to aversive (unpleasant or harmful) stimuli can be transmitted transgenerationally (Yehuda et al., 2015). My grandparents' experience therefore might have led to a disproportionate predisposition in me to react to the same or similar stimuli in a certain way. This could mean that I may have inherited some predisposition for depression or addiction. But even if this is so, I am only ever interacting with events that are happening inside of me now – because my reality today is only ever created in this very moment.

The events my grandparents had experienced had long passed, and the patterns passed on to me from my parents and grandparents were re-enactments in my unconscious mind in the here and now. After all, a pattern is only a pattern if you constantly re-create it. Or in other words, the hot potato I was holding in the present was made up of thoughts and feelings I had about other people's thoughts and feelings. The insight that the hot potato is an event that I am creating myself within me right NOW was disturbingly simple and at first somewhat disorienting. Seeing my family as the source of all my unhappiness and the hot potato as their real and tangible legacy had at least been a plausible explanation, even if it hadn't led to contentment.

This being said, I do not mean to belittle anyone who is struggling with the demons of their own or their family's past. The nature of our minds is such that as long as we believe in the story and the power that it holds, the consequences of this story are painfully real. In other words, the hot potato is real – *inside* of us. Once we expose it for what it is – a cognitive illusion, a shadow on the wall with no object to cause it – it stops being a powerful influence because we no longer experience it as real internally. The past is done with us when we are done with it.

Letting go of the hot potato

Whatever we believe to have shaped or perhaps even determined the person we have become, from our genes to our upbringing, is, ultimately, a story. Since the mind is such a powerful storyteller, and the images it produces are so persuasive, the stories we tell are amazingly convincing and feel utterly real. Because we think our life into existence moment-by-moment, that which we perceive to be an issue *is* an issue because our mind has created it as such.

It took me rather a long time until I met teachers who brought to my attention the fact that the hot potato I thought I was holding was only present in my mind. And it took even more time until I fully believed it. Part of me hated this insight – hated letting go of the story, letting go of the logic that had for so long ruled my life. Somewhat embarrassed, I had to admit that identifying myself as a 'third generation victim' of the Third Reich had had certain benefits, especially in Germany. The story of my father's family was so horrific that nobody could help but express deep sympathy for me. Additionally, it freed me from investigating more deeply the passivity of the German side of my family during the years of the war. My stories, as limiting as they were, had also been my allies. They had kept me safe and they had provided something important for me: identity. Once I got over the shame of having clung to these stories, I was able to define my identity on my own terms, all the while honouring my family's history. This history has in fact led me to my personal mission: to use my work of making people more conscious as a tool to help prevent another holocaust. Today, I am my own person, influenced but not determined by my family's past – nor by my own.

In the many *aha!* moments I have been privileged to witness as a coach during my 6,000+ hours of coaching, I have noticed that most of us have a hidden (or not-so-hidden) potato-lover inside of us. This part of us is a firm believer that the past has the power to determine our future. To the potato-lover, the past is an unchangeable fact, especially when the past presents itself as a uniquely tragic melodrama. The potato-lover will explain any suffering in the present as having been caused by other people's actions (parents, grandparents, partners, etc) or events that were seemingly beyond our control (anything ranging from divorce, death or war).

I have seen the potato-lover in my clients become defensive, resistant, or angry because it felt threatened by the idea that we – not our parents or some tragic event – are the creators of our reality in the present. When this is brought to our attention, our potato-lover can feel blamed or even shamed. And all too often, our inner critic uses this opportunity to raise its finger and yell at us: 'See? I knew it all along. It's all your fault. You thought this mess up – it's not even real!' If you have such a reaction while reading this, just acknowledge the judgements and feelings that arise, and rest assured: I have been there too, and so have many of my clients. There is no need to hide, prevent, suppress, or apologise for any of the mental constructs or feelings you may have. They served you well and were put in place to shield you from further harm. But it might be worth exploring how your life might be different if you were to accept the reality that you are the one creating you own reality inside of yourself right now.

Post-insight hangover

During one coaching conversation, my client Angela had an *aha!* moment that challenged how she had looked at her life for as long as she could remember. Instead of being happy or excited about her insight, she exclaimed, 'Oh God, please tell me that it is not really that simple?'

I was confused by her response, since I had just witnessed a powerful revelation, during which she realised how she had successfully created her painful reality for most of her adult life. In my mind, this insight should have been liberating, but Angela looked anything but liberated. My puzzlement must have been written all over my face, because Angela said, 'What I mean is I feel so stupid! I have wasted all these years trying to push against a mountain of pain only to suddenly discover that the only place where this mountain exists is in my head; that I dreamed it up! Why didn't I see this earlier? Why did I have to feel all this sadness, all of this anger and resentment, when it would have been so easy to be happy?'

I now call what Angela described a *post-insight hangover*. During my conversation with her it dawned on me that all the seemingly illogical reactions to profound insights that I had experienced in myself and witnessed in my clients — from depression, anger, resistance, and walling-off, to shame — were rooted in essentially the same thought:

....

If I see a different reality and accept that in any given moment I am creating the reality I experience inside of me, it means that I could have stopped being stuck in unhappiness (substitute with a complaint of your choice: addiction, loneliness, depression, anger, etc) years ago. This is testimony not only to my having been wrong for a long, long time, but worse, it proves that something is wrong with me: that I am stupid, a slow learner, ignorant, selfish, bad, or something worse.

....

23

When we believe *this* thought, it can seem easier to stubbornly stand our ground, grind our teeth, and refuse to move. Even if *here* is not a happy place, it is safer than *there*, with all the unpleasant implications about our character or intelligence and the uncertain future benefits of changing our paradigm. For a time I did in fact resent myself for not *getting it* quicker. But I found relief in knowing that if it had been possible for me to understand this fact earlier – that I am creating my reality from the inside out – I would have. It appears that insight happens when it happens. We can't will it.

You are a hero

The good news is that even if a part of us firmly believes we are beyond rescue, disempowered, helpless, and emotionally crippled by our past, the findings of neuroscience over the last ten years have proven that this is not actually true. Our brain has the unexpected ability to adapt, heal, rewire, and find different and creative solutions until we take our last breath. Therefore, the age-old argument of *that's just the way I am* is simply not true. Transformation is a part of our very nature and happens constantly – with and without our conscious participation.

Granted, from where we are sitting, it doesn't necessarily feel as if progress, much less transformation, is taking place. Our process of self-discovery and self-transformation can be slow and tedious. We often feel more like Sisyphus – condemned for eternity to push a boulder up a hill only to watch it roll down again – than an evolving being. When we seemingly encounter the same drama for the umpteenth time, it is as if the only movement we see is backwards.

I would like to offer a more rewarding angle through which to understand our lifelong journey towards consciousness.

In the 1940s, the American mythologist and author Joseph Campbell first coined the term 'hero's journey' in his book *The Hero With a Thousand Faces* (1949). Campbell observed that most mythical narratives appear to be variations of the same story, irrespective of the culture or time in which they were created. According to him, humans have always used stories to connect us with the universal truth, a truth that simultaneously pre-empts and transcends language and speaks to the most sacred of human qualities and values. Through metaphors in stories, we give form to the intangible yet eternal universal wisdom, share it with others, and teach it to our children. Most cultures have a version of the hero's journey, a story of one or more people who, due to a crisis, are forced to leave the known world and embark on a perilous quest for a resolution. On their journey, they are confronted with risks and challenges that nearly result in their defeat. Only because of their endurance and bravery are they finally rewarded with the potion or answer they were seeking. Our heroes return home and, enlightened by their newfound wisdom, wield the power to not only change their own fate but that of many.

Why not tell our own life as a hero's (or heroine's) journey? If we did, it might sound like this:

In the **first act**, we receive the call to adventure. At the beginning of our journey, we are largely unconscious about most aspects of our life and ourselves: we don't know yet what we don't know. At some point we receive, often repeatedly and unwelcomed by us, a call to leave behind the old and familiar world. What used to work does not work any longer. This demand for change can originate from within ourselves or from the external world and most likely comes in the form of a crisis, a threat, or a vision. Initially, we might be in shock and resist out of stubbornness or out of fear of having to leave behind our comfort zone and challenge the status quo. The turning point of the first act is when we accept the inevitability of change and embark on the mission, regardless of how dangerous and unknown the outcome might be.

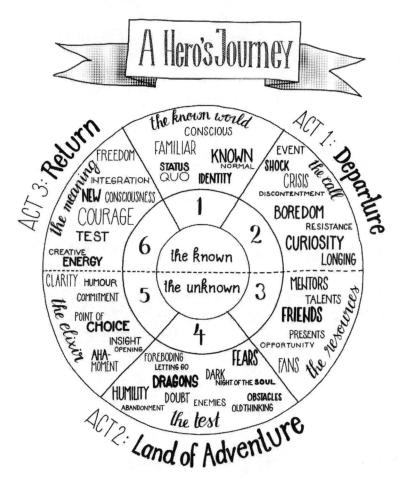

The **second act** focuses on the adventure and the journey itself. It is here that we face challenges we cannot be sure we will be able to master, or even survive. We grieve for the world we have left behind and enter the dark night of the soul. Confronted with near impossible trials and the most terrible demons, we are pushed to our limits and are ready to declare defeat. In a moment of humility we surrender and thus prove that we are worthy to receive our answer from the source of wisdom. By enduring the dark night of the soul, we acquire new, valuable insights and behaviours, transcend our old self and ego, and reach the next level of development.

The **third act** describes our return from the unknown back to the known world. Equipped with the answer, we embark on the strenuous journey back home, where it is our destiny to apply our newly found insights for the greater good. On our return journey, our dedication to the new path is often tested multiple times. And even once we have returned home, we are required to defend and protect the 'new way' against those who doubt and who want to see us fail. Nevertheless, in the end it is the wisdom we acquired that brings relief and healing to our old world.

In essence, the hero's journey describes the journey back to ourselves, during which we face our inner demons and rediscover clarity by connecting to timeless wisdom. The journey ends where we began – yet, to put it in the words of Marcel Proust:

THE REAL *voyage* OF DISCOVERY CONSISTS NOT IN SEEKING *new* LANDSCAPES, BUT IN HAVING *new*

eyes

Admittedly, the path of our journey across time often feels more like an endless progression of valleys. We invariably experience numerous moments of anger, fear, and confusion and suffer through more than just one dark night of the soul. Progress appears unreliable and a demon we expose as a self-created illusion in one moment feels terribly real and scary in the next.

Every valley we cross is followed by yet another valley that appears to be just as dark and dismal as the one before it:

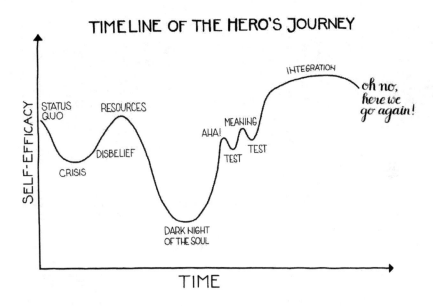

TIMELINE OF THE HERO'S JOURNEY

Throughout our lives, most of us are indeed confronted with similar challenges and familiar demons, and seemingly encounter the 'same landscape' over and over again. What we often fail to recognise is that every rendition of our personal hero's journey equips us with 'new eyes' that guide us through familiar territory with greater ease. Every call to adventure we answer has the potential to make us conscious of the very thing we were previously unaware of. Becoming more conscious means choosing sight over blindness and elevating ourselves to a new level of awareness. And even if at times we feel as if we have learned nothing, every true insight provides us with a slightly better view and with more options to choose from. If we were able to zoom out of our timeline and look at the journey of our life from a distance, I find that most journeys would look like the following graph.

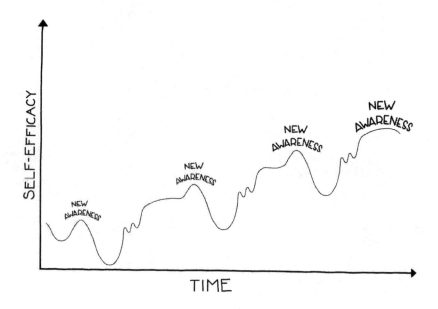

I like the metaphor of the hero's journey. For one, I much prefer to picture myself as the brave heroine slaying dragons than as the hapless Sisyphus pointlessly pushing a boulder up a hill. But more importantly, I find the hero's journey a charming reminder that I am both the narrator and the heroine of my own story. I simultaneously create and experience my own story. The more I am able to see this, the more humorous and less frightening life appears to me. Like anyone else, I still receive 'a call' at times and like most people, I tend to initially ignore or resist this call. I still forget to dance with my dragons and battle them instead, and I still experience glimpses of the dark night of the soul (see more about this in 'Dance with Dragons'). But because today I know with great certainty that the dragons I face are creations of my mind, cycling through the three acts of the hero's journey, which used to take me years, now takes days and sometimes only a few hours.

Old story vs. new story

Along the path of the hero's journey, we are confronted with the need to learn new things, to acquire skills that were previously alien to us, and to learn to dance with dragons. The steps of learning seem to follow a simple and familiar principle. This process has been described as the so-called 'ladder of learning'.

On the first spoke of the ladder, we are unconsciously unable; we don't know what we don't know (a blind spot is a blind spot exactly because we don't know it's there). Then, something happens, something challenges us to question our reality or makes us aware of something we don't know and our own inability becomes glaringly obvious to us. This catapults us to the second rung where we are now 'consciously unable'. Needless to say, this is not the most comfortable place to be, since this is the moment when we must make a choice: to continue as we have or to deepen our understanding and ability through persistent practice.

The reward for staying awake and continuing to look towards what we don't know yet (vs. looking for evidence of what we do know) is achieving new abilities and being able to use them at will. Eventually, what we once accomplished only through rigorous attention becomes an unconscious ability, one that flows effortlessly from our hands and minds. For the brave ones who continue to climb the ladder, mastery is the prize – although this level of understanding may neither be wanted nor needed, it is available. A different way to look at the hero's journey is to see it as a process of climbing different ladders and acquiring new abilities along the way.

When it comes to consciousness development, climbing the ladder has little to do with acquiring a new skill but rather with increasing our ability to see life in a different way, to see the 'hot potato' for what it is. The trickiest part of any journey is making the invisible visible, uncovering the narrative that has been running our life. It is a tricky process because our narrative is, for the most part, unconscious. Uncovering our unconscious narrative means seeing that our life today is the direct consequence of the stories we have told ourselves (or believing in the stories we have been told). Luckily, whenever there is a moment of awareness, a moment of true insight, we reach a 'point of choice' that represents the potential beginning of a new story. As the journey up the ladder continues, we experience reality from a slightly more elevated perspective.

This is what transformation means to me: to progressively wake up to my self-created narrative – to become conscious in areas in which I was previously unconscious, see the old story in which I had gotten lost, and to marvel at the new story appearing through my new eyes.

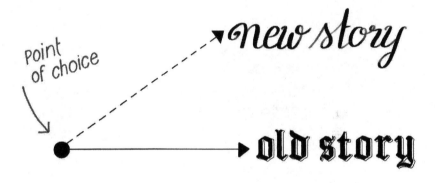

This book is aimed at helping you gain a different interpretation of your own hero's journey and to start telling a new story. You are a hero. You made it here. I challenge you to rewrite your story from (potentially) a tale of crushing disasters or repeated disappointments to seeing yourself as a 'hero' or 'heroine', who dances with dragons and eats hot potatoes while diving with curiosity and boldness into this marvellous adventure called life.

The chapter in a nutshell

The 'hot potato' of trauma and grief passed to you from your parents and grandparents is a mirage in your mind. The past is done with you when you are done with it. The potato lover within you tends to clutch to stories of past pain and suffering in order to explain what is wrong with your life today.

Why not tell our own life as a hero's (or heroine's) journey? On your path, you will climb the *Ladder of Learning* more than once. You may sometimes feel as if you are not making any progress, even though you are. As you climb further up, you progressively wake up to your self-created narrative – and become conscious in areas in which you were previously unconscious (your blind spots). Every time you become conscious of something that used to be unconscious, you have the choice to remain where you are or to investigate this blind spot and subsequently develop a new awareness. The journey up the ladder continues, but each time you see reality from a slightly more elevated perspective.

From your higher vantage point you will understand your 'old story' and marvel at the new story appearing in front of you.

On your journey, you may experience the occasional 'post-insight-hangover' that is the consequence of an insight that makes you question the necessity of all of your previous suffering. It is normal to experience this; be kind to yourself and wait for the hangover to pass.

ENDNOTE

1. Post-traumatic growth refers to positive psychological changes following an experience of adversity. These changes are of such fundamental nature that the person displaying post-traumatic growth rises to a higher level of functioning than before the event (or series of events).

REFERENCES

Campbell, J. (1949). *The Hero With a Thousand Faces*. Pantheon Books.

Yehuda, R., Daskalakis, N. P., Bierer, L. M., Bader, H. N., Klengel, T., Holsboer, F., & Binder, E. B. (2015). *Holocaust Exposure Induced Intergenerational Effects on FKBP5 Methylation*. Biological Psychiatry Journal.

We walk through ourselves
meeting robbers, ghosts, giants,
old men, young men, wives,
widows, brothers in love.
But always meeting ourselves.

James Joyce

CHAPTER 3

Look Who's Talking

Emily, a creative director at an international advertising firm, wanted to explore a looming sense of frustration she felt with her life. 'My life has turned into one big hamster wheel of work! I feel lost between the endless demands of my job and keeping everything together at home with Joe and the kids. I have noticed that lately, I seem to have zero tolerance for Joe's "inability" to run the household in a way that I find appropriate. I mean really, he is a stay-at-home dad and can't even manage to keep the kitchen clean half the time.' Emily impatiently wiggles her leg up and down. 'To be fair, he is great with the kids and they adore him. But playing with them is not everything that is needed here. I come home, and the first thing I have to do is clear up the pigsty that is our kitchen. After I've spent ten hours in the office with overworked teams, or travelled halfway across the world, or handled clients, he can tell me he didn't really notice the crumbs everywhere. I mean, REALLY?'

One of the tools I have found most useful in my work is an approach called Voice Dialogue, where clients come to understand how some of their conflicts and patterns arise from the drives of different inner 'voices', which we experience frequently in the form of seemingly contradictory thoughts and emotions. Emily and I tackled the subject directly from the emotion she felt most strongly, by exploring who within her (which voice) was so frustrated. In order to talk with this part, I asked Emily to sit or stand in a different location within the room, the location associated with that part of her. This helped her to physically and energetically differentiate that particular voice from any others. We referred to her original starting point, the chair right across from me, as the driver's seat, the place where she was integrated with all of her different voices. When Emily sat in that chair, and only when she sat in that chair, would I be referring to her as Emily. As soon as she moved to another position in the room I would talk to her *about* Emily, since she was then representing only a part of Emily and not everything Emily felt or wanted. For the same reason, I encouraged Emily's voices to speak *about* Emily in the third person as well.

The first part that emerged turned out to be a familiar voice for Emily: her *inner perfectionist*, who referred to herself as *Miss Perfect*. She chose a spot right next to the *Emily* chair and remained standing. When prompted for her perspective, Miss Perfect immediately listed all the expectations she has of Emily and every aspect of her life and performance. Miss Perfect went on to share her annoyance at the 'uselessness' of Emily's husband Joe, who clearly wasn't performing to Miss Perfect's standards. Emily had extensively explored the viewpoint of this part in previous dialogues, and Miss Perfect clearly felt comfortable giving me her opinion on Emily and Joe. When Miss Perfect had no more to say, I thanked her for her input and asked to again speak to Emily.

Emily left Miss Perfect behind and went back to her original chair. She suddenly appeared tired, and her eyes were filled with tears.

I asked Emily to immediately move to a place in the room where she could connect with the energy that felt like crying. Emily got up and sat down on the floor in a corner of the room.

'Hi. Who are you?' I inquired, once she had made herself comfortable on the floor.

The part of Emily I was now talking to nervously nestled with her sweater, crying quietly and avoiding my eyes. 'I am so tired. I am so sick of having to do everything at home. As Miss Perfect said, Joe never notices anything – not the crumbs on the floor, not the sticky surfaces, not the pans in the sink. When I come home after a twelve-hour workday, I begin to clean and cook for the next day. If Emily (she points at the empty chair opposite me) has to travel for a few days for work, I will pre-cook all the meals to make sure the kids are fed properly.' She started to smile bitterly.

'Why do you smile like that?' I asked.

'Because I was thinking about who I am. What came to my mind is that I am the part of Emily that is the *housewife* – but then I was thinking of Emily's sister-in-law, who is such an impeccable homemaker, and I am nothing like that. I have no eye for beauty or design, the only thing I am good for is cleaning and cooking. So then I thought I should be called *House Slave* – that sounds about right. That's what I feel like, anyway. Sometimes, I am just exhausted; I am tired of Joe, the kids, my life, I mean, Emily's life. I wish I could take a break, but it is like Miss Perfect doesn't let me. She is like a slave master. In her book, there are no breaks, ever.'

House Slave cried, 'And really, I don't even want to be so uptight all the time, I want Emily to not worry when she is on a business trip, I want her to trust that Joe is feeding the kids. And I really want her to stop giving a damn about crumbs on the floor. I want her,' she pointed at Emily's chair, 'to keep the awful Miss Perfect in check. She is always yelling at me. Nothing is ever good enough. I want Emily to tell her to leave me alone. I want a break, and for Emily not to be disappointed or angry with me. It's not even that I mind working hard. But Miss Perfect turns everything into a chore and sucks all the fun right out of it. I am sick of doing chores. Why can't Emily just relax and play with the kids when she gets home?'

House Slave stared at the floor, and I asked her if she had anything else to say to, or about, Emily before we brought Emily back. House Slave shook her head, and I thanked her for talking to me so openly. I asked House Slave to leave her place in the corner and for Emily to come back to the chair right across from me.

When Emily landed on her chair, I invited her to gently disconnect fully from her house slave energy. Quietly, Emily looked at her fingers.

'What are you thinking?'

'I mean I did know about Miss Perfect obviously. But I didn't know that House Slave is a part of me as well. I had no idea that House Slave suffers so much because of Miss Perfect. But it does make sense. The strange thing is that I now realise how House Slave sometimes hijacks me when I am at work too. Of course I know I am smart. I have a master's degree, for Pete's sake! It's like if I don't do something good enough according to Miss Perfect, she gets so angry that all of a sudden House Slave takes over, and I feel small, insignificant, invisible, and put upon. And when House Slave takes over, it is impossible for me to work with anyone in my environment at eye level. Then I feel like I need to kneel before everyone and just do as they say. Obviously, I know this is not where I need to be when I give a presentation in front of the board.'

Emily sighed. 'It is helpful, though, to know why I sometimes feel this way. And I do feel sorry for House Slave. I don't want her life to be so hard. I can see how Miss Perfect is never satisfied and how hard she is driving House Slave. So, I guess I have to hold Miss Perfect at bay sometimes and give House Slave a break. I see that, as much as Miss Perfect helps me to perform at a high level of quality, she does have the tendency to turn everything into a chore. And maybe the crumbs are really not the most important thing to take care of when I get home. And of course I know that Joe will feed the kids, even if I don't prepare a meal for the following day.'

Emily looked directly at me and laughed. 'Okay, so no more picking up crumbs first and wiping down counters and cooking until midnight. Freedom for House Slave! I'll have a word with Miss Perfect.'

Who am I anyway?

Rather than thinking of ourselves as having *one* coherent personality, it might be closer to our subjective experience to think of ourselves as made up of many different selves or parts, which collectively create what we may call 'I'. Instead of imagining 'I' as one consistent set of thoughts, beliefs, emotions, and physical reactions, there might actually be many different facets to this 'I'. We hear our inner parts argue and debate and comment inside our head all day long:

'You should have done the shopping before work – I knew it was going to be too late to get this done in time before dinner. Now look at the mess. We'll have to do frozen pizza again, and this is exactly what you promised you wouldn't do anymore.'

'Hello gorgeous! You are looking amazing today. I must say the blue really suits your hair colour well. Do remember to call the hairdresser, you need a trim before the meeting on Thursday!'

'She hasn't called... I can't believe she hasn't called: the paper wasn't good enough. You didn't go the extra mile – you just *had* to cut corners, didn't you!'

'Do you see the dress on that woman? Makes her bum look big. Ah – now look who's talking. The scale this morning didn't exactly give you the green light for the croissant you gulped down with the cappuccino, did it!'

What we call 'I' is the combination of all of these voices or selves and the interactions among them. It is this multifaceted nature of personality that Drs. Hal and Sidra Stone, the creators of *The Psychology of Selves*[1], explore with the methodology they coined *Voice Dialogue* (Stone, 1998).

Before you get concerned that speaking in 'voices' could mean you're schizophrenic, or that acknowledging different selves could trigger multiple personality disorder, let me assure you that Voice Dialogue has no such power.[2] The different selves as explored through Voice Dialogue are metaphors. The process of dialogue, of speaking with these selves, can bring astonishing insight into the *what* and *why* of our thoughts, feelings, and actions.

Many years ago, my first Voice Dialogue session as a client left me hungry to know more about my own inner 'orchestra' and eager to learn the art of conducting these dialogues, so that I could introduce this powerful technique to my clients. What I understood during the first session was that everything I feel, think, want, or fear is rational from the particular perspective of *one* of my selves. This insight resulted in a deep feeling of being at peace with myself and at peace with what I had previously experienced as my many contradictions.

When we describe a person we often depict them as having a particular *character*. What we label as their character seems to be a stable set of personality traits influencing that person's thoughts and actions. However, the model of a fixed character does not explain why we are at times so out of character. We often observe others behaving in ways that are just not like them ('I don't know what got into her. She was not being herself!'). It is even more irritating when we catch ourselves thinking or wanting things that are in direct opposition to the things we *really* think or want. This leaves us with the puzzling question of *Who am 'I'?*

The explanation Voice Dialogue offers is that there are different selves, parts, or voices in all of us, which influence who we are at any given moment in time. Going forward, I will use the words *self, part, or voice* interchangeably, since they refer to the same phenomenon.

43

Most of us will be able to attest to not always being exactly the same person, with the same consistent reactions, beliefs, or moods. We can feel and behave very differently depending on the context we are in or the people we are with. A person can be loving and patient with their child one moment, and aggravated and judgemental with their spouse the next. We often become aware of the presence of different voices or selves whenever we have an important decision to make. Faced with a consequential choice, it can feel as if we are literally being pulled in different directions; one part of us wants to turn left, and the other wants to turn right. In the end the cacophony of the voices in us can grow so loud that we are left confused, depleted, and incapable of moving forward.

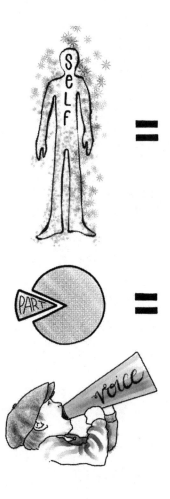

The touch of an angel and the evolution of I

According to the Talmud, right before birth an angel gently touches us in the place between our nose and our upper lip (where it causes the little dent). It is this touch, the story goes, that causes us to forget what we knew before we were born: that we are complete, a perfect and unflawed individual expression of life. We begin to believe that we are imperfect, broken, or unworthy. The rest of our life is dedicated to reclaiming what we had at the beginning, and is expressed through our longing for a sense of peace, belonging, and completeness. The touch of the angel is a metaphor, of course, but a beautiful one.

Human babies have the longest period of dependency of any mammal. As infants and children, we rely on someone else to fulfil our physical and psychological needs. We would be incapable of survival without help until we are old enough to provide for ourselves. The assimilation of different environmental and archetypal personalities can therefore be seen as a natural and inevitable part of the adaptive learning process. Inner voices are by no means negative or counterproductive; we simply internalise and synthesise whatever we've experienced. The explanations in this chapter focus solely on the parts of our personality that are formed through social interactions. In the on-going debate about the share of nature vs. nurture, depending on the source, the balance seems to be roughly 50/50. This means that we are all born with certain character traits, which can only be tangentially altered by outside events. The remaining 50% of our personalities is still hugely receptive to nurture – the way we are raised and educated.

Using another metaphor, imagine that all of humanity originates from the same 'pond' or source. Within this pond, you will find all human needs, thoughts, feelings, and behaviours. As children, our connection to the pond or source is undisturbed, and we access and express the full spectrum without inhibition; one moment we are giggling with joy, the next we bump our knee and are in a world of pain – until we glimpse a butterfly passing by and follow its movements, mesmerised. When we don't get what we want we are sad, angry, or stubborn. We give gifts of love abundantly. We are envious, generous, mischievous, funny, coy, loud, and quiet. We are everything a human being can be. Life flows through us and we never hold onto any thought or emotion for very long.

Eventually however, we learn how the expression of some of these qualities leads to being more loved, praised, or rewarded, and the expression of others leads to rejection, shame, or punishment. Wanting to be loved and accepted, we begin to mould ourselves into the shape most likely to be rewarded by our environment. Like our environment, we now label behaviours, thoughts, and feelings as good, bad, right, and wrong. How we sort these qualities into the different categories is heavily influenced by our cultural and socio-economic background. We might learn that being friendly, courteous, studious, and quiet are good qualities; whereas being loud, angry, envious, and self-centred are considered undesirable by the people around us. Thus begins the journey of disassociating ourselves from the unwanted qualities and identifying with those that best guarantee the attention and affection of our primary caregivers.

In effect, out of the limitless pool of possibility, we assemble a small army of selves with qualities bearing the highest likelihood of fulfilling our needs. This process of adaptive learning is automatic – nearly or even completely unconscious. Each self ultimately stands for a distinct strategy of how to fulfil our needs, buffer us against fear, attack, or failure, or let us experience joy and connection. In our adult reality, the different strategies we employ are more or less effective, healthy, or even rational. Rarely do we take care to upgrade our strategies based on newer events and situations; instead, we continue to exercise particular ways of thinking, feeling, and acting, which are based on realities that have long passed.

One of my clients, Doris, discovered she had a self that made her eat and grow fat. She felt limited by this in many ways, particularly in her quest to find a new lover/partner. In dialogue with this *fat self* she came to understand how this self created a rather complicated protection strategy. Fat Self observed Doris being used and humiliated by men in her past and decided that *no* man could be trusted because in the end, male attention was always hurtful. In order to prevent future abuse, Fat Self had emerged with the strategy of keeping Doris safe by making her physically unattractive. Being fat led to being less attractive, which allowed her to avoid drawing any male attention which could potentially result in more humiliation and pain.

Our selves have a strong preference for pre-emptive strikes. Sadly, the very behaviours they inflict on us with the intention of keeping us safe often make us even more vulnerable and out of control and remove us further from the state we desire.

Copy and paste; the creation of selves

The selves follow, in essence, the strategy of a chameleon; they allow us to adapt to our environment. Each self acts in order to fulfil or protect a need that we sense is unfulfilled or at risk. Depending on the situation at hand, a different self steps to the forefront and takes over. How each self tries to protect our vulnerability may not always be evident at first glance.

The different parts of our personality form during different stages of our lives, and are strongly influenced by the role models we were exposed to. Although, traditionally, our parents play a pivotal role in the formation of our selves, our grandparents, siblings, teachers, friends, or cultural role models may have been equally influential. We are social animals, and we learn by observing and copying. As we grow up, our predominant caretakers turn into our primary attachment figures. We turn to them for emotional support while we go off to explore; we seek their approval when we experiment with new behaviours; and we yearn to be loved and accepted by them.

By observing how they act and how they respond to our signals for closeness and separation, we learn how we need to be, and even who we need to be in order to survive and have our basic human needs met (please see chapter 'Dance With Dragons' for more information on needs).

The disapprovingly raised eyebrow of my mother and harsh remarks of my father might have nourished my *inner critic*. My inner critic learned *how it's done* and subsequently took it upon herself to criticise me even without further need for external input. My *inner critic*, like all selves, does so with good intentions; the harsher the critical self-judgements are, the more prepared I am to weather future criticism by others. My inner critic might also be fuelled by the wish to please my mother and father and gain their acceptance, by treating myself just as they treated me. Likewise, my inner perfectionist may have been modelled after my hyper-organised grandfather, or could have been created as a response to the experience of a chaotic home environment in which we were constantly struggling to instil a sense of control and predictability.

In addition to ensuring our survival and protecting our vulnerable core, the selves we summon may serve the purpose of keeping us psychologically close to these important people from our past. We achieve this by modelling the characteristics of a specific self after people and relationships that mattered to us. The actual modelling appears to occur through three copy processes (Benjamin, 1993): Identification (we behave just like he/she behaved), Recapitulation (we behave like we did around him/her, as if he/she was still in charge), and Introjection (we treat ourselves just like he/she treated us).

FEARLESS SUPERHERO

CRITICAL MOTHER

VULNERABLE CHILD

THE SHY ONE

GRUMPY MONSTER

SCARED BUNNY

SOMETHING THAT HAPPENED

IDENTIFICATION
(I ACT JUST LIKE SHE/HE DID)

RECAPITULATION
(I REACT AS IF SHE IS STILL AROUND)

INTROJECTION
(I TREAT MYSELF AS SHE TREATED ME)

Anyone who has ever had anyone tell them, 'You are just like your mother', or, 'Don't treat me as if I was your father', has likely experienced someone else reacting to a self, created through one of the three copy processes. The copy processes are completely normal developmental learning processes, indifferent to the content of what is being copied. They are simply tools that allow us to translate recurring external events (how we were treated by important others) into internal patterns (how we interact with the world and ourselves). Luckily, since the copy processes work in all directions, positive messages we received from important others are also patterned into our personality.

The psychologist Lorna Benjamin calls behaviours formed through a copy process a 'gift of love' (1993). According to her, gift-of-love behaviours allow us to maintain a psychological closeness to important people in our past. More specifically, these behaviours are gifts of love to the *internalised representations* of important others that we have created within ourselves. These internalised representations are somewhat like imaginary friends or ghosts of our subconscious who can comfort or haunt us; even if my parents are no longer alive, I can still be locked in a pattern of pleasing my mother, show the same submissive behaviour I learned in order to be acknowledged by my father, or criticise myself with the same harsh language my grandmother used with me. Behaving like them, behaving as if they were still around or treating ourselves like they treated us, is our (futile) attempt to finally gain their love, approval, and validation. Note that positive behaviours and attitudes that we experienced are written into our internal dialogue the same way; if I was loved and acknowledged, my internalised representations will love and acknowledge me. If I was treated with good-spirited humour, I will be able to laugh at myself. We simply create copies of what we experienced to be true at the time – and we will go to great lengths to replicate these early experiences throughout our lives.

Mother Maria

About 10 years ago, I experienced first-hand what it was like to be hijacked by one of my selves. I was travelling to a client in Luxembourg with my colleague, Peter, a very handsome man with a boyish energy and a contagious smile. When we arrived at the front desk of our five-star hotel, Peter immediately started to joke and flirt with the receptionist – who clearly enjoyed the attention. With a raised eyebrow I observed their banter. Then Peter made *the move*; he leaned on the desk, and with all the innocence he could muster up, he asked the receptionist if there was any way she could upgrade his room to a higher floor of the hotel with a view of the old town of Luxembourg. After all, it was his first time in this beautiful city and after a long day of work nothing would make him happier than to enjoy a gorgeous view with a drink in his hand.

At this point, I was livid. I could not believe the blatantly obvious and unashamed manipulation of the 'poor girl' behind the counter. When the blushing receptionist finally handed him the key to one of their suites on the top floor, I had lost all faith in and respect for humanity, and women in particular. Tight-lipped and cold as ice I took my turn at the check-in desk and, with what I felt was a very dignified look on my face, received my key – to my second floor room. Opening the door to my room, I found that my window not only lacked a view of Luxembourg but faced the parking lot at the back of the hotel.

As I was unpacking my suitcase and playing out in my mind all the things I would like to say to Peter and the naïve receptionist, Peter rang: 'You have to come up and see this! I have two rooms and a spectacular view! It is so cool, let's have a drink together.' Needless to say, I turned down the generous offer to celebrate the fruits of his unethical seduction and instead settled into a restless night, tossing and turning to the sounds of the parking lot traffic.

At the time, I didn't know what had hit me. When I observed Peter and the receptionist, I was completely overtaken by a sense of self-righteousness and indignation. Although I believed I was right to be appalled, even I could not understand why Peter's behaviour triggered such a strong response. During a Voice Dialogue session a few years later, I found my answer: I discovered one of my parts, that called itself *Mother Maria*. My inner Mother Maria was in fact modelled after Maria, my late grandmother. She had always credited her long and healthy life (she passed away a few months after turning 100) to her Prussian virtues of self-discipline, humility, and prudence. My grandmother had exercised daily until she was 96 years old and had cared for old people (all 20 years her junior) until she could no longer walk. She had been the most Protestant Catholic I ever met. As with many women of her generation, my grandmother had seen the little she had grown up with dwindle into even less with the start of World War II. Her life was marked by a tight regime of hard work and little compassion for herself or for her four children (amongst them my mother). My grandmother had nothing but disdain for people who acted entitled, who manipulated others for favours, or who felt it was their right to cut in line.

She had been one of my main caretakers while growing up, and I copied many of the values my grandmother exemplified. I owe much of my success to her role model. I was surprised to discover that I had apparently made her immortal by creating my own internalised representation of her: my internal Mother Maria. When I got to know this part through Voice Dialogue – her views on life, her values, and her wishes for me – I discovered that Mother Maria's moral high ground was only half of the story. During one of my Voice Dialogue sessions, Mother Maria revealed how much she envied people who were not ashamed to try to better their conditions. Since she had never felt that this had been an option in her life, the only thing she had to her name was at least to be morally superior to everyone else. Understanding the qualities Mother Maria brought to my life – as well as her secret desire – allowed me to invite her energy more consciously, instead of being hijacked by it. One of the gifts she brought was the lesson I learned during the Luxembourg incident: dare to be like Peter more of the time. Ask for what you want. And enjoy what you may receive.

Dominant selves and our operating ego

The selves are not only psychological re-enactments of relationships with important people in our lives; our various parts are archetypal[3] in nature because they represent universal human qualities expressed through our individual personality. The particular expression of these qualities is shaped by our personal experience and by the role models we learned from, but the essence of the selves is rooted in simply being human. Amongst the usual subjects of archetypal selves is the ever-present *inner critic* who is never satisfied, the *judge* who hardly has a kind word for others, the *pleaser* who is always concerned with everyone's comfort and happiness, the *achiever* or *pusher* who relentlessly pushes us to work harder, the *realist* who only trusts facts and numbers, the *artist* who engages with the world through creative expression, and the *rebel* who chafes against conformity, authority, and rules.

As we grow up, we learn that love, acceptance, and in some extreme cases, even our survival, are more easily secured by identifying with some selves than with others. For example, if you grew up in a white middle-class household in Europe or North America, you might have learned that being a good student/achiever and pleasing others wins you more brownie points with your parents and peer group than stepping into your inner free spirit or artist. Conversely, if you had the experience of growing up in a neighbourhood marked by gangs and violence, your survival might have relied much more on your ability to develop a strong connection with your inner rebel, or a part comfortable with being cunning or even violent. From an early age, we learn to identify with the subset of selves who receive the most external validation and thus keep us safest under the given circumstances. These parts of our personality are called our *dominant selves* and together they form of our *operating ego*. Confidently, our operating ego declares 'This is who I am,' as well as 'This is who I am not.'

Most of the time, the energies of our selves play out without much conscious involvement on our part. In effect, our selves hijack us, if and when they feel like it. As a result, we go from being pleasing to being hostile, from being easy-going to being controlling, and from being happy to angry in a split second. Each self forces the others into the background until the internal power dynamic changes and another part of us takes over. When we allow our selves to run the show without any conscious intervention, the quality of our relationships can suffer and our well-being diminish; life begins to feel limited. Our dominant selves shape our world: from the perspective of a distrustful self, life appears filled with deceitful people; a self who puts reliability as the highest human virtue will set us up for constant disappointment; a relentless pusher self will drive us to the brink of exhaustion; and a judging self will alienate us from others by criticising them constantly. To be stuck with our dominant selves is like being the conductor of a beautiful orchestra – but allowing only two instruments to play, the flute and the drums. Unless we, the conductor, invite other parts to play as well, the flute and drums begin to assume they are the orchestra. Despotic as they have become, they will not think twice about pushing the conductor off the pedestal. The flute and drums may be wonderful instruments, but we clearly diminish the beauty of the symphony of life if we perform it with only two instruments and no conductor!

Opposites attract

Each self has a twin, a polarity representing the other side of the same coin. For every *driver/pusher*, there is a *hedonist*, for each *pleaser*, there is a part that is *withdrawn* or even *antisocial* and doesn't care about anything or anyone, for each *dreamer* there is a *realist*, and for each *social butterfly*, there is a *hermit*. Whatever the nature of our dominant selves, they point us in the direction of their opposites: parts of us we may scarcely know, parts we like less, or whose existence we deny entirely.

The polarity of a *dominant self* is either an *uncharted self* (not yet discovered by us), or more often, a *disowned self*. As the name suggests, disowned selves are largely unwanted, since they represent values, beliefs, and qualities rejected by one or many of our *dominant selves*. Because they don't fit with the definition of our *operating ego* as to who we are or who we should be, they are reduced to a shadow existence in the basement of our figurative inner house. For example, the values upheld by the dominant selves forming my *operating ego* may require me to be modest, studious, self-disciplined, reliable, and kind. Therefore, any parts in me that are egocentric, lazy, laid-back, unreliable, or unfriendly are destined to be hidden, shamed, and rejected.

Our disowned selves are the basement-children of our soul because they make us feel ashamed, helpless, or overwhelmed. They symbolise human qualities that once made us feel unsafe while growing up because they were forbidden, sanctioned, or ridiculed. Today we find them undesirable or even repulsive. Our *operating ego* will go to great lengths to prohibit these characteristics from emerging – but as with all contained energy, this energy is also looking for release. The more we attempt to lock these selves away in the deepest dungeon, the more creative they become at making their presence felt. When we are tired, weak, or feel attacked, our operating ego can lose control and our basement-children unexpectedly burst their chains and break free with a raw and unmediated energy (please refer to 'Don't Panic' for an explanation of the *Amygdala-Hijack*). A normally quiet and peaceful person turns into a madman, livid with anger. A warm and understanding person suddenly grows cold and judgemental. A strong and composed person breaks down, sobbing helplessly. At the same time, a normally passive and indecisive person can become practical and proactive.

The dominant self of one person is the disowned or unchartered self of another. That is why opposites attract. We are often fascinated by and drawn to qualities in others that we seem to lack; a fact that is responsible for much pleasure and pain in relationships. We are mesmerised by those qualities in others which we have difficulties expressing ourselves. At the same time it is precisely those qualities which our dominant selves judge most harshly if they feel overwhelmed in any way. A very driven and self-disciplined person might fall for someone who is happy-go-lucky, carefree and fully in the *now*. They will find this way of being refreshing – until their vulnerability is triggered and suddenly the very behaviour they once found endearing has become intolerable. The qualities we are attracted to or repelled by are, to a large degree, determined by our context: our family, peer group, and our culture, as well as the social, political, environmental, and economic conditions we are exposed to.

It is fascinating to witness a Voice Dialogue process in which the selves, free of censorship and safe from judgement, reveal their unique personality. Each self has a distinctly different energy, mood, way of thinking, set of rules, and bodily position. Their different natures result in divergent opinions, viewpoints, and emotions, and the dynamic between the selves is not unlike the dynamic between members of a real team. The most complete version of 'I' would therefore encompass our full orchestra: all aspects of our personality including our dominant selves, disowned selves, and uncharted selves.

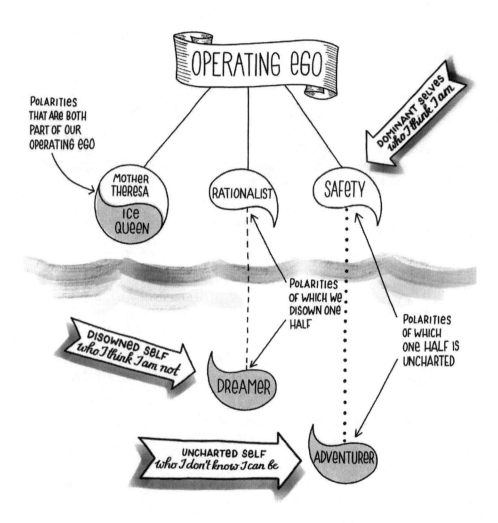

Learning not only to see, but to welcome the qualities of our disowned and uncharted selves is nothing less than the evolution of consciousness. Returning to the angel's touch, as described in the Talmud, we could argue that reclaiming our selves means remembering what the angel made us forget. By integrating our selves we regain access to the full spectrum of the human existence. As the conscious and empowered conductor of our own orchestra, we know which instrument is the most appropriate in any given situation. We can choose either to be continuously hijacked by a few dominant voices and helplessly flip-flop between extremes – or to deepen our self-awareness until it becomes self-confidence. One self at a time.

Sorting the spaghetti

Initially, when we first become aware of the selves, it can feel like being caught in the middle of a pile of entangled spaghetti. We have trouble identifying distinct voices and our thought process feels conflicted and confused. This feeling of confusion usually passes, once we have made contact with the first self and begin to see the distinct perspective of each of our selves.

When dialoguing with our selves, it is helpful to physically change location. The starting point for any exploration is the driver's seat – the first position in which we name the topic of our exploration. In the driver's seat, we are as much owner as conductor of our voices. By shifting to another physical location when engaging with a different part, we signal two important bits of information to our subconscious: a) whichever part speaks from that new position is *not 'I'* but is *a part of 'I'*, and b) whichever part wants to come out has permission to speak freely and uncensored. Once a part has found its location in the room, we engage it in a curious and non-judgemental dialogue. At this point, our only interest is to get to know this part: what the world looks like from its perspective, the purpose it serves, what it believes in, when it first appeared, and why it was formed.

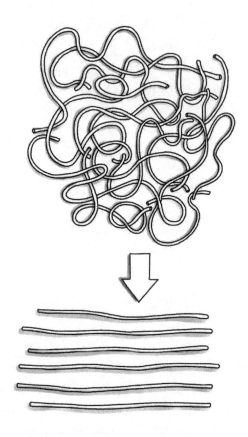

Our emotions are the consequences of our thoughts. Since most of our thinking happens without the involvement of consciousness, our thoughts are largely opaque to us. By engaging in the dialogue with our selves, we begin to discover what *this* part is thinking and which emotion is created as a result. The parts are often astonished and relieved when they are invited to speak uninterruptedly and without being judged. What each part has to say can sound familiar, surprising, and sometimes shocking, but hearing the 'truth' of one of our parts nearly always furthers our sense of clarity and understanding. Once we return to the driver's seat, we gently disassociate from the part we dialogued with. Now, we can look *at* the thoughts and emotions of this part from a balcony perspective instead of being locked into its experience of reality. To understand that this is *one* perspective within us and not everything that we are, believe, or want, can feel incredibly liberating. Each self we make peace with enables us to reclaim another human quality in the big pond of the human existence.

The philosopher Sydney Banks once said in a lecture, 'This is why the great sages and mystics throughout time have told us to look within for the answer we sought. They knew that wisdom wasn't discovered, but uncovered from the very depths of your own soul; here lies the truth,' Voice Dialogue is one of the fastest approaches I know to connect us to the depths of our soul and to help us to unearth the wisdom that lies within.

The Aware Ego Process

A Voice Dialogue Process is often most helpful when we feel hijacked by one of our selves, when we are locked in a feeling and don't see a way out. As the process begins, we first identify our current position in the driver's seat. Next, we physically shift positions to explore the reality of one self, usually the self already occupying our thoughts and feelings. When this self has nothing more to say, we shift back to the driver's seat, gently dissociating from the energy of that self, settling back into a new awareness. Being back in the driver's seat, we frequently feel less burdened by the feeling, and see more options of dealing with the situation at hand.

This dance between associating and dissociating is aptly named the Aware Ego Process. To experience the Aware Ego Process is a quantum leap in consciousness; instead of operating on autopilot and being victim to the different selves hijacking our thoughts and feelings, we develop the ability to be aware of and play with their different energies. The Aware Ego Process thus consists of three interwoven stages: awareness (to observe our selves), experience (to feel and be in the energy of our selves), and action.

The Aware Ego Process is not another self, not a fixed state to be achieved or mastered, but rather a life-long process that is continuously in flux. We move in and out of awareness, in and out of experience, and in and out of conscious choice. Experimenting with awareness, experience, and action allows us to connect with our full orchestra instead of being stuck forever with one or two instruments. From the place that is simultaneously suspended between the selves and encompassing the selves, we connect with our wisdom and clarity. I often find that after the exploration of two polarities I experience a deep stillness. After exploring the part of me that always wants to be helpful and liked, followed by the part that couldn't care less and is fiercely independent of other peoples' judgement, I notice that I am neither one nor the other. By realising that I am in fact both, I more frequently know the appropriate response for myself in any given situation.

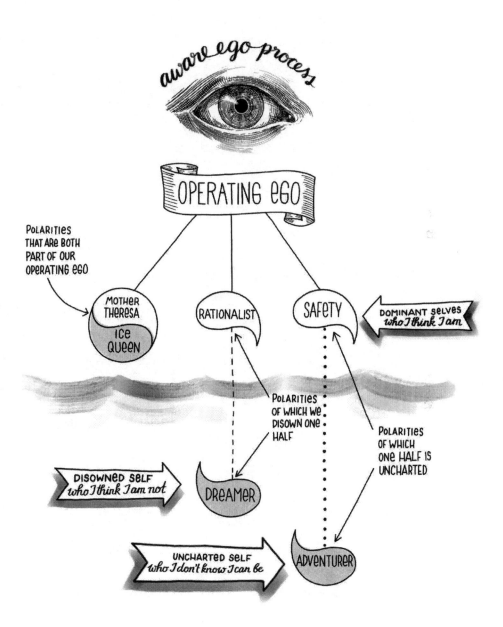

aware ego process

OPERATING EGO

Polarities that are both part of our operating ego

MOTHER THERESA / ICE QUEEN

RATIONALIST

SAFETY

DOMINANT SELVES *who I think I am*

Polarities of which we disown one half

Polarities of which one half is uncharted

DISOWNED SELF *who I think I am not*

DREAMER

UNCHARTED SELF *who I don't know I can be*

ADVENTURER

Looking *at* my voices instead of being stuck *in* them, I transform that which was subject (this is me) to object (this is a part of me). This wondrous sensation of becoming witness to my own inner processes relieves me from the compulsion to act on every voice's whim. The parts or energies within me are constantly expressing thoughts, feelings, and wants, but I do not have to act on them. I acknowledge these internal stirrings with more compassion and begin to relax into myself, knowing that no singular perspective or self holds the key to freedom. The goal of working with my selves is to reclaim the dissociated parts of me, thereby empowering me to act from a position of choice. I can only consciously manage the energy of a self if I don't deny its existence. If I insist in *never* being angry, anger might break out of me unexpectedly or with inappropriate force. If I connect with the angry part within me, I can learn to listen to its complaints and needs and act on it out of awareness. Additionally, the Aware Ego Process allows us to experience how every human quality has a *light side* and a *dark side*. A person who is caring can shift from the state of being empathic and connected to being clingy and enmeshed. One who is self-reliant can maintain a healthy distance without getting entangled – or can come across as cold and egotistical. How a quality is perceived by ourselves and others depends on the context: no human quality is inherently better or worse than the next.

Hal Stone once described the goal of Voice Dialogue in a lecture as '...the awakening of the Aware Ego Process which allows us to live our life between ever-widening and ever-deepening oppositional energies, and thus gradually neutralize our ideas and feelings about what is good and bad. In this way we are led to a gradual lessening of judgment and the chance to live what is, rather than believing our judgments about how they should be'. The exploration of our selves thus brings more awareness and freedom not only to us individually but also to how we engage in relationships with important others in our lives: our spouses, children, siblings, parents, friends, and colleagues. When we dissociate, by choice, from one overpowering voice in order to enjoy the more subtle energy of another, we bring more flexibility and range to how we engage with the world. Being able to perceive but not be overtaken by the different energies within allows us access to the wisdom and competency of each self.

Effective exploration involves an interest in and empathy for our own emotions, awareness of our thinking, and determination in adapting our behaviour. A genuine interest in understanding the motivation of all of our selves (even of those we don't like) permits us to embrace the gifts they bring to the full spectrum of our being-ness. It is an experience of grace to get to know our polarities – the two sides of our coins – and to be able to empathise with each perspective, its specific fears and wishes for us. Having compassion for our various selves means to have compassion for our complete/unified self. We learn that we are not the voice in our head, since this is merely one of our voices, which has hijacked our consciousness.

Discovering wholeness

Our ability to adapt to our environment by identifying with selves that allow us to be who we think we need to be ensures our survival. However, the more we divide qualities into good or bad and distance ourselves from the bad, unwanted qualities, the further we move away from feeling complete in our imperfection, loveable and belonging.

In the *Harry Potter* novels, Lord Voldemort achieves immortality by fragmenting his soul and locking the parts into objects. Eventually, he is no more than a ghost of his former self. In a way, we do the same; we fragment our soul and forget that we are born whole. As our consciousness matures, we may feel more clearly the internal conflict which dissociation creates, and sense that we are not accessing our full potential. This tension can prompt us to reclaim what has been ours all along: part by part, voice by voice. Through considering and balancing polarities, we experience an awakening, a growing sensation of becoming more real. We rediscover oneness when we realise the shimmering facets of *I* to be an illusion. To live in this awareness all the time is not the reality of most people – but it is a reality accessible to all of us at any time.

Real-world examples

Sue: baby blues

My client, Sue, a woman in her late thirties, had already met a number of her different selves in previous sessions. In this particular session, she wanted to explore what different parts of her had to say about her wish to get pregnant. At the time of our conversation, Sue had been trying to get pregnant with her partner for about five months. The first attempt resulted in a pregnancy that was beset with complications and terminated naturally after six weeks. Since then, nothing had happened.

Sue was aware of one part feeling sad and rather frustrated about not getting pregnant, while yet another part of her was not keen on being pregnant and therefore felt rather relieved that it was not working out. Although Sue heard the *not wanting to be pregnant* part quite clearly, she felt that the *wanting to be pregnant* part was still stronger. Sue wanted to get a better sense of who in her wanted what and if the part of her which didn't want to get pregnant was possibly even interfering with her ability to become pregnant.

The first part we explored was Sue's inner *protector*. We had already been in touch with this self in our previous explorations. Her protector went by the name of *Cloak* and came forward willingly. I wanted to make sure Cloak was comfortable for Sue to speak with me about this very personal topic. When I asked Cloak which of the other parts she was interested in hearing from, Cloak didn't want us to explore either of the two parts Sue had named. The arguments for and against having a child were well known to her. Instead Cloak suggested we speak to Sue's *lower belly* since this part of her body had been tense ever since the first failed pregnancy.

After moving back into the driver's seat, Sue was surprised at hearing how clearly Cloak recommended we speak to Lower Belly instead of engaging with the parts she had intended to explore. Sue agreed with Cloak, since her lower belly had indeed felt bloated and often painful ever since the failed pregnancy. Sue quickly located a position on the floor in which she could connect with the energy of Lower Belly. Once Lower Belly was present on the floor, her body appeared smaller. When I asked Lower Belly to tell me about herself, she began to cry. 'I am so overwhelmed and confused. Ever since we got pregnant, Sue has been scrutinising me, and I feel pressured to perform. I don't even know what exactly I am doing, I have never done this before, and when I don't deliver, I feel as if I have let everybody down.'

When I asked Lower Belly who *everybody* was, she reported on a number of different voices invested in Sue getting pregnant. 'There is the critic who is clearly disapproving of my performance. Then there is the part in Sue *who wants to be pregnant* so much. And the part who turns *Getting Pregnant!* into yet another task on Sue's to-do list. To this part, getting pregnant is what a woman is supposed to achieve. It would be the icing on Sue's successful life. Then there is this part that drives me crazy; it is constantly worried and makes Sue all worried. It keeps telling Sue she is probably much too old to get pregnant. Or, if she does get pregnant at her age, the chances she could bear a handicapped child are very high. Or, even if the child is healthy, the stress that comes with raising a child will wreck her relationship. By the time this worried part is done talking, the part of Sue that *doesn't want to be pregnant* anyway has grown. Sue then feels it might just be easier to not get pregnant. It is all too much for me. The pressure to perform on the one hand and hearing all the doubts on the other hand make me really tense. I don't know what Sue wants. I don't know what I am supposed to do!'

When Lower Belly had no more to say, I invited Sue back into the driver's seat. Sue was stunned at how stressed Lower Belly was by the different forces pulling at her. She decided it might be best to speak to the worried part, since this part seemed to exert a rather large influence over Lower Belly. Pushing it out of her awareness had apparently not been successful.

Sue quickly found a position where she was able to connect with the worried energy. The worried part showed up at once, confirming all the concerns Lower Belly had already alluded to. When I asked her how long she had been a part of Sue's life, she replied, 'For a long time.

Since Sue was seven. I came when her parents got divorced. It was a very worrisome time for us then. Sue cried all the time and nobody was paying much attention to her. I took care of Sue, and I haven't really stopped worrying for her since. Sue doesn't listen to me much. She has made many choices I was very uncomfortable with – but she made them anyway. I don't really expect her to follow my advice, I can see that she has been doing well for herself – but I would like her to pay more attention to me. I want her to see me.'

I asked this part what she felt her role in Sue's life had been. After a long pause, the part started sobbing quietly. 'I think Sue has built her entire life on fixing me, trying to make the worry and the sadness go away. I can see how good Sue is at this in her job, with her partner, with her friends. She makes everyone feel better but me. She never has much patience for me, and when I do get her attention by worrying, she just tells me how unreasonable I am being. She only likes the part in herself who sees the glass as half full. But the glass is not half full! I say the glass is definitely half empty, but Sue doesn't want to know this.'

I inquired what this part needed from Sue and she replied, 'I don't want her to fix me. I want her to be there for me, to hold me, to keep me safe and comfort me. I don't know how she will ever be able to be there for a child if she can't be there for me. That's why I don't want her to have a child.' The part concluded our conversation by naming itself *Sula*. After thanking Sula for speaking to me so openly, I asked to speak again to Sue.

Sue moved back to the driver's seat and sat quietly for a while before taking a deep breath. 'I thought the worried part was going to be this

75

old nagging woman. Instead it was me! Me at age seven. I called myself Sula when I was little, and I remember well how worried and scared I felt during this period of my life. I guess Sula is right, I have been trying to make the pain inside of me go away by helping others to deal with theirs – and I have completely forgotten about her. I see why she feels that having a child is not a good idea if I can't even take care of her.'

Finding her inner seven-year-old through the Voice Dialogue Process helped Sue to feel compassion for herself. Sue saw that her wish for a child was partly driven by wanting to create the kind of home for a child that she never had. Having met Sula, she re-evaluated her wish and felt more at ease with nature taking its course – which included both the possibility of getting pregnant and the possibility of not getting pregnant. In the weeks following the session, Sue made a point to pay more attention to her body, and the pain in her lower belly slowly disappeared.

Clive: money or the meaning of life

When I started working with Clive, a private investor in his mid-forties, he wanted to prioritise the different areas of his personal and professional life. He had already achieved everything, or so it appeared: he was happily married to a woman who was a successful lawyer, he had three healthy boys who adored him, he had published a highly acclaimed business book, and he had made a name for himself with his small but thriving mergers and acquisitions business. Despite this impressive list of accomplishments, Clive had reached a point where his life felt stale and lacking purpose. Attempting to give himself direction, he had drawn up a list of goals which included: writing another book, volunteering for an NGO to drive political change in his home country, spending every breakfast and lunch with his boys, taking his family to the country estate on a regular basis, and acquiring a family-run business that had gone bankrupt. Yet, instead of moving proactively towards any of these goals, Clive felt stuck. Notwithstanding his past successes, and what looked like boundless supplies of energy to any outside observer, Clive was unmotivated and found himself wasting time ruminating and endlessly surfing the internet.

Through coaching, Clive sought to understand why he had been unable to make progress on any of his plans and develop a strategy to move forward. In our first Voice Dialogue session, we encountered three distinct parts, each of which revealed a very different perspective on Clive's life.

The first voice quickly identified himself as Clive's inner *achiever*. He had a strong and slightly impatient energy about him. He shared with me his belief that Clive just needed to get his head out of the sand and start moving. To the achiever, Clive's dreams of bettering the political situation of his home country and writing a new book were a waste of time, since neither of them would make money in the short run. To him, the acquisition of more wealth was the only worthwhile pursuit in life; money equalled freedom and secured the future of his children. His agenda for Clive was to buy the business and focus on expanding his mergers and acquisitions business instead of fantasising about the meaning of life.

The second voice was much softer in his demeanour and called himself the inner *idealist*. He empathised with Clive's wish to have a life that amounted to more than just making money. The idealist felt sad that Clive did not seem to value the many contributions he was bringing to Clive. When I asked him to share his view of what life was all about, the idealist named 'doing good things' and 'spending time with loved ones' – but not 'making more money'. From his viewpoint, Clive had enough money for a lifetime and would find happiness in raising his children, donating time to an NGO, and making progress on his book.

The third voice was the inner *hedonist*. As he began to speak, he leaned back comfortably in his chair and explained how he didn't understand why Clive was so stressed. From his viewpoint, the only thing missing for happiness was for Clive to get out more, do some of the things he had enjoyed before he had a family, and spend time with his male friends. He reminded Clive of how much he loved to explore the mountains on his motorcycle, to go sailing, or even do nothing and lie on the beach with a good book. The hedonist feared the achiever would drive Clive into the ground with his endless list of demands. He advised Clive to get more pleasure by embracing his wild side and re-charging his batteries with fun activities, to celebrate life now instead of later.

When Clive returned to the driver's seat and reflected on the parts he encountered, I asked him to 'sense' again the distinct energy of each of the three parts. He was surprised how different they each felt; the achiever was cold, restless, and impatient. The idealist warm, caring, and quiet. The hedonist simultaneously energetic and laid-back. Suddenly, Clive understood the source of his ruminations: he felt stuck amidst the three powerful selves, who each prescribed a very different remedy to his problem. Back on the driver's seat, Clive was able to see how each self held part of the solution but how no voice by itself *was* the solution. Clive decided that he wanted to give more room to both the idealist and the hedonist, since the achiever had been driving his life for the past twenty years. This did not mean discarding the achiever – after all, he had been a huge contributor to Clive's success – but rather to turn up the volume on the other two voices. To start with, Clive elected to dust off his motorcycle, went on a trip without his family, and planned to look at NGOs representing values he was invested in. Life began to feel fluid again. Instead of losing himself in the internet, he resumed his writing. In subsequent sessions, Clive discovered more selves, amongst which were the *Buddhist* (who has a very philosophical outlook on life), the *pleaser* (mainly active in his relationship with his wife and children) and the *explorer* (who loves to be out in nature). With each self, Clive discovered another facet of his life. And with each self, he found himself better able to make conscious choices about how to spend his time and create a life that is meaningful to more than just one of his selves.

The chapter in a nutshell

We are born complete and whole. At all times we have access to the full spectrum of human existence.

Each human characteristic comes in the form of a polarity: for example, kind-unkind, intelligent-foolish, patient-impatient, slow-fast, etc. We experience and express the quality of each polarity through our different selves or voices.

Each self is like an autonomous being with its own specific set of behaviours, feelings, thoughts, values, and needs.

If we learn, through the process of socialisation, that certain human qualities are unwanted, we disown or forget them.

The selves are constructed at different stages in our development as we adapt to our life conditions. The selves are formed through the three copy processes of identification, recapitulation, and introjection.

The selves which we associate most highly with ('this is who I am') are our *dominant selves*. These selves form our *operating ego*. The selves we do not access are either disowned or uncharted.

Being able to witness and experience the energy of our different selves – to appreciate their vulnerability without judging, controlling, or submitting to them – is the *Aware Ego Process*.

I *have* my selves but *I am not* my selves. *I am not* the voice in my head. I am whoever is witnessing the voices in my head.

ENDNOTES

1. Although most of this chapter is based on the teachings of Hal and Sidra Stone, this chapter is my interpretation of this powerful process. I have combined it with some of my personal observations whenever I felt they would add a helpful perspective or clarity. There is a selection of marvellous books on the topic available for anyone who feels drawn to learn more about the different selves or the teachings of Drs. Hal and Sidra Stone.
2. Most Voice Dialogue practitioners will only use the Voice Dialogue Process with 'healthy' clients. There is, however, some compelling evidence that dialoguing can be healing for patients diagnosed with schizophrenia or

other illnesses associated with hearing voices. Please watch the outstanding TED talk 'The Voices in my Head' by Eleanor Longden.

3. I am using the term archetype as defined by dictionary.com: 'the original pattern or model from which all things of the same kind are copied or on which they are based; a model or first form; prototype' vs. the traditional categories of archetypal energies such as *king, sage, lover, alchemist*, etc.

REFERENCES

Benjamin, Lorna, *Every Psychopathology is a Gift of Love*, Psychotherapy Research, Volume 3, Issue 1, 1993.

Stone, Hal and Sidra, *Embracing our Selves*, New World Library, Nataraj, 1998.

FURTHER RESOURCES

Longden, Eleanor (2013). TED talk: 'The voices in my Head'.
https://tinyurl.com/EleanorLongden

More information about Voice Dialogue and its creators Hal and Sidra Stone:
https://tinyurl.com/VoiceDialogue

For more insight into how the selves affect our daily life, I recommend John Kent's excellent book *Selves in Action* (2012) which you can order via https://tinyurl.com/VoiceDialogueUK

You can not have
exterior development
without interior
development
to hold it
in place

—Ken Wilber

CHAPTER 4

The Transformation Map

'What are you unhappy about?' I ask my client.

Alistair looks at me puzzled, as if this question has caught him by surprise. 'Well, that is a good question. Actually, I find it hard to say, right now; everything seems like a mess. Let me vent for a moment. Our organisation recently went through a change process. We paid a lot of money to have all of our processes overhauled and streamlined. The leadership team received feedback, which was supposed to make us more efficient leaders. But somehow, since the change initiative started, everything is worse than before. The atmosphere throughout the organisation is tense, everyone is dragging their feet and is moaning and complaining about anything they are asked to do differently. And frankly, I can't blame them.

'Part of the change initiative was to strengthen leadership within the organisation. Which is great in theory – and so I also received feedback about my leadership style and what I need to change. But I don't think the process was fair, and they simply dumped all the data on us and left us to our own devices to make sense of it. As a result, I mainly feel put upon and right now I have absolutely no motivation to figure out how to turn myself into the *inspirational leader* they want me to become. And on top of everything, I am frustrated with how my team is resisting the change. Even when it comes to steps that actually do make sense.' His voice trails off... 'I sure as hell don't like how things are right now, but I wouldn't even know where to start to fix it.'

The dance between the individual and the collective

Whenever life feels stuck, somehow not in flow, it can be helpful to understand the location and nature of the blockage before rushing to change random aspects of our life that may or may not be the cause of our unhappiness. Instead, we can hit pause and enquire as to where we experience the biggest gap between our current and our desired reality. If we were in possession of a map, we could even systematise our exploration and conduct a thorough diagnosis. Then, once we had identified *where* something appears to be stuck, we could proceed to investigate *what* seems to be stuck, and eventually create some ideas about *how* we might be able to fix it. With this deepened understanding of the situation, we could focus our efforts and energy in the right direction and identify the lever that would result in the biggest shift towards the desired direction. That would all be wonderful.

Half of the time, however, we feel bad but either have only a vague idea about the origin of our unease, or else mistakenly suspect a source in the wrong place. This is why buying a Ferrari and getting a 23-year-old girlfriend is, at best, a temporary fix for a midlife crisis. Now, I am not saying that this wouldn't bring joy to your life on some level, but it is unlikely to resolve the issues that might be at the root of your dissatisfaction. The model I will share with you in this chapter has proven to be a very useful map in understanding more about the territory I am interested in: the landscape of the human experience.

We human beings are social animals, each of us embedded in a number of different collectives or groups. A *collective* is hereby defined as any number of individuals who interact in order to form a whole and share an identity, whether temporarily or permanently. Some of the different collectives we belong to might include our relationships, our family, the team we work with, the team we do sports with, an interest group we attend, the organisation we work for, the nation we were born into, and humanity at large.

Human experience unfolds in the constant dance between the individual and the collective. As individuals, we are part of a nearly infinite number of more or less permanent collectives. These include, for example: my family of origin, my religion, my nationality, the relationship I am in, my gender, whether I am a stamp collector, artist, or train conductor. In every moment, I am simultaneously separate (I am me, distinct from anyone else) *and* a part of different collectives/ groups (me in interaction with one or more other individuals).

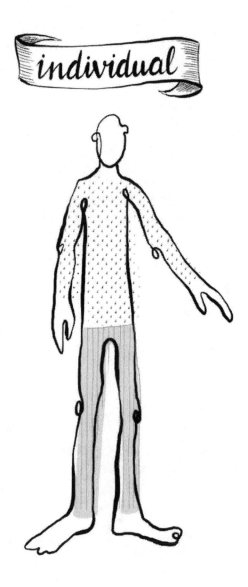

There are aspects about each perspective – the individual and the collective – which are observable, measurable, and/or quantifiable. Because we can observe them, let's call them *exterior*. At the same time, the individual and collective perspectives each have aspects that are experiential (they are experienced internally) and mostly intangible. These aspects are much harder to observe, and we will call them *interior*. When we combine the individual/collective and exterior/interior perspectives we get a four-quadrant matrix that can serve as our map for transformation.[1]

	INDIVIDUAL	COLLECTIVE
EXTERIOR	can be seen OF THE INDIVIDUAL = OBJECTIVE REALITY	can be seen OF THE COLLECTIVE = INTEROBJECTIVE REALITY
INTERIOR	is experienced BY THE INDIVIDUAL = SUBJECTIVE REALITY	is experienced BY THE COLLECTIVE = INTERSUBJECTIVE REALITY

The *top-left quadrant* allows us to relate to what can be known of an individual through observation: their behaviour (what they do) and their physical body (their *objective reality*). The *bottom-left quadrant* encompasses what is mostly invisible to the outside observer, yet known to the individual: reality experienced and expressed through thoughts and feelings (their *subjective* reality).

The *top-right quadrant* relates to what can be seen or measured about a collective: its structure, systems, and processes (their social or *interobjective* reality). The *bottom-right quadrant* encompasses that which is experienced collectively: culturally shared values, norms, and ways of communicating (their *intersubjective* reality).

	INDIVIDUAL	COLLECTIVE
MEASURABLE QUANTIFIABLE **EXTERIOR**	BEHAVIOURAL BODY PHYSIOLOGY BEHAVIOUR SKILLS INDIVIDUAL OUTPUT	SOCIAL ENVIRONMENT SYSTEMS STRUCTURES PROCESSES COLLECTIVE OUTPUT
EXPERIENTIAL **INTERIOR**	INTENTIONAL PSYCHE MINDSET CONSCIOUSNESS	CULTURAL CULTURE RELATIONSHIPS SHARED VALUES NORMS COMMUNICATION

If you wanted to study me, Nadjeschda, you could quantify and measure my body and physiology, track my behaviour and the results I produce, the skills I master and those I don't. By doing so, you would create a report of my top-left quadrant (the exterior-behavioural quadrant).

However, what happens inside of my consciousness, my feelings and thoughts, is not directly accessible to you as an outside observer (the bottom-left quadrant). What is going on in this quadrant determines how I experience others and myself. For me as an individual, the bottom-left quadrant is the centre of my subjective reality; what is created here is my concept of 'I', my thoughts and feelings – the way I experience the world.

If you now want to investigate any particular collective I am a part of, you could, for example, zoom in on a project team I work with. Through observation, you could quantify the top-right quadrant of this project team: how are we structured, the systems and processes we use, and what the output of our combined actions appears to be (exterior-social quadrant).

To you as an observer, my team's bottom-right quadrant is equally as elusive as my individual-interior quadrant. Within my team we experience a shared reality that is called *culture*. This culture is expressed through our shared norms and values and the way we communicate with each other (interior-cultural quadrant).

If this explanation of the four quadrants feels a bit dry and theoretical, consider how each of the four perspectives allows you to explore another aspect of your own world. Every quadrant brings light to another fragment of your reality. The contents of each individual quadrant can also change depending on which of your different collectives you look at. For example, if you look at yourself in the context of your family you might see habitual ways of feeling, thinking, and behaving which are very different from those you experience when in the context of your organisation.

Enquiring into the four quadrants within the specific context of one collective allows you to gain a different perspective on your life. You may feel stuck at work because you are lacking a skill that you need (upper-left, behavioural), or because you feel isolated in your team and at a loss how to create more meaningful connections with your co-workers (bottom-left, intentional). Or, possibly, you feel upset that your team doesn't have the right systems and processes in place to work effectively (upper-right, social) or because the culture of your team, the way you communicate, is lacking mutual appreciation and respect (bottom-right, cultural).

When working with Alistair, the frustrated manager you met at the beginning of this chapter, looking at the four quadrants of the transformation map helped him to resolve his confusion. We first looked at his team and identified which structures and processes were effective and which he felt were missing, or even hampering the team. We went on to identify what the current shared culture was and what needed to shift, on a values level and in the team's shared communication, to improve the general atmosphere. Eventually, Alistair was ready to look at his individual two quadrants, and it became clear to him how the mindset he was holding was causing his frustration.

In this way he identified a behaviour of his that was contributing to the problem – and that he subsequently committed to changing. The four quadrants allowed Alistair to deepen his understanding of the situation before designing a strategy that considered all, not just one, of the quadrants. Encouraged by the results this approach created in his own team, Alistair brought the four quadrants as a perspective to the leadership team of his organisation. The transformation map guided their analysis of where and why the recent change initiative had worked and where it had failed.

What lies beneath

Let's imagine our four-quadrant map as one giant iceberg.

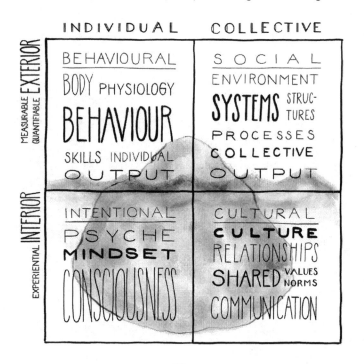

Only about 10% of the actual mass of an iceberg is visible above the waterline. The iceberg as a metaphor brings to our awareness just how much there is lurking below the surface. Because the bottom quadrants are less accessible they are too often overlooked as the root cause of the sinking ship.

When I am called into organisations which are undergoing change processes, I often observe how the lower sections of this map have been forgotten entirely. There seems to be a belief, stemming from the industrial age, that all it takes to make a company more successful or productive is to optimise its systems or structures (eg introduce better software or re-arrange who is reporting to whom), and to train people in new skills so they can be more effective at their job. Organisations that are narrowly focused on improving the two exterior quadrants (everything above the iceberg's waterline) eventually produce employees with severe change fatigue. Employees are tired of being rushed through one new system after the other and often develop resistance to new structures and procedures – even if they are sensible. I have heard countless complaints from employees who feel that new is not better but worse, because it does nothing for them but add to their confusion and sense of being overwhelmed.

Obviously, it makes sense to influence and optimise the upper quadrants, but as the management consultant Peter Drucker famously pointed out, 'Culture eats strategy for breakfast'. Unless we consider what lies below the waterline (the interior quadrants), sustainable structural change in individuals and collectives is unlikely. Change is more peaceful and takes less of a toll when driven by individuals operating from a higher level of personal awareness or consciousness.

As much as I believe it to be necessary to affect social change, to invest ourselves in creating social justice, gender equality, and affirmative action, I believe that these endeavours are more successful if we are able to acknowledge our part in having co-created the very system we seek to change. Social change leaders such as Gandhi, Martin Luther King Jr., Rosa Luxemburg, or Rosa Parks are all examples of the power of consciousness in action. The bottom quadrants of our four-quadrant iceberg (our individual mindsets and our shared mindset expressed through culture and communication) are at the heart of individual and collective transformation. They deserve a lot more attention than we typically grant them.

Some leaders believe that the saying 'you can't teach an old dog new tricks' expresses how resistant to change their employees seem to be. And they are right to a certain extent; humans will continue to do what they have always done unless they are touched at a deeper level, unless the new is embraced as sensible and meaningful, unless their thinking shifts profoundly. I believe most people are very much capable of learning new tricks and are willing to do so — if the new trick makes sense to them.

The ripple effect

Each of us holds the power to exercise true choice for one person and one person alone: ourselves. Beyond this chapter, I will therefore concentrate my attention on the individual and interior experience, the lower-left quadrant. What we think and feel — what happens in our internal reality — is the key for personal transformation. But since none of us is an island, disconnected from other people, collectives, or groups, I want to at least demonstrate how being mindful of the right-hand quadrants of our map can help to fundamentally shift our understanding of life.

For some time Andreas, a retiring CEO of an automotive supply company, had been plagued by recurring nightmares. Andreas was in his early seventies, and had been brought up during post-war Germany. In his dreams, he was haunted by images of his early childhood; he saw himself wandering anxiously through his destroyed hometown of Dresden or having unsettling interactions with his overwhelmed and disconnected mother or his angry and violent father. It was evident to me that much of what Andreas had experienced was shared by a whole generation of post-war children. To give context to the memories that haunted him, I recommended he read a book called *Die vergessene Generation: Kriegskinder brechen ihr Schweigen* (The Forgotten Generation: Children of the War Break Their Silence), which is about children born during or shortly after World War II.

During our next session, Andreas shared how reading the book had touched him deeply. 'For many years I have been so incredibly angry with my parents and how they had brought me up. I was angry at my dad's uncontrollable rage and how he beat me and my siblings, I was angry with my mother for her inability to communicate and connect with us, I was angry about how emotionally unavailable they both were and that the only thing that ever gained their acknowledgement was my success.

'But when I read this book, I was absolutely dumbstruck by how many of my most personal feelings about experiences I had with my parents were reflected in the stories of others. I realised that what I thought had just been my parents' ineptness at raising children was actually the experience of a whole generation. After all this time, I can read these stories and I feel deep grief for the life my parents – and all these parents – had. I suddenly understand that they really didn't know any better. They simply tried to make the best of an awful situation.'

Andreas and I worked on helping him release the emotional charge still connected to his memories. Very quickly, the nightmares subsided. Andreas had realised how powerfully the living conditions present at the time had influenced his personal experience. Our individual reality is embedded in a collective reality, and this reality is shaped by the existing living conditions. Whether we live in peace or in war, whether there are enough resources or not, if there is a balanced climate or natural disasters strike – the living conditions we experience will influence the systems and processes and will affect the culture, the way people interact. Every change in one quadrant has a ripple effect in all other quadrants.

If you, like me, are among the privileged few (globally speaking) to have been born during a time of peace in a democratic country, your experience may not have had the same intensity as the one that had continued to influence Andreas. But even then it can be informative or even freeing to understand the interconnection between our own internal experience, our behaviours, and the collectives we belong to and interact with – whether they are our family, our team, our organisation, or our nation.

The four-quadrant map can not only guide our understanding of a current situation, but it can also help us to articulate what change we would like to effect in the future. As stated previously: no quadrant is in itself more important than any of the others, and change in any quadrant will reverberate in all other quadrants. In order to start somewhere, we can enquire: What are the challenges I am experiencing at the moment, and therefore, what is the perspective I need to pay particular attention to?

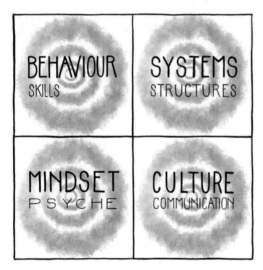

In the following real-world example, I will share with you how one of my clients, headmistress of a secondary school, used the four quadrants to guide her inquiry into her current and her desired reality for herself and the school she leads.

Real-world example

My client, Mrs Schiller, is the headmistress of a 400-pupil high school. During our coaching, she had repeatedly expressed her frustration with her faculty. To organise her thought process, we designed questions for each of the four perspectives that helped her to deepen her understanding of herself, and of herself in relationship to her faculty team:

INDIVIDUAL	COLLECTIVE

EXTERIOR

Behavioural Quadrant

1. What is my measurable contribution within the team?

2. What behaviours do I see in myself that I experience as positive and that I believe contribute to success?

3. How are my core strengths and values reflected in my current behaviour?

4. What could I do to integrate my strengths even more?

5. Which behaviours do I want to stop (what feedback have I previously received from others)?

6. How well am I taking care of my body/health in the context of my team?

Social Quadrant

1. What do I assume we want to achieve together?

2. Which systems, structures or processes are supporting or enabling us?

3. Which processes, rituals or structures do I believe would strengthen us (what is missing)?

4. Which processes or structures do I believe we should let go of (because they are limiting us)?

INDIVIDUAL	COLLECTIVE
Intentional Quadrant	**Cultural Quadrant**
1. What is my dominant emotion in the context of my team?	1. How would I describe our 'culture' based on how we choose to communicate with each other?
2. What do I believe/what assumptions do I have that are leading to this emotion?	2. What do I experience as positive?
3. What positive or empowering mindset (beliefs) do I have about my colleagues and myself?	3. What do I experience as negative?
4. Which of my need(s) do I want to focus on more, moving forward (see 'Needy Icebergs')?	4. How do we feel when we are together (positive and negative emotions)?
5. What is important to me, what do I value?	5. What do we seem to believe/ assume that leads to this feeling?
6. What do I want to create?	6. Which values do we share?
	7. What do I believe we want to create together?
	8. Which 'rules of engagement' (behaviours and communication we commit to) do I believe would support us in creating this?

INTERIOR

Mrs Schiller wrote her answer to each of the questions into an empty four-quadrant sheet and began to create some *Froms* (what is our current status quo?) and *Tos* (where would I like us to be instead?). She decided to share her reflections during the next faculty meeting and began to explain to her team how she felt, the things that made her happy, and those that kept her up at night. She talked about the unproductive behaviours she noticed in herself: the tendency to complain and blame others, the focus on the negative or the lack of sufficient resources, but also the sense of being overwhelmed, as well as her thoughts about the state of the faculty team. She spoke about realising that she wanted to work less, but with more joy. She shared her intention to focus her life on what worked instead of putting all her energy into what didn't work. Finally, she declared her wish to work as part of a team which would take joint ownership to create a school they felt excited to enter each morning.

Through the coaching, Mrs Schiller had learned to distinguish between instances where she had created problems in her mind and blown them out of proportion with her own thinking, and instances that presented tangible challenges, to be jointly addressed with her team. She painted a powerful vision of the school she wanted to lead, and the team she wanted to be a part of.

Her faculty team was touched by her openness and her willingness to be vulnerable, especially since the previous headmistress of the school had fostered a culture in which any form of personal sharing amongst colleagues felt inappropriate. Inspired by her vision, the team decided to use the four-quadrant map for a collective reflection and invited me to facilitate the process.

Based on the team's perception of their current reality, we jointly formulated questions to help them define an appealing vision of the future of their school and their team. The questions allowed them to bring to the surface what they currently experienced as positive, to determine aspects they desired to integrate, and to identify things they needed to change.

After reflecting on these questions, the next step was to define what they felt they wanted to continue in each quadrant (because it worked), what they wanted to stop (because it was limiting) and what they wanted to start (because it was missing). Each team member began to share around the question of continue, stop and start. Soon some common themes began to emerge and they recorded what felt most relevant to the process of moving forward.

The faculty team decided to use their description of their desired future during a school event at which students, teachers, and parents worked together on expanding the vision of the school they wanted to learn and be in. Their school now applies the lens of the four-quadrant map regularly to assess progress and define the next steps in their development journey. My client, Mrs Schiller, continues to base her self-reflection on the four quadrants to discover what works and to delineate actionable steps for what she wants to achieve in all areas of her life.

	INDIVIDUAL	COLLECTIVE
	Behavioural Quadrant	**Social Quadrant**

EXTERIOR

Behavioural Quadrant

Continue: Being supportive and offering help, being friendly, asking solution-oriented questions, expressing appreciation.

Stop: Complaining, nagging, taking over what someone else started, making our own contribution small.

Start: Letting others speak uninterrupted, making time for personal or deep conversations.

Social Quadrant

Continue: Monthly big team meetings.

Stop: Delegating problems or conflicts upwards.

Start: Creating smaller teams dedicated to one cohort of students (instead of teaching subject). Weekly small team meetings. Introduce listening circles into team meetings. Assign rotating meeting roles (moderator, scribe, pacer) for every meeting. Regular exchange with teachers from other teams. Invite students and parents to participate in meetings on regular basis.

	INDIVIDUAL	COLLECTIVE

INTERIOR

Intentional Quadrant

Continue: Investing in my personal growth in order to be more content and successful in this team.

Stop: Limiting mindsets:
I don't have the time. It's because of lack of resources that I am unhappy. 'The glass is half empty.'

Start: Strengthening mindsets:
I have the potential to change. You have the potential to change. I mean well. You also mean well. We have the potential to be awesome. Working together energises.

Cultural Quadrant

Continue: Sense of humour & frequent laughter. Our shared values of learning, creativity, empathy, humour, respect.

Stop: Interrupting each other, not listening/allowing ourselves to be distracted.

Start: Greet each other with eye contact every morning. Sharing more about our feelings and wishes. Taking time to truly listen to each other.

The chapter in a nutshell

Human experience unfolds in the constant dance between the individual and the collective. As individuals, we are part of numerous collectives (for eg: relationship, family, family of origin, team, organisation, sports club, nation, humanity).

There are aspects about individuals and collectives that are observable, measurable, and/or quantifiable; they are *exterior*, and elements that are experiential (they are experienced internally) and mostly intangible; they are *interior*.

The *top-left quadrant* allows us to organise what can be known of an individual through observation: their behaviour (what they do) and their physical body.

The content *bottom-left quadrant* is mostly invisible to the outside observer, yet known to the individual: reality experienced and expressed through thoughts and feelings (their subjective reality).

The *top-right quadrant* relates to what can be seen or measured about a collective: its structure, systems, and processes (their social or interobjective reality).

The *bottom-right quadrant* encompasses that which is experienced collectively: culturally shared values, norms, and ways of communicating (their intersubjective reality).

Every quadrant brings light to another fragment of our reality. There is a ripple effect: change in any quadrant triggers change in all of the other quadrants. The contents of each individual quadrant can also change, depending on which of our different collectives we look at.

Inquiring into the four quadrants within the specific context of one collective allows us to gain a different perspective on our life. The four quadrants can serve as a map for the transformation we would like to bring about.

ENDNOTE

1. The four quadrants depicted here are a simplified variation of the four quadrants developed by integral philosopher Ken Wilber (2001, 2007). Integral theory offers other highly valuable models that go beyond the scope of this book.

REFERENCES

Bode, S. (2010). *Die vergessene Generation: Die Kriegskinder brechen ihr Schweigen.* Klett-Cotta

Wilber, K. (2001). *A Brief History of Everything* (2. ed.). Shambhala.

Wilber, K. (2007). *The Integral Vision: A Very Short Introduction to the Revolutionary Integral Approach to Life, God, the Universe, and Everything.* Shambhala.

FURTHER RESOURCES

Download a PDF of the 'Transformation Map' here:
https://tinyurl.com/TransformationMap

Until you make
the unconscious
conscious
it will direct your life
and you will call it

— C.G.JUNG

CHAPTER 5

Needy Icebergs

'I am so frustrated. I do want to make this work with Frank, but it seems that every time we speak, we end in the same stalemate. Neither one of us is willing to compromise. By the end of every conversation, we are both angry and annoyed.' Elaine sighed deeply and shrugged her shoulders. 'I just don't understand where he is coming from.' She laughed bitterly and added, 'I am not even sure why everything about him feels so wrong to me. It just does. If we don't find some common ground soon, our marriage is over.'

The human iceberg

In 'The Transformation Map' we discovered how our human experience unfolds as a dance between individual realities and collective realities.

	INDIVIDUAL	COLLECTIVE
MEASURABLE QUANTIFIABLE EXTERIOR	BEHAVIOURAL BODY PHYSIOLOGY BEHAVIOUR SKILLS INDIVIDUAL OUTPUT	SOCIAL ENVIRONMENT SYSTEMS STRUC-TURES PROCESSES COLLECTIVE OUTPUT
EXPERIENTIAL INTERIOR	INTENTIONAL PSYCHE MINDSET CONSCIOUSNESS	CULTURAL CULTURE RELATIONSHIPS SHARED VALUES NORMS COMMUNICATION

The left-hand side of these four quadrants describes the individual experience, with both its exterior and interior aspects. Ever since becoming self-aware, humans have sought to understand why people behave the way they do, what motivates them, and how their self-concept is created and organised. The obscure territory below the waterline of our metaphorical iceberg, the intentional space of our psyche, has captured the attention and imagination of researchers, philosophers, and writers alike. There are as many different definitions of what defines our psyche or what constitutes *I*, as there are researchers and schools of thought. The *human iceberg* model presented in this chapter is not to be mistaken for a scientific model of the human psyche; rather it is a metaphor that allows us to shed some light onto our internal reality and how it drives our behaviour.

The iceberg analogy reflects the fact that what we can physically see of ourselves – our body and our behaviour – is only a fraction of what we are. Just beneath the waterline, hidden from direct observation, is what only we can know about ourselves from the inside out. Let's attempt to structure this unseen territory of our psyche by investigating four central components more closely: *thoughts*, *feelings*, *values*, and *needs*.

Needs

We will begin at the bottom of the iceberg by exploring our so-called psychological needs. Most people are familiar with our physiological needs (such as food, water, air, etc), but unaware that there is a set of psychological needs whose fulfilment (or lack of fulfilment) has an effect on our well-being. Humans are born with a set of psychological needs that exist irrespective of our culture and that are therefore distinct from *learned values*, which we acquire through observing our parents, grandparents, siblings, peer-groups, and society.

There are five core needs[1] that shape much of our behaviour because we go to great lengths to secure their fulfilment:

1. the need to belong/be loved;
2. the need to express ourselves autonomously;
3. the need for growth/stimulation;
4. the need for predictability/safety, and
5. the need for meaning and significance.

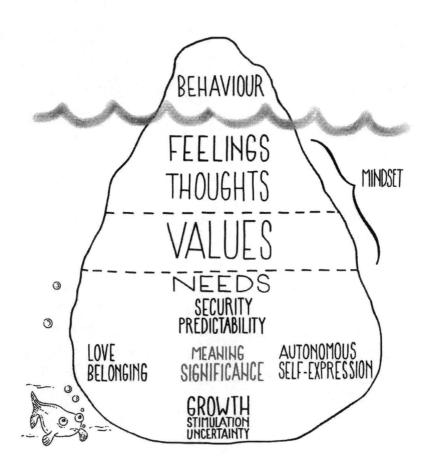

As infants we are helpless and defenceless, and our survival depends on our ability to form a stable attachment to a primary caregiver[2] (Bowlby, 1977). We are genetically programmed to attempt to create a bond with the people that nourish us and, if at all possible, even to be loved by them. Love becomes the simplest measure for the strength of the attachment we have with someone, which is in turn a survival advantage. The stronger the emotional attachment a caretaker feels, the more likely they will do everything in their power to care for us and protect us from harm. But even when we are no longer physically dependent on another to feed and protect us, this need for belonging and love continues to influence us.

While it is simple to recognise how this need plays out in our personal relationships, it is less obvious how the need for belonging and love influences us in the workplace. We usually express this need in a way that is more suitable to the professional context – instead of saying that we want to be *loved* by our boss or co-workers, we say we want to be *appreciated* or *liked*. In the end it all boils down to the same thing: as humans we are social animals, and as such we are on a life-long quest for community, closeness, acceptance, and love.

As important as *belonging/love* is to us, we are also all explorers at heart. For a child to flourish, it needs not only to know that it is loved and belongs, but needs equally to have the opportunity for *autonomous self-expression*. This parallel striving for attachment (being with) and detachment (moving away from) can be called raising a child *with roots and wings*. As babies, we express our autonomy by putting things in our mouth in order to feel and taste them, eating sand, or pulling on everything within reach. Even in infancy, we want to do things the way we want to do them. Later in life, we test our emotional range and revel in experiencing and expressing our emotions fully, whether through joy, anger, sadness, or fear.

The process of socialising a child into society usually limits the degree to which autonomous self-expression is permitted. However, depending on the specific culture, family norms, or peer group, the degree to which the child is expected to suspend autonomous self-expression varies greatly. In some cultures, the 'societal corset' is bound tightly, whereas in others the norms are looser, allowing for more room to breathe. Although we can argue that, to a certain degree, moderating the need for autonomous self-expression is the foundation of any functional society, the constant external regulation of our explorative behaviour comes at a cost. A child that is constantly corrected, stopped, shamed, or punished for expressing itself freely receives the message that its free self is unacceptable and needs to be constrained.

Given our need for belonging/love, we can't afford to risk being rejected, and we learn to turn our attention outward, instead of inward. We sense what others might want from us and shape ourselves into whatever we believe we need to be in order to be loveable – instead of expressing how we feel, what we think, and what we want. Not a few of my clients realise during coaching just how much of their autonomous self-expression they have sacrificed in order to remain accepted by their parents, peer group, and later in life by their spouses, as well as within their teams and organisations. A child that is allowed more autonomous self-expression while feeling loved is more likely to develop a greater sense of self-efficacy – the degree to which it believes it is competent to achieve desired outcomes in the real world.

Which brings us to the next central need: the *need for safety and predictability/certainty*. The need for safety and predictability is a physical survival need. On a cognitive and emotional level, we crave predictability and a sense of safety, which is not always the same as actual safety. This drive in us is so strong that we attempt to fulfil it with all kinds of things, some of which are inherently safe: a relationship, having kids, having a house, having money in our bank account, or habits and routines. Depending on our age, level of development, and contextual factors, we lean on some or all of these to make us feel safe. This notion of security is strengthened through routines and rituals that add another layer of predictability to our world. Children take great comfort in hearing the same bedtime story for the hundredth time and protest vigorously if even one word is changed. To experience the world as a predictable place and to feel safe has as many emotional benefits as it has physiological benefits. Routines and predictable events can be soothing because they allow our brain and body to relax by freeing us from constantly having to process and integrate new information.

Depending on our context and our life conditions, as well as on our own level of development, we find security, safety, and predictability in different things. Under conditions that have the potential to threaten our physical survival, we gain security from knowing there will be enough food and water. Once our physiological needs are met, we seek to create a sense of psychological certainty or safety that has little to no correlation with our physiological safety. At this point, anything can serve as a projection screen onto which we project this desire to feel safe: our relationship, our income, the savings we have in the bank, or any routines that we repeat on a regular basis.

This is not to say that relationships, a regular income, money in the bank, or routines are not pleasant to have – but we are mistaken if we believe that any of these things have the inherent power to *make* us safe. If they did, then every married person with a secure job and money in the bank would by definition feel safe – and we can surely find examples in our own environment which prove that this is not necessarily the case. Projections are a part of being human. The goal is not to dismantle all of our projections and rid ourselves of our material possessions, but rather to create an awareness of the fact that the things we believe make us feel safe do so because we have assigned this function to them – not because they actually provide safety.

Juxtaposed with our need for security and safety is our *need for growth and stimulation.* The cells and nerves in our body and brain require input in order to develop and grow. Colours, smells, sounds, movement – anything that tickles our senses or challenges our mind is stimulating to our body and deepens our experience of being alive. At the same time, an environment that is constantly in flux and requires us to adapt without pause can be disorienting and overwhelming. We need stimulation so that we can grow and differentiate, but not so much stimulation that our body goes into emergency mode and shuts us down. Fortunately, today it is no longer in vogue to break down complex work processes into minute actions that require workers to perform the same three tasks for eight consecutive hours. Even in traditional assembly-line environments like the automotive industry, manufacturers have caught on to the benefits of varying stimulation and challenges for their workers. Modern assembly lines require employees to perform a variety of tasks that keep them stimulated, alert, and engaged.

The final need is the *need for meaning and significance*. As human beings we are unique in the sense that we are fully aware of being alive in an infinite cosmos. The notion that we are, in relation to all of existence, nothing more than a speck of dust, is a potentially disorienting insight. In order to come to terms with the relative insignificance of our existence, millions of people on this planet struggle to demonstrate that our life here, now, on this planet has meaning. We build, write, paint, perform, pray, produce, and go to war, all in order to feel relevant within our context (there is a more thorough exploration of this need in 'Dance With Dragons'). The search for meaning and significance can propel a person to create and contribute in outstanding ways – or it can launch them into a toxic spiral of megalomania. But the bottom line is that most of us will suffer in environments that allow no space for our need for meaning and significance. We thrive in environments that invite us into deeper dialogue and which challenge us to create connections between our personal sense of meaning and the meaning of an organisation, project, or endeavour.[3]

As human beings we share these five core needs. However, depending on how the expression of our needs has been promoted, regulated, punished, or even ridiculed, we each develop a different centre of gravity. We might have learned to please others and suppress our need for autonomous self-expression in order to feel we belonged/ were loved by our family. Or we were expected to grow up and be independent, and any signs of wanting to belong/be loved were branded as clinginess, whininess, and neediness. Or, perhaps, we were expected to be orderly and reliable at all times, and therefore forced to repress our need for variety/stimulation. We all learned to adapt to our environment as best we knew in order to survive, even at the cost of ignoring or even disowning one or more of our core psychological needs. Although we fundamentally share these five needs, each person has naturally different intensities of needs based on their upbringing and biochemistry. Rediscovering some of our neglected needs can add a whole new side to our personality, and creating balance among the five needs brings a wonderful richness to our experience.

Values

Moving up one level in our iceberg, we reach the level of values. Whatever was deemed appropriate within the collectives in which we were raised (our parents and culture – the right-hand side of the four-quadrant iceberg) has not only influenced which *needs* we prioritise, but has shaped the rules by which we operate: our values. Values describe what is important to us – to pursue or avoid, to gain or keep. In a social context, values are, for the most part, interchangeable with norms: they define how we are expected to conduct ourselves in order to be a worthy member of a certain group/collective.

Most of our social values are shaped by *going along with or by going against* a way of thinking and being that is accepted as normal in our specific cultural context and under our existing life conditions. For example, one family might endorse the values of modesty, hard work, and dutifulness, while another family deems assertiveness, independence, and competitiveness as essential. In either case, the implicit promise is that if you live according to these values, you will belong and possibly be rewarded by having some of your other core needs fulfilled as well.

To consciously value something, an idea or a way of behaving, is a wonderful thing; the trouble starts when we forget that values are ultimately nothing more than beliefs we have acquired through role models. They are not things, they are concepts made of thought. The values I hold make sense in my particular context – but this does not necessarily make them applicable or sensible in all contexts and under all conditions. For example, in most places in Germany, you will thrive if you uphold punctuality as a value. People respect you for being punctual, and often, they simply expect it. In Brazil, however, being punctual is simply not a culturally expected behaviour. The relative importance we assign to certain values does have consequences. But what we refer to as values are words devoid of inherent meaning. The precise meaning assigned to a value is dependent on a multitude of factors. If you ask five people with different cultural backgrounds to describe what *respect* means and how to express it, you are guaranteed to get five very different definitions of the same word. This does not imply that we should not have values or not value anything. It merely points to the fact that we can improve the quality of our communication with others if we acknowledge that our values do not define us, but that we define our values.

Thoughts and feelings

Tools for developing self-awareness are unfortunately not taught in most schools, and thus many of us struggle through life entrenched in unexamined feelings and thoughts.

When things are going well for us, we see no need to examine the source of our well-being, because life is in flow and fortune appears to be kind to us. When things are not going well, we often accept our feelings as an inevitable consequence of outside events: our unreliable spouse, our bad-tempered boss, or our misbehaving children. The one thing we have not learned to consider as the cause of our feelings is our thinking. But think of it (pun intended): our mood can shift in a split second, the moment a new idea enters our mind. We have the ability to go from tears to ecstatic laughter in mere moments – all because of a thought.

Imagine this situation: Your boss says something to you and you don't quite catch it, but you think you heard her say something dismissive or even critical about you. The moment you think this thought, you get a feeling – it might be fear (a sinking feeling in your stomach) or it might be anger. You then decide to double-check if what you thought you heard her say was really what she said. To your relief, you find out that you had only misunderstood her. Your feelings change again; you begin to relax. In the outside world, nothing has changed. In the inside world, everything has changed.

What complicates our expression of feelings is that often, when we attempt to describe how we feel, we are actually describing what we think. Here are some examples of thoughts mistaken for feelings:

- I feel you don't trust me.
- I don't feel understood.
- I don't feel heard.
- I feel judged.
- I feel let down.
- I don't feel appreciated by you.
- I don't feel safe.

Just because we pre-empt a statement with 'I feel...' doesn't make it a feeling. The psychologist and emotion researcher Paul Ekman determined that there are actually fewer than twenty basic emotions:

1. Amusement
2. Anger
3. Contempt
4. Contentment
5. Disgust
6. Embarrassment
7. Excitement
8. Fear
9. Happiness
10. Guilt
11. Pride (in achievement)
12. Relief
13. Sadness
14. Satisfaction
15. Sensory Pleasure
16. Shame
17. Surprise

While we have many more nuanced words and phrases for different affective states, they are all derived from the same emotional building blocks: frustration has an element of anger, feeling depressed is a form of sadness. If we use the above list as a starting point for describing what is real for us emotionally, we create more clarity in our communication and make it easier for another person (and often for ourselves) to understand how we truly feel.

For example, if I feel upset with a colleague, the first step towards a constructive communication is for me to recognise what I really feel. Do I feel anger? Contempt? Or perhaps even embarrassment? Only when I know how I feel can I begin to share with the other what is true for me. Communicating our feelings is a powerful way to bridge the gap to the heart of another person, because humans have the natural capacity to understand and relate to emotion.[4] Moreover, to express ourselves, to put words to our internal mumblings, requires us to 'see' our own thought processes, which is again essential not only to understanding ourselves but also to giving another person the chance to understand us.

Since the majority of our thoughts are subconscious (just below the threshold of our full awareness), it often seems as if our feelings come out of nowhere, as if they are a direct and inevitable consequence of the external reality we are confronted with. We will explore the connections between thought, feelings, and reality on a much deeper level in the chapters to come (especially in 'The Butt-Naked Emperor' and 'This Too Shall Pass'). For the time being, consider the possibility that our feelings are not caused by events outside of us, but instead are the result of what happens inside of us.

Behaviours

Our thoughts are not only the source of our feelings, but they also guide our behaviour. The quality of the behaviour of any person is a reflection of the quality of their thinking. From the acting person's perspective, within the realm of their logic, their behaviour makes perfect sense.

Tragically, as long as we are unconscious about what we feel and why we feel what we feel, our icebergs are blindfolded, crashing into other icebergs adrift in the rocky sea of life. Decked out in protective armour and equipped with deadly weapons, we brace ourselves for confrontation with other, often seemingly hostile, icebergs. We act out with language, or, in some instances, even physically, because we feel that our needs or values are threatened or our feelings are being hurt by someone else's behaviour.

As long as we operate from the assumption that the other person is the problem, while remaining blissfully unaware of what is going on in our own iceberg, confrontations with other icebergs often erupt into conflicts and rarely result in a mutually satisfactory resolution. Even though it may not appear like this at times, we are all trying to do our very best, given what *we think* it takes to fulfil or protect our needs and values. The more core needs/values my behaviour *appears* to fulfil, the more likely I am to repeat it, and the more likely it is that it becomes habitual – even if it doesn't really contribute to a sustainable solution (which would require me to also consider other people's needs and values).

For example, if I observe that screaming gives me control over my chaotic environment and protects me from others invading my autonomy, I will continue to scream. Now, screaming is usually not appreciated by those around me, since they may perceive it as violating their core needs, such as their need to be loved/to belong (aka: be respected), or their sense of control or autonomy. But even if I only experience momentary relief through screaming, my brain's reward system is triggered, which in turn will make it more likely that I will scream again.

Understanding the causal chain of thought, feelings, and behaviour empowers us to transform this process. Getting 'onto the balcony' allows us a bird's-eye view of our life — instead of remaining 'on the dance floor', where we execute the same mindless motion over and over. It brings us to a point of choice to see how our thoughts create feelings and how these feelings result in behaviours that in turn create consequences in our life. Awareness of the infinite cycle of thought-feeling-action is the essence of conscious living.

Benefits of diving deeper

In the chapter 'Look Who's Talking', we discovered that what we call 'I' is actually a construct made up of rather different facets or parts. Each of these selves functions like an independent iceberg, equipped with its own set of thoughts, beliefs, values, and even behaviours. When exploring our selves, we are therefore really exploring icebergs: the particular way that each of our selves experiences life and the strategies that this self has employed to cope.

The consequences of our actions and thoughts in our lives have tangible benefits and costs. When we begin to examine what we do and why we do it, we may begin to notice more than a few gaps in our logic; what we thought to be essential to fulfil and protect our core needs/values, may in fact have the opposite effect – or come at a great and hidden cost. Upon closer investigation, we may discover that our behaviour is only serving the fulfilment of our needs on a very superficial level, that we are fulfilling one need at the expense of other core needs, or that there could be easier and healthier ways to meet our needs altogether.

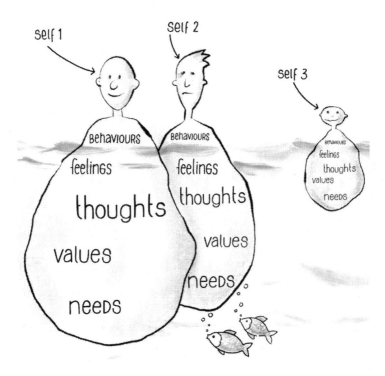

Do you remember Elaine from the beginning of the chapter? She was at a loss as to how to save her marriage. Every interaction she had with her husband Frank ended in conflict, and she was unable to understand him and felt incapable of liking him for who he was. During our conversation, Elaine began to see that not only was she lacking insight into who he was and what he wanted, but that she had very little understanding of who *she* was, what beliefs were driving her own behaviour, and what she wanted. When we looked at some of her less constructive behaviours, Elaine was able to unravel the hidden logic behind them. She was flabbergasted at discovering some of her underlying assumptions and how she had formed them, but was even more touched when she could finally find words for her own feelings and wants.

Understanding her own iceberg allowed Elaine to communicate to Frank what was true for her, what she thought and felt, without having to attack or blame him. Not surprisingly, Frank responded to Elaine's vulnerable self-disclosure much better than to her previous accusatory rants, which had focused entirely on his shortcomings. Eventually, Frank agreed to come to coaching with Elaine. In the couple's coaching process, Frank began to voice what was true for him, and they deepened their mutual understanding even further. Frank and Elaine's newfound insights into their icebergs re-kindled their love and admiration for each other, and they ended up saving their marriage.

Diving below the waterline of our own iceberg is a pre-requisite if we want to improve our relationships with others. Other people can't read our mind (or at least I haven't met anyone who can) and therefore it is our responsibility to communicate what we think, feel, value, and need. The more we understand our own iceberg, and especially understand how we are seeking to fulfil our values and core needs, the easier it becomes to make our intentions and motivations transparent to others. If we do this, we create the opportunity for others to respond to us in a similarly constructive way. The resulting deeper mutual understanding is the foundation for constructive communication between people.

At the same time, knowing that each of us has different levels to our icebergs may allow us to understand how someone else's behaviour makes perfect sense within the logic of *their* thinking. The next time your spouse, child, or co-worker does something you don't understand or approve of, you can try to see which need they might be trying to protect with their behaviour. Do they crave appreciation? Autonomy? Do they want to regain a sense of control? Are they yearning for growth and stimulation? Or is their quest for meaning and significance driving them? You can test the validity of your assumption by asking directly what is at stake for them. Asking with empathy may even help them to challenge their thinking *and* discover more effective ways to get what they want – whether it is appreciation, control/safety, freedom, growth, or significance.

Real-world examples

Why do I always say yes when I actually mean no?

Karen, a consultant in her mid-thirties, was feeling constantly overwhelmed at work. It seemed that regardless of how many things she crossed off her to-do list, the list kept getting longer. When I asked which one of her behaviours most likely contributed to her experience of the pile of to-dos always increasing instead of shrinking, she immediately had an answer: 'I never say no. My colleagues know that I am friendly, helpful, and dependable. If anything needs to get done, they come to me and ask for support. I have a reputation for never turning anyone down.' In order to produce more clarity for Karen, we looked at what happened on each level of her iceberg when she found herself saying yes even when she really wanted to say no.

Level by level, Karen came to appreciate how her behaviour made sense: she said yes (her behaviour) because she believed (her thoughts) that she was a helpful person by nature (and helpful people don't turn others down) but also because she believed that she had to prove her value to the team. The progression of thoughts and feelings connected to this yes-behaviour looked roughly like this: directly after saying yes to someone, she felt proud of herself (because her saying yes pleased the other person or made them grateful). Very quickly, however, the feeling of pride would give way to frustration and even resentment towards this person.

When I asked her what thought preceded her frustration, Karen was puzzled 'I am not sure I follow. What do you mean? What thought?' 'Well, if we assume that our feelings are triggered by thoughts, then frustration was triggered by a thought. So what are you thinking about yourself and/or about your colleague that makes you feel frustrated?'

Karen paused before speaking again. 'Two things. I guess I believe that I caved in. That I am weak because I said yes again even though I actually don't have the time. And I am resentful towards my colleague because I think that he shouldn't have asked me to do this. He saw how much I already have on my plate. Therefore, if he asks me to do this, he is knowingly taking advantage of me.' Listening to her own reasoning made her grin. 'Okay, I see how these thoughts make me feel frustrated.'

Karen continued by identifying the two main values she served by saying yes: being helpful and promoting harmony. At the very bottom of her iceberg, Karen realised that saying yes served no less than three of her core needs: to belong/to be loved, security/predictability, and meaning (which for her meant to make a contribution to the team). To discover the structure of her iceberg helped Karen to understand how her current behaviour was sensible – in line with how she believed she needed to act in order to fulfil and protect her core values and needs.

I asked Karen where she believed she had learned that, in order to belong or be loved, she needed to say yes to every request. She thought for a moment and then her face lit up. 'I can't remember ever being different. I have always done this! When I was little, my mother was very ill. My siblings and I learned that to please her we had to do two things: firstly, to not fight and to keep harmony among us at all costs and secondly, to do as we were asked to without complaining. Saying no wasn't really an option. As long as I stuck to these rules, I was rewarded. If I didn't, I was shunned, which usually meant being sent to my room alone for the rest of the day while my siblings could play next to my mother's bed. I hated being in my room by myself.' Karen grew quiet.

'What are you thinking now?' I enquired.

'I am thinking that my mantra of *Yes, I can!* is clearly not working.'

Karen had realised how her implicit strategy did not really produce the results she wanted. Given her frustration and resentment, the harmony she appeared to create by saying yes now appeared shallow and fake.

Underneath her waterline, she felt anything *but* harmony. I challenged her to consider the costs *and* benefits connected to her current behaviour and write them down in a matrix. As she filled in the columns, she was surprised by the number of costs and benefits that saying yes produced simultaneously. She was mostly surprised to see that the three needs she had put into her gain-category were actually only met superficially.

Karen summarised her insights by saying, 'How can someone love or appreciate me when I am pretending? I am not saying the truth half of the time, so whatever they are appreciating, it is not *me*. I know that saying yes gives me a sense of security because it feels as if I can control what is happening, but in fact I am constantly letting myself be directed by others people's wishes and agendas, and I exercise very little control over my own life. By doing all these bits and pieces here and there, I am not making the most meaningful contribution I could. It is as if I have been hiding behind all these menial tasks in order to avoid creating disharmony – or worse, being excluded.'

It had become clear to Karen that she had hoped to buy a sense of belonging and appreciation by being helpful, when in fact she was making it impossible for anyone to love her for who she truly was. Additionally, she wasn't contributing at the highest level, because she was constantly draining her energy on tasks that were not driving her greater vision, and she actually felt out of control because the demands of others were running her life. Stunned by the consequences of her yes-strategy, she exclaimed, 'This is silly! I don't want this anymore!'

We now turned our attention to how she wanted her iceberg to appear instead. Starting with the tip of the iceberg, I asked her what she would like to be able to say or do (instead of automatically saying yes). 'I guess there are situations when saying yes is actually okay. But I know when I would rather say no. In those cases, I want to say no with conviction, which means not drowning my no in long justifications. And I want to continue to be warm and friendly when I say no. In the past, it felt as if the only no I was able to produce came from a very cold and defensive place.'

In order to find more support for her new behaviour, we went to the bottom of her iceberg. Karen decided that focusing on autonomous self-expression would make it more likely that she could say no with conviction and warmth. 'I realise now that if I want people to truly like and accept me, I have to be authentic; to say what I think and share what I know to be true for me.' I prompted her to identify which of her other values would support her in this new way of being. All of us have an entire treasure chest full of values: principles we believe in and priorities that we have defined for our life.

So far Karen had chosen to give priority to helpfulness and harmony, and she decided that going forward, her values of honesty and clarity might serve her more powerfully. When I asked her to imagine what she might think and feel when acting from the foundation of her values of honesty and clarity while being firmly grounded in autonomous self-expression, she replied, 'I would feel energised! Obviously, saying no does not mean I am a bad person. It just means that I am honest, and I can even imagine that people will respect this more. At least I respect people who are honest. I would certainly simply feel happier because I am expressing integrity whenever I say no.' Through gaining new awareness about a very old pattern, Karen had shifted her thinking, and new possibilities of being emerged naturally.

In order to increase the momentum for this new way of being, we again looked at the costs and benefits that were associated with the new behaviour. The benefits flowed easily onto her page: 'I will have more time because I will not spam myself with stuff I don't want to do. I actually stand a real chance of being loved or at least appreciated. I will have more control over my life because I am monitoring what gets onto my agenda. And I might finally make progress with the project that I have been thinking of for so long and truly make a contribution!' When I asked her about what she thought she might risk or lose by saying no more often, it boiled down to, 'They (colleagues/clients) might not like me as much because I am less helpful and accommodating'. This thought made her visibly anxious. When I asked her about the evidence she had for this being true, Karen had none. On the contrary, she realised how deeply she respected people in her environment who were clear about their boundaries. Also, since Karen hadn't even tried saying no to anyone, she acknowledged that she was making herself anxious with an untested assumption. Eventually, Karen agreed to test her new behaviour and observe the actual reactions of people around her (instead of the imaginary reactions of the people in her head) as well as her own feelings and thoughts.

During our next session, Karen was pleased with her own progress and shared her two most important insights. 'The first time I said no to a request, I was terrified. It wasn't anything big that my colleague had asked for, it was really just a favour, but I didn't feel like doing it. And then I said that I was not available. And nothing happened! My colleague didn't even appear to give a second thought to my no – he just went on doing what he was doing.' Karen laughed, 'I was so flabbergasted that I tried it again immediately. This time, I said no in an e-mail. And again, nothing terrible happened. The person took note of my no and that was the last thing I heard. So, what I realised was that I have been making up a lot of stories about how people might feel and respond if I said no. In reality, hardly anyone seems to challenge a no. When I noticed that people just accepted my no, I stopped giving long-winded justifications about why I wasn't able to do something. There was no drama!

'Here is what really blew me away. As you know, I had dreaded letting anyone down. Sure enough, one of my colleagues did express her disappointment when I declined her request for support. She actually challenged my no. And even though there was a part of me that urged myself to just give in, I decided not to budge. And guess what? I managed to stand my ground without feeling like I was a terrible person! I had to think about our iceberg exploration, and how everyone is creating their world from the inside out through thought. That everyone's feelings are the result of their thinking. So I thought, it is not my job to make her feel good, and I am not responsible for her bad mood. I didn't feel I was the right person for the job, so I was just being authentic. To experience not feeling responsible for her feelings was so freeing.'

A few days after the interaction with her colleague, her boss insisted on Karen contributing to a project that she had not been involved with from the start. Instead of saying immediately yes, as she would have before, Karen asked for the specific expectations her boss had and for clarification as to why her involvement was vital. During this conversation they came to the agreement that some of the tasks her boss had added to her list could in fact be taken on by someone else in her team. At the same time, Karen understood why her involvement was vital for the project.

Over the course of a few weeks in which she challenged her thinking and actively changed her behaviour, Karen learned that the world did not come crumbling down just because she stopped pleasing everyone. The experiences she had, and her insights into the dynamics of her own iceberg, equipped Karen with more choice. She made the choice to take responsibility for meeting her own needs in a way that was congruent and authentic.

The lopsided iceberg

Christian, a successful entrepreneur in his late fifties, had accumulated substantial wealth with his company, which produced supplies for the automotive industry. He had come to me for coaching because he had lately been plagued by a general restlessness and dissatisfaction with his life. His dissatisfied state had caught him by surprise, and he could identify no logical reason for his feelings. On the contrary: he had reached a point in his life at which he could finally enjoy the fruits of his labour. His company was running smoothly, the kids were nearly out of the house, and he finally had free time to spend with his wife and on the golf course. 'I don't know what is wrong with me. It is as if the colours have been drained from my life. I have been looking forward to this point in my career a long time and I feel I have sacrificed a lot to get here. But now, it all feels stale.'

Christian had seemed tired and disengaged at the beginning of our conversation. As I walked him through the levels of the iceberg, explaining the connection between our behaviours, feelings, thoughts, values, and needs, he became more and more animated. As soon as I had finished explaining the last need, Christian's finger went straight to meaning/significance. He exhaled deeply. 'This is it. This is why everything seems so pointless. For the longest time in my life, I was focused on creating stability and safety – for my company, my employees, my customers. But somehow, this doesn't feel meaningful anymore. I am just not sure if making plastic casings for car headlights is my purpose. I think my iceberg is lopsided.'

Christian and I talked about, how over the course of our lifetime and depending on our circumstances, the focus of our needs changes.

In our twenties, autonomous self-expression may be the driving force for most of our actions. Once we have a family or other people who depend on us, creating safety/predictability may become more prominent. And once we have achieved sufficient stability, the need for meaning/significance may become more prominent. Every person experiences this shifting of priorities in different ways. But usually, we will observe change over time, and with the focus on different needs, our values will shift as well. And although fluctuations are natural, we need to attend to all of our needs in some shape or form in order to feel our life is balanced. So far, every one of my clients who felt dissatisfied with their life was able to pinpoint one or more needs they had neglected for too long.

Upon understanding that he did not feel his life was meaningful or that his activities were significant, Christian's energy surged. In order to identify what would feel meaningful/significant to him, we talked about the values he stood for. He identified two core values he wanted to use as his North Star: community and future generations. Christian began to think about ways he could benefit his organisation by applying these two core values. Very practically, he began to re-design the layout of the cafeteria in the building, and he hired a caterer specialised in organic food. He created a physical space which invited people to engage as a community, to meet and speak while nourishing body and soul with healthy foods. In order to promote more cross-generational communication, Christian initiated a two-way mentoring process: the most senior workers and leaders in his organisation were invited to dedicate an hour every two weeks to one of the younger employees, and the most junior hires were asked to mentor one senior in whatever they felt was important in their world – from social networking to the use of technology.

Slowly but surely, Christian noticed the changes in the company's culture; there was more communication in the hallways and in the cafeteria, which allowed for a more fluid and informal approach to problem solving and innovation. People simply talked more, and with more openness. Inspired by all the change he witnessed, Christian made the decision to postpone his golfing career and instead signed up with a foundation supporting the development of NGO-leaders worldwide. In our last session he concluded: 'I feel I am now the captain of my iceberg, perhaps for the first time in my life. I am much more conscious about where to invest my energy, and I have realised just how important *making a difference* is to my personal sense of purpose.'

The chapter in a nutshell

Our behaviour (above the waterline) is driven by our psyche (below the waterline).

Our psyche is comprised of our thoughts and feelings, our values and our needs.

Our core psychological needs are: to belong/be loved, autonomous self-expression, security/predictability, growth/variety, and meaning/ significance.

Everyone's behaviour makes sense from his or her perspective. We act how we believe we need to act in order to fulfil or protect our values and needs.

Every behaviour has specific benefits and costs. Investigating into the 'why' can help us to let go and engage with a different self that offers a different perspective.

We make assumptions about other people's icebergs (why they act this way, their future behaviours, how they feel and think). It's worth it to test our assumptions.

The more we know our own icebergs, the more we can make our intentions and motivations transparent to others – which will encourage them to interact with us more positively in the future.

Our focus on specific needs and values can change over our lifetime. If the iceberg of one of our selves feels lopsided, we have most likely lost connection with a core need that this self feels responsible for realising.

ENDNOTES

1. Depending on which author you follow, you might find much longer lists of needs than the five I refer to in this chapter. Since I believe that many so-called needs are actually acquired values, I have condensed the list to five key needs that appear to be non-negotiable, irrespective of our specific cultural context. And remember: this is a model, not a final truth!
2. John Bowlby coined the term 'attachment theory'. The theory describes how children form attachments to a caregiver, and the developmental consequences when this bond is severed or not fully formed.
3. I am aware that the acceptance of inherent meaninglessness is a marker for relativistic and systemic thinkers and fundamentalist Buddhists alike. However, since these are not majority movements, I feel it is safe to

generalise that the rest of humanity is still struggling to come to terms with this.

4. With the exception of people who have certain psychological illnesses such as narcissistic personality disorder or socio-/psychopaths and who are unable to empathise with others.

REFERENCES

Bowlby, J. (1977). *The making and breaking of affectional bonds. I. Aetiology and psychopathology in the light of attachment theory.* An expanded version of the Fiftieth Maudsley Lecture, delivered before the Royal College of Psychiatrists, 19 November 1976. Br J Psychiatry, 130, 201-210.

FURTHER RESOURCES

Download a PDF version of the iceberg illustration here:
https://tinyurl.com/Full-Iceberg

Empty FROM-Iceberg
https://tinyurl.com/FROM-Iceberg

Empty TO-Iceberg
https://tinyurl.com/TO-Iceberg

Short biography of John Bowlby:
https://tinyurl.com/JohnBowlby1

Short summary of Attachment Theory:
https://tinyurl.com/AttachmentTheoryWiki

Fear is a question:
what are you afraid
of, and why?
Just as the seed of
health is in illness,
because illness contains
information, your fears
are a treasure house
of self-knowledge if
you explore them.

— MARILYN FERGUSON

CHAPTER 6

Dance With Dragons

'She is driving me absolutely and entirely crazy. What is up with this woman?' Liam exhaled deeply and rolled his eyes.

I was coaching Liam as part of a conflict resolution process. For the past year, tension between Liam and Amber – his fellow team leader in an IT company – had worsened until it had finally reached the breaking point.

'You've heard that we have been preparing to present this new product to one of our big clients, right? As far as I am concerned, we're ready to deliver an outstanding performance. Yesterday, Amber finds out that most of the client's representatives are part of their top team. Since then, she has been frantically trying to get everyone on our end onto another team call to spin the presentation differently. No doubt she will want to create yet another one of her hyper-detailed action plans for the presentation. Amber is prepared for anything – except for things going differently than she had planned. This woman doesn't have one flexible bone in her body – her fixation with detail is off the chart! When I only so much as alluded to the possibility of her over-preparing for this presentation, she recoiled as if mortally wounded.'

Although it often doesn't seem like it, at the root of conflict with others lies fear: fear that we will not get what we want or need. Although fear is just an emotion like any other, it is one of the less popular ones, because it is connected with vulnerability and loss of control. Most of us, both unconsciously and consciously, devote a lot of time and energy to avoiding feeling fear. But being unaware of or denying fear has consequences.

Unacknowledged fears erect an invisible wall between ourselves and others. When we are unaware of how fear drives our actions, it becomes impossible to resolve conflict because we are busy fighting proxy wars instead of speaking about what we are really afraid to lose.

What if we discovered that we do not need to be afraid of fear, any more than we need to be afraid of a pillow, laughter, a knee, a brick, or a happy thought? One natural consequence might be expending a lot less energy on trying to avoid feeling fear. From a physiological perspective, the ability to feel fear has been hardwired into our system in order to protect and remove us from physical harm. This fear response is quick because it triggers our organism to fight, flight, or freeze. Fear evolved as an emergency switch, a way to protect us from imminent physical harm – not as a fire alarm that is always on. We seem to believe that our physical body is not the only thing that can die. We carry the misconception that we might not survive emotional pain, that we could somehow break. In response, we shield against attacks that threaten our emotional and mental integrity. Fear of psychological pain has the intention of protecting us from situations in which we anticipate experiencing such pain again. Yet, even if we lock ourselves in an internal catacomb we can't avoid pain, hurt, or disappointment: as long as we are alive, we feel.

Like most of you, I have experienced deep pain around situations in my past. At times, the pain was so intense that I felt nothing could protect me from certain death or damage. Most of us will have seen dramatic examples of people who appeared so damaged by abuse that they were never able to recover. So, you may ask: 'Given Nadjeschda's personal experience, and given that some people seem to be irreparably broken by their past, how can Nadjeschda claim that the 'I' of a person can't be destroyed?' Psychological research has shown how many people who have experienced abuse during their childhood can exhibit an array of different symptoms in adulthood. Research also shows that not every person responds to abuse the same way. On a physical plane, cause and effect is much easier to predict: if I cut off your arm, it is gone and won't grow back. But if I abuse you verbally, or manipulate you, or treat you like dirt – there is no way of knowing how you will respond and how long it will take you to recover.

Viktor Frankl, holocaust survivor and psychotherapist, observed that some of his fellow survivors had recovered remarkably well from their experiences. He started researching this phenomenon by investigating deeper into the nature of the emotional and mental well-being of holocaust survivors. What interested him was the very fact that not every person who had survived the horrors of the Nazi regime ended up irreparably damaged. Many did, but some displayed a remarkable ability to withstand and overcome the immense suffering they had endured. Today we call this resilience. Resilience does not mean not feeling pain or suffering in the face of adversity. It describes our ability to bounce back, like a piece of bamboo that has been battered by a storm. Even simply thinking *I am a resilient person* has the power to increase a person's resilience. Why? The ability to withstand and recover is ingrained in us.

Imagine that what we call 'I' is just an idea and not a fixed entity. If 'I' is indeed an idea and not a thing – what are we afraid could be damaged in an argument, by someone insulting or criticising us? Fear is certainly useful when it comes to moving our body out of physical harm's way. When it comes to relationships, the damage we believe could be inflicted by someone's words is imaginary. However, the trouble is that thinking and feeling are inseparable. To fear means to feel it in our body. The moment we have a physical reaction it is no longer imaginary, even if the threat was not real. We are so afraid of someone destroying this formless energy of 'I' that we hide behind physical or emotional walls, numb ourselves with substances, or attack others before they attack us. Our unconscious fearful thinking creates physiological stress-reactions in our body, as well as consequences in the outside world.

The wars we fight with others often have little or no connection to the original source of our fear: our imagined vulnerability. With our spouse we argue about unfaithfulness, when we are actually afraid they might not love us. We yell at our children for being messy, when we are actually afraid of losing control of our own life. We arrogantly dismiss the attempts of others to be close to us, when we are really afraid we might not be able to protect our autonomy. We fight against orders and rules, when we are afraid of getting stuck or not expressing our creativity. We sue our company for not giving us a raise, when we are actually afraid of not being appreciated. The fear triggered by our insecure thinking is at the root of all of our self-destructive behaviours. If we want to live in a more peaceful world, we have to acknowledge that we have fears, speak about what makes us feel vulnerable, uncover our erroneous assumptions, and see fear for what it is: just another emotion caused by a thought.

To stop being afraid of fear and to see how it is created by our thoughts rather than by outside circumstances means to transform our experience of life. For this reason, I have dedicated a whole chapter to the topic of fear. In this context, the fear I speak about is the constraint of our unconscious fearful thinking that restricts our ability to interact freely with life. This chapter will hopefully help you to understand how fearful thinking shows up in your life and how, instead of running away from your fears, you can use them as a guide pointing you in the direction of your transformation.

Needs and fears

In 'Needy Icebergs', we explored the psychological/emotional needs at the bottom of the icebergs of our different selves.

Growing up, we not only learn which ways of meeting our needs are approved of and rewarded, we also learn which are discouraged or punished by our parents, our peer group, and by society at large. The energies of four of the five needs are polar opposites in nature, and fulfilling them simultaneously can seem impossible.

On the one hand, it is essential we learn to trust life, the world, and other people, and to let others be close to us and allow for intimacy (love/belonging). On the other hand, we need to become mature and autonomous individuals, accept and embrace our independence, and differentiate ourselves from others (autonomous self-expression).

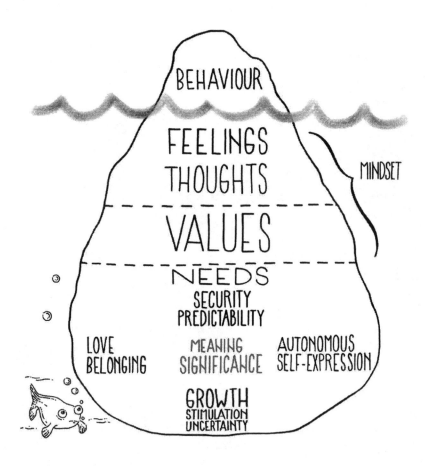

To meet our need for stability and security, we learn to be consistent, make plans, and follow them reliably (security/predictability). Yet, if we want to grow and enjoy life, we need to remain spontaneous and creative, be willing to embrace the unknown, and let go of the familiar in order to be open to change (growth/stimulation).

Our inner selves assign different importance to these needs, depending on the interaction of our biology, our upbringing, and our current stage in life. Quite often, we invest a huge amount of energy on fulfilling a need that appears crucial under our current life conditions, while neglecting the rest. The longer we (or one of our selves) serve this one need, the more readily we dismiss the other needs – and sometimes we even begin to react against people who place more importance on a different need. In order to feel balanced, we have to find some way to express and fulfil all of our needs, not just one or two (as you may notice, this is analogous to the idea of discovering and leveraging different aspects of our personality as described in 'Look Who's Talking').

While still young, we naturally depend on other people to fulfil our physical and emotional needs. However, it is a costly error to continue this dependency into adulthood. If we continue to hold others responsible for the fulfilment of our needs as adults, we make our happiness dependent on their willingness and ability to take care of us. Since they often fail to do so in the way we deem appropriate, we begin to distrust their motives and end up feeling disappointed and let down. To accept our inherent responsibility to take care of our own needs also means to reclaim our innate capability for fulfilling them better than anyone else ever could.

Now, there was a time in each of our lives where the fulfilment of our needs was indeed dependent on one or more people: as infants, toddlers, or even as young children, we needed our caretakers to fulfil our needs – physical and emotional alike. There is a connection between our needs, the fears we experience when we think this need is not being met, and patterns of behaviour.[1] If one (or more) of the core needs were not sufficiently provided for by our earliest role models, we probably developed fearful thinking and behaviours aimed at securing what we lacked. We will begin by exploring first the need/fear connection of the four needs of *love/belonging, autonomous self-expression, predictability/security* and *variation/stimulation*, before looking at *meaning/significance*.

If your life has been dominated by the need to belong and be loved, you will most likely fear rejection or separation. If your strongest need is for autonomous self-expression, you will want to run screaming when others encroach on your autonomy, smother, or engulf you. If you need a high degree of order and certainty to feel safe, loss of control and chaos are your worst nightmare. If your main objective is a life of growth and stimulation, the possibility of stagnation or being stuck makes you gasp for air.

Whatever need we put at the centre of our attention, most of us react to the associated fear as if it was a life-threatening dragon we need to run from or defeat and slay.

The 'fear dragon' unconsciously driving us can trigger rather rigid or even bizarre behaviours, of which we ourselves are often blissfully unaware. Whenever driven by our dragon-fearing thoughts, we slide into a shadow response, a behaviour that quickly becomes a liability for ourselves and others. Sometimes we may even be aware that a particular response is unhelpful or irrational, but somehow we can't help doing it anyway. The less conscious we are of the connection between our fears and our automatic shadow behaviours, the less likely we are to stop them, and the higher the risk of alienating others. Ironically, it is often precisely that shadow behaviour aimed at avoiding the fearsome dragon which creates more of what we are trying to avoid.

Dance With Dragons

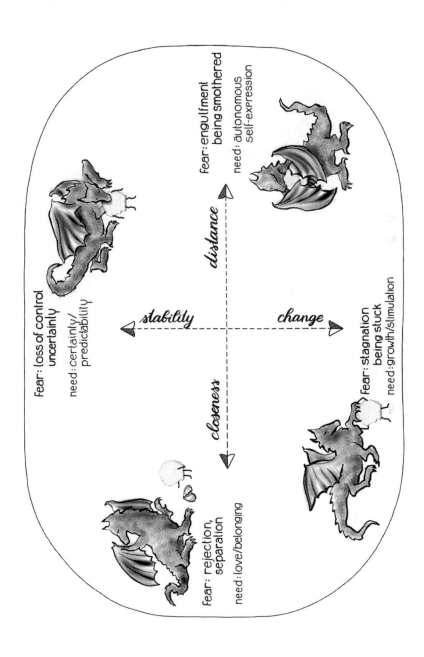

149

Let's look at how we unconsciously create what we fear the most:

If I am focused on being loved and liked, and my fear is being rejected, I might come across as a people-pleaser, acting clingy or needy. I try to be everything to everyone by suppressing my authentic self. As a result, people move away from me, because they sense my incongruence and are put off by my neediness.

If I vehemently insist on protecting my autonomy, and accuse others of engulfing or smothering me, I push them away by over-emphasising my independence. In return, they try to get my attention and affection and run after me in the attempt to elicit an emotional response. My ability to move freely is restricted.

If I try to eliminate uncertainty or potential loss of control by micromanaging my environment, I lock myself in a cage of structure and rules, and disempower others with my fixation on details and process. As a result, I experience a constant sense of being overwhelmed, because the more I try to control, the more I notice how little control I have and the more others will rebel against my rules.

If I pursue constant growth and stimulation because I am afraid of being stuck or stagnating, I repel anyone or any system that requires me to conform to agreements and rules. My stream of incessantly changing creative ideas frustrates others and stalls progress. The more I resist, the more others feel compelled to make me follow the rules, and I am left feeling restrained and lifeless.

All of these counterproductive behaviours are triggered by the assumption that behaving this way will get us what we need. In reality, our shadow behaviour very rarely gets us what we need, and quite often, it gets us precisely what we want the least.

Let's go back to Liam, the frustrated manager at the IT company whose situation I described earlier: I interviewed his fellow team leader Amber to get her point of view later the same day. When Amber began to share how the interaction with Liam had impacted her, she was shaking all over. 'I guess Liam told you how he and I had a blow-up? I am completely lost. It honestly feels as if we are speaking two different languages! I simply don't understand why it is so hard for him to be just a little bit friendlier, just a little more accommodating towards me. I mean, I get that he doesn't share my need to be prepared. At the same time, I really don't think I am asking too much if I want to have a team call prior to one of our most important presentations. But every one of my requests hits a wall and every offer is rebuffed. I don't know how to say things to Liam anymore because he is so cold and distant. It actually feels as if he is going out of his way to not talk to me, and that really makes me anxious. After all, we are in this together.'

The next day, Liam, Amber, and I met together for a conversation. In order for them to see their conflict from a different angle, we looked at the connection between needs and fears. I then asked each of them to identify where they would locate themselves on the dragon chart.

Liam spoke first. 'Well, I guess I spend the majority of my time on the right-hand side and the bottom. I really do value my autonomy, and I absolutely hate it when people run after me for approval. And I need room to be spontaneous, for new and unexpected stuff to happen. Life is full of unexpected stuff and I like that.'

Amber nodded and pointed to the left-hand side of the field. 'I suppose it's fair to say that I spend most of my time being concerned about being liked and making sure that others feel appreciated. I think I do a lot to make others happy...' Her finger wandered to the top of the drawing. 'I try to be as prepared and reliable as I can. I think that a certain degree of discipline and orientation to detail is really important. It really bugs me when people wing it and then claim that not being prepared is somehow creative – I think they are just being unprofessional.'

Based on where they gravitated to most often, I asked them to describe their understanding of the dynamic between each other.

Liam laughed. 'It appears that we truly are each other's dark twin. We are on the polar opposite on each axis.'

'Yes, that's right. I think I get it.' Amber drew a circle around the four poles with her finger. 'In many ways, we are playing cat and mouse. I am asking for attention and approval from Liam, and he runs away or blocks me. The faster he runs, the less loved I feel and the more energy I invest in running after him.'

Liam chimed in. 'Exactly. And when you run after me, it freaks me out. I feel suffocated because you are so freaking needy. All I need from you is a little space.'

I step in. 'So Liam, it seems that your credo is *if you leave me alone, I might acknowledge you did something right*, and Amber, your credo is *if you show me that you appreciate me and what I am doing, I might give you some space*. Does that sound about right?' I ask.

'Yes. Spot on.' Liam pointed to the vertical axis. 'I believe that Amber should just relax, let go and play a little. And I keep telling her that we will be fine. But of course, the more I say that, the more she worries about details. And I assume that Amber believes I have to finally grow up, be reliable, and prepare appropriately. That pretty much explains why we push each other's buttons. Clearly that's not working very well for either of us, is it? So, what are we going to do about it?'

Hidden gifts

Most of us gravitate towards one or two of the needs in particular. With each need, there is not only an associated fear and a shadow behaviour, but also a particular strength, a way to behave that comes easily to us and that is often seen as one of our natural talents.

When I asked Amber and Liam to write down what they saw as each other's strengths, they came up with the following list:

Amber's strengths:
- Always helpful
- Good at making people feel comfortable and appreciated
- Eye for detail
- Reliable
- Consistent

Liam's strengths:
- Independent thinker
- Gives people a lot of responsibility and freedom
- Creative
- Unorthodox
- Unfazed by a change of plans

Recognising the gifts and talents they saw in each other created an energetic shift in the dialogue between Amber and Liam. Instead of staying stuck in their corners and labelling the other wrong for being different, they were now open to exploring how their opposite patterns could be leveraged as complementary strengths, and open to learning what they needed from each other. To be fair, the discovery of their opposing need-and-fear pattern did not eliminate their cat-mouse (or dragon-vs-dragon) dynamic immediately. But getting onto the balcony and observing the game they played from a distance introduced a sense of humour into their relationship and enabled them to address this dynamic before it turned into a conflict.

Putting it all together, we see a complete pattern: our dragons (what we fear), the shadow behaviours we have developed to avoid or defeat our dragons, and the particular strengths or gifts corresponding with each of the four needs.

Not unlike many women I know, I grew up believing that in order to be appreciated by those around me I had to be nice, make no trouble, and be good at school. In order to do and be what I thought people expected of me, I learned to disown my need for autonomous self-expression. I became so skilled at being anything to anyone that I turned myself into a social chameleon. Driven by my craving to be liked and accepted, I sensed what was required or rewarded in a specific environment: I was the gifted artist, the intellectual student, the compassionate classmate, the witty cool girl, or the silent and obedient daughter. After a while, I lost all sense of what I thought or wanted independently of people around me. I wanted what they wanted and appreciated or snubbed things they appreciated or snubbed.

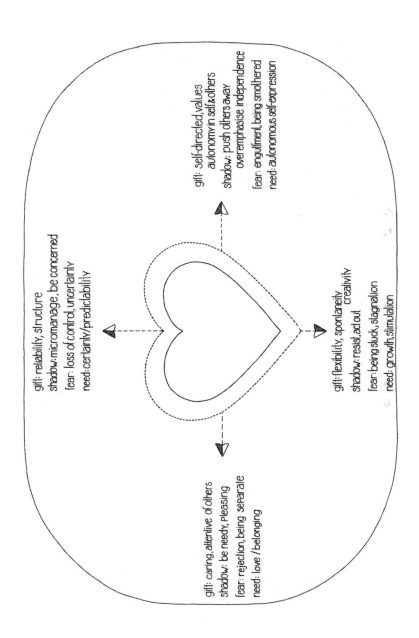

gift: reliability, structure
shadow: micromanage, be concerned
fear: loss of control, uncertainty
need: certainty/predictability

gift: self-directed, values
autonomy in self&others
shadow: push others away
overemphasise independence
fear: engulfment, being smothered
need: autonomous self-expression

gift: flexibility, spontaneity
creativity
shadow: resist, act out
fear: being stuck, stagnation
need: growth, stimulation

gift: caring, attentive of others
shadow: be needy, pleasing
fear: rejection, being separate
need: love / belonging

I was hyper-adaptable – and completely spineless. In addition to expunging my need for self-expression, I tried very hard to re-introduce a sense of structure and predictability, which my life had lacked after my parents' separation. Instead of acting out, I developed an overly strong sense of discipline and reliability that helped me establish control over my environment as well as securing the admiration of others. In some respects, this survival tactic of over-adaptability and merciless self-discipline served me well: it had a big part in getting me where I am today. At the same time, I paid a high price. In order to be accepted by the right people, I learned to be disingenuous, saying and doing the things I felt would buy me their attention. My need to control my environment manifested itself in rigidity and a tendency towards self-righteousness, which sometimes drove others away. For years, I was blind to the potential of the other two poles of the playing field (growth/stimulation and autonomous self-expression) because I could not see how to align them with my personal survival strategy.

My old patterns worked well enough until I became a self-employed coach. Suddenly it was obvious that being the nice and studious girl was not a viable strategy for professional success. To be an effective coach and give straight feedback to clients, I needed to let go of wanting to be liked and instead develop the courage to be honest and learn to articulate my opinion. And in order to run a business and offer my services, I had to stop playing small in the hope that someone would accidentally discover my greatness. I had to stand tall and promote myself. To cooperate effectively with colleagues on bigger projects, I had to be more flexible and allow for people to do things differently than I would have done them.

Whatever pattern you may detect in yourself – view it with kindness. Your survival strategy has helped you manage your fear and has got you to this level in your life. But it will probably not get you to the next. Every one of your shadow behaviours points you towards a blind spot, an area where you have been operating – consciously or unconsciously – from fearful thinking. If you learn to develop more ease in playing in all four corners of the playing field, you will unleash your full potential and become more of yourself.

Take your dragon for a spin

Virginia Satyr, a famous family therapist, once said, 'The greatest need is to experience the familiar.'

The dread of the unfamiliar – the opposite of whatever happens to be our personal centre – is what keeps us locked in our comfort zone. Our comfort zone does not necessarily represent a happy place, it is simply a familiar place where we choose to stay, even if it is toxic and even if we are unhappy. To create security through predictability is at the root of all kinds of seemingly irrational human behaviour: battered wives stay with their abusive husbands, people stay with their constantly nagging partners, and disillusioned employees stay at companies they hate working for. When I was first introduced to the idea of thinking of fear as an acronym – F.E.A.R. = False Expectations Appearing Real (see more about F.E.A.R. in the chapter 'Don't Panic') – I found it to be a clever play on words, but it didn't seem relevant in my life. Since then I have come to understand the deep wisdom contained in the F.E.A.R. acronym.

Moving through my own Hero's Journey (see 'The Tale of the Hot Potato') meant that life challenged me to become conscious of my unconscious false expectations. Once I found the first one, they kept coming. It seemed as if there was no end to the number of unconscious false expectations that were at the very core of my world. In the process of uncovering false expectations, I found one question especially useful: *What is the worst that could happen?* Looking at my answers to this question, I was rather amused by the image of doom my mind had created. The scenarios usually ended with me dying on the street as an anonymous bag lady, deserted by anyone who had ever loved me. Once I had dragged my fear dragon into the bright sunlight and investigated it more closely, I discovered that I was indeed looking at a creation of my own mind, not at Reality.

Even though a part of me seriously believed that my life could end in poverty and isolation, I had to acknowledge the utter improbability of this scenario. Most of the time I scared myself with consequences that would likely never happen – and on the rare occasion that they did happen, I was able to deal with them much better than I had anticipated. Now, even before I started down the 'what is the worst that could happen?' road, I wasn't even aware of the many things I was afraid of: being abandoned, being a failure, disappointing people, hurting someone, etc. Like a strong undercurrent, my fears had influenced me from below, confining me in an ever-shrinking comfort zone, the walls of which were decorated with embroidered sentences such as: 'I am who I am', 'This is not my cup of tea', 'You can't teach an old dog new tricks', or 'Better safe than sorry'.

To have fear is not bad or wrong. It's natural. Fear is simply a signal by our subconscious to be cautious, based on the assessment that something dangerous is happening or will happen. But the thing we are afraid of is a dragon created by our own mind. If you find your fears suffocating and want to experience something different from your current reality, this means it is time to move beyond what is familiar. Open your mind to new perspectives, discover your F.E.A.R. If you are unsure which particular dragon you might be running from, ask someone who loves you. People who know us well can, often with embarrassing accuracy, point out our blind spots on the playing field.

This makes me think of an old German joke (yes, Germans do have jokes!). A man driving on the motorway hears an announcement on the radio: 'Drivers on the A3 motorway are cautioned to proceed with extreme care! There is a car driving in the wrong direction.' After hearing this warning the man angrily shouts: '*One* car going in the wrong direction?! There are *hundreds* of 'em!'

In other words: If people who know you well point out that you are unnecessarily afraid of rejection, of being smothered, of losing control, or of being stuck – they probably know what they are talking about. If they perceive you as emotionally needy and intrusive, or inflexible and controlling, or impertinent and unorganised, or emotionally shut down and distant, there is probably some truth to that. But even if another person can see something about your behaviour or mindset that you haven't yet discovered yourself, this does not make you wrong or a bad person. You did what you thought you had to as well as you could. And now it might be time to update your GPS and step outside of your comfort zone!

When it comes to relationships, we are often amazingly skilled at attracting people into our life who are comfortable in the corner of the playing field that is uncharted territory for us. It is quite easy for us to fall in love with someone *because* they are different, but it is not so easy to stay in love with someone *despite* them being different. We are attracted to someone very independent with a free spirit – until we feel rejected by them, which is when we will try anything to break their will. We are touched by the warmth and attentiveness of a person – until we find them smothering, and start pushing them away. We admire the structure and discipline of someone – until we feel they want to put us in a box, and we begin to ridicule them for being rigid and inflexible. We are enamoured with a creative person who creatively dances with life – until we feel they broke a commitment, and we attack them for being unreliable and flimsy.

Our closest relationships are often our most challenging relationships – whether this is with our spouse, our parent, or our child. Often, these people push our buttons because we feel threatened by them acting out a pattern opposite to our own. If this is the case, our position on the dragon field can help us identify where to head next. The quality that can enrich us and expand our skillset most, our growth opportunity, usually lies in the space opposite to us. If we meet a person who represents our opposite pole, this person has the potential to become our greatest teacher; they already know how to do what we struggle to learn. Curiously, when we dare to leave our home turf instead of embracing our strengths, we sometimes drop into the *shadow behaviour* of the pole opposite us.

For example, if my dragon tells me I won't be loved and appreciated, I may pre-emptively close up and push people away to demonstrate

I don't need them anyway! If I catch myself doing that, I can recognise the F.E.A.R.-dragon driving my behaviour. Instead of acting from this shadow, I can make the conscious choice to explore the other side of the dragon field. If I can discover what people who spend a lot of time 'over there' do well, I can begin to integrate this strength or gift into my own repertoire; by expressing myself autonomously, acting more independently, speaking my mind, and doing my own thing. And just in case you wonder: this doesn't mean I urge you to become a different person or that everyone should be equally comfortable and skilled in the four corners of the playing field. However, stretching the boundaries of your comfort zone will allow you to move more joyously through life and will give you more options to choose from. Take your dragon for a spin and see what happens!

The master dragon

According to the philosopher Ernest Becker (1971), there is one ultimate fear, deeper and older than all the fears we have explored so far: the fear of non-existence – or, in other words, the fear of the death of ego. Because of its existential nature, we could call it the 'master dragon'.

As far as we know, humans are the only species with the consciousness of being alive as well as having the consciousness that we could (and someday will) not exist. The notion of *I could not exist* is distinct from the knowledge of *I will die*. Theoretically we know that all living things will die. Non-existence confronts us with the question of the ultimate relevance of our life. What if there is not a higher purpose to our existence? What if, in the grand scheme of things, in the vastness of the universe, it doesn't matter if we are or if we ever were?

Becker proposed that being fully aware of the potential of our non-existence and with it the potential meaninglessness of our life strikes a terror so deep it has the power to overwhelm us. In order to avoid feeling this terror, humanity has created buffers to shield itself against this disempowering and ever-present fear. We seek solace in a shared cultural worldview, a socially structured fiction, which connects us to other members of our 'in-group'. Our cultural worldview provides a blueprint for a meaningful life that embellishes our existence with purpose and is the source of our self-esteem. Through the ages, we humans have thought up contexts and stories in which belonging to our particular in-group makes us meaningful, powerful, or even immortal. To protect ourselves from the void we build empires, fight wars, invent religions and worship god(s), build temples, believe in life after death, destroy unbelievers, write books, amass riches, and found nations. It might be an oversimplification to claim that all cultural and religious achievements are founded on the avoidance of fear of non-existence – there are many other theories offering alternative understandings of the origins of human drive and motivation. But there is no denying that humans have pondered the question of the purpose of their existence for as long as they have possessed self-awareness, and that the quest for an answer is at the centre of all religions and philosophy.

For some people, the notion of a fear of non-existence immediately rings true while others will claim never to have felt afraid of not existing. Whether you have ever been aware of this fear or not, you might be surprised to know how it probably impacts you unconsciously. Based on the ideas of Becker, a group of social psychologists developed what they coined the *terror management theory* (Rosenblatt et al., 1989). On the hypothesis that everyone is subconsciously affected by the fear of the void, they came up with some rather entertaining experiments to test how people would change their beliefs and actions when they were reminded of their own mortality (which is how they operationalised the fear of non-existence for experimental purposes). What they found was that prompting people to subconsciously think about their mortality does in fact have the power to change their worldview and behaviour, an effect that could be replicated across different cultures and religions. They also found that people who deny being afraid of not being or of dying (in other words: who suppress the inevitability of their own demise) think and act very differently from people who consciously reflect about their own mortality and the fears this brings up.

In one of their famous studies they recruited unsuspecting students to participate in an experiment about creativity. While the students were waiting for the start of the experiment, a researcher different from the one who recruited them walked into the room and asked if they minded filling out a questionnaire to gather data for a different study. Of course, the questionnaire they received was in fact part of the experiment, but they wanted to ensure that the participants did not make a link between the questionnaire and the task they were asked to complete later. The questionnaire asked them a bunch of innocent questions about their preferences for leisure activities. But half of the group received an additional set of questions that ever so subtly prompted them to think about their own death (interestingly, none of the subjects later recalled having answered questions about death). According to the researchers' hypothesis, the participants who had previously been reminded of their own mortality should feel a greater need to identify with cultural or religious symbols because those anchor our individual life in a meaningful collective frame of reference.

Upon completion of the questionnaire, each participant was led into a room in which they had to solve a problem creatively. In one experiment, the participant was given a crucifix and a nail, and was asked to hang the crucifix on the wall. Since there were no other tools in the room, the only solution was to use the crucifix as a hammer. The students who had subconsciously been reminded of their mortality needed significantly more time to come up with and choose the crucifix-as-hammer solution than the students who had not been reminded of their mortality. As the researchers had predicted, the symbolic significance of the crucifix to those participants had become inflated by their being reminded of their own mortality.

In another setting the creative task consisted of separating out black ink, which was mixed with sand in one container, by pouring the ink into a second container. The only object in the room that could be used as a makeshift strainer was an American flag (in other countries, they obviously used the flag of that respective country). Participants who had been reminded of their mortality again took significantly longer to use the flag as a filter to separate the sand from the ink. For them, to soil the Stars and Stripes had become sacrilege, since the flag had increased in meaning for them when they were confronted with their own mortality. Even more than before, it had become a symbol of their identity and belonging.

In yet another study, random people passing by on a street were interviewed either while facing a department store or while facing a funeral home. The interviewer inquired about their views regarding topics such as equality of same-sex marriages, diversity, integration, and immigration. When interviewed in front of the funeral home, people became more conservative in their political views, more nationalistic, less accepting of different life-styles. At the same time, triggering their mortality made people more likely to accept violence as an acceptable measure to enforce their cultural or religious rules and norms on others.

In the terror management studies, the topic of their own death never consciously registered for any of the participants, but they still adapted their beliefs and behaviours based on this inkling of non-existence. Terror management studies have proven how even a subtle reminder of the fragility of our existence is enough to have people barricade themselves behind cultural and religious symbols, because these bestow our lives with meaning and purpose and give us a sense of belonging.

To my great relief, the researchers also discovered a very simple cure for our unconscious reaction to this master dragon: look at it, talk to it, be kind to it. It seems we change for the better when we face the big questions about life, death, and meaning head on instead of hiding from them. The terror management data showed that people who deliberately engage in deep conversations about death, and the meaning of life and the universe, become measurably more open-minded, more accepting of diversity, more empathic towards the disenfranchised, more willing to help others in need, and less ready to see violence as a solution for cultural or religious conflict. So, here as well the same principle applies: dance with your dragon, drag it into the sunlight, tickle its belly, and show it to others. It might just become your favourite pet.

Soul need

We have already discovered that behind every fear there is a deeper yearning. The yearning behind the fear of non-existence is connected to the need of our soul: to know our life has meaning and that we matter. In the life of many of my clients, this fear shows up as the nagging feeling that they are not yet doing their thing, that they are somehow not delivering on their purpose. As a result, their lives feel flat, devoid of a deeper meaning. To listen to our need for meaning and significance can be a powerful and positive driver for creativity and change.

At the same time, being blind to the need for meaning, and therefore blind to the fear of non-existence, can create unpleasant results. On a personal level, the drive to qualify the relevance of our existence can inhibit our ability to enjoy the moment. We work towards ever-increasing levels of influence, power, and wealth, hoping for peace of mind as a reward. Compelled to leave a mark in the fabric of history, we are much like teenagers carving 'I was here' into the trunk of a tree. Even worse outcomes can entail, if whole groups of people are blind to this fear in their hearts. Terror management theory is based on the assumption that in order to avoid facing the dragon of non-existence, humans have created cultural and religious reference points against which we can measure the meaning of our life. By these standards, the *right life* is one that obeys the rules and furthers the established way of life. The more I live by the book (whatever the book may happen to be), the more meaning I am promised in return.

The bearers of this kind of institutionalised meaning see anyone who does not defer to the written (and unwritten rules) of the book as a potential threat. They will ridicule, persecute, and sometimes even kill people who think outside of the box of their cultural or religious boundaries. Because if there are no absolute truths, then how can I measure the significance of my own accomplishments? How do I know that I matter? In this light, the recent surge of young European men and women joining the cause of the Islamic State and the rise of popularism in the West can be seen as a desperate outcry for significance and meaning by people who otherwise feel disempowered, marginalised, and irrelevant.

If we allow the fear of non-existence to drive us subconsciously, we turn life into a struggle for power and personal relevance without ever really getting away from our fear. Paradoxically, terror management research has demonstrated that nothing makes us feel more alive and more connected to others than when we relax into the inevitability of our non-existence (at least to the inevitability of our non-existence in this physical form – who knows what happens next?). The more we accept that we, in this body, are but a very temporary expression of life's energy, the more contentment we find in being alive in the here and now and being connected with the world around us.

In her book *My Stroke of Insight* (2009) the neuroscientist Jill Bolte Taylor describes her astounding experience of observing her own brain during a stroke, and her resulting shift in perception and experience. As her left hemisphere (which is responsible for much of our logical reasoning and abstract thinking) was slowly shutting down, the notion of 'I' began to dissolve while at the same time the experience of being *one* with everything became a tangible reality for her. What Taylor's experience points to is that the illusion is our 'I', rather than our *one-ness*. My own understanding of oneness is based on the rather prosaic fact that *I am* an inseparable part of life. I already belong because I am part of the miracle unfolding in the universe on this planet. When my physiological existence ends, my energy is funnelled back into the big pool of everything that has been and everything that is yet to be.

To think that our existence is both utterly insignificant *and* utterly meaningful at the same time seems contradictory at first glance. On the one hand, it is highly unlikely that any individual existence will affect the course of the universe. On the other hand, each of us matters. Because we are alive. Because there are people around us whose lives we affect every single day. Because we affect the fate of humanity and the fate of all life on this planet. Because we are an expression of life itself and need to believe we matter in order to protect it. And although I don't believe that I have a predetermined purpose, I believe that choosing my purpose based on the talents and gifts I have is a worthwhile quest. The question therefore is not 'what is my purpose?' but rather 'what do I choose my purpose to be?'.

Putting all the parts together, our needs, fears, the associated shadows and gifts/strengths, we end up with a 'self-realisation compass'. On it, our biggest growth opportunity may lie directly opposite to us. We can choose to leave our comfort zone and our familiar dragon behind. If we embrace the gifts of our opposite pole and discover strengths in us that maybe most unlike us, our options in life will increase.

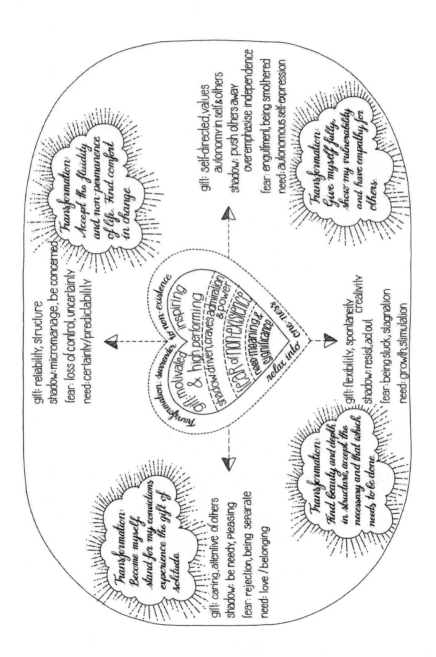

gift: reliability, structure
shadow: micromanage, be concerned
fear: loss of control, uncertainty
need: certainty/predictability

Transformation:
Accept the fluidity
and non-permanence
of life. Find comfort
in change.

gift: self-directed, values
autonomy in self & others
shadow: push others away
overemphasise independence
fear: engulfment, being smothered
need: autonomous self-expression

Transformation:
Give myself fully,
show my vulnerability
and have empathy for
others.

Transformation: surrender to non-existence
gift: motivated, inspiring
& high performing
shadow: driven, craves admiration & power
FEAR OF NON-EXISTENCE
need meaning &
significance
relax into

Transformation:
Become myself,
stand for my convictions,
experience the gift of
solitude.

gift: caring, attentive of others
shadow: be needy, pleasing
fear: rejection, being separate
need: love / belonging

Transformation:
Find beauty and depth
in structure, accept the
necessary and that which
needs to be done.

gift: flexibility, spontaneity
creativity
shadow: resist, act out
fear: being stuck, stagnation
need: growth, stimulation

Real-world example

Eric, the CEO of a medium-sized company, wanted to speak about the panic attacks which had plagued him his whole life and that had become more frequent in recent years. He described how the panic would descend on him without any apparent warning signs, leaving him fighting for air, frozen with fear.

The topic clearly made him nervous, and he paced up and down the room until settling in one of the chairs. I asked him to describe what he knew about his panic attacks.

'Well, I guess am afraid of a lot of big issues of the world and the universe, meaning, death, and afterlife. Those sort of things. I worry about holding it all together. Since I turned fifty-four, it makes me feel more vulnerable than ever to think about these questions. When I do, I get really anxious, my breathing changes, and I feel as if I will faint.'

When Eric got up, he leaned on the window frame, looking at the tree outside. 'I noticed that when there is more uncertainty in my life, these panic attacks caused by metaphysical questions come more frequently. It is usually in the quieter, more meditative moments when my thoughts begin to wander that I suddenly notice how the tightness in my chest sets in. Other than that, there seems to be a long fuse from any actual event in my life to my feelings of panic. I am not entirely sure how they are connected.'

'So, what is the connection you see?'

'When I was thirteen years old, my mom passed away, and I never really grieved for her until I was twenty or twenty-one years old. It was around that time I had the first panic attack too. That certainly was a long fuse – from her death to the first panic attack. Now, as I grow older and get closer to death myself, I begin to worry. Because I can see the end of my life and there are some new issues to manage, such as illnesses that weren't there before. All of a sudden I am not sure I can hold all of it in anymore.'

'What do you mean?'

'Since my first panic attack at twenty-one, it seems like I have managed to hold it all in. I believe that a lot of the drive and ambition I developed was actually a way of managing my fear. I worked very hard and achieved a lot by most standards – it seemed the only thing I could do in order to feel tethered. At the time of my mother's death I felt so alone and abandoned, everything was pointless. And by getting the approval and appreciation of others, my teachers, my dad, I somehow felt less disconnected and alone. But then came the first panic attack.

'Since then, I have been afraid of having a mental breakdown, perhaps having to be institutionalised, or to become homeless, or that I would turn into a vegetable.' Eric paused. 'I guess it's not a very realistic fear, is it?' He looked at me, shrugging his shoulders.

'Why do you shrug your shoulders?'

'Well, I am realising that by doing what I have done, I may have actually kept myself safe and sane all of these years. Perhaps I did the right thing for myself?'

'If you think about it like that, that what you did kept you safe and sane – how does that feel?'

'I guess I feared that underneath all that is the real me. I saw the panic attacks as proof of what would happen if this real me had a chance to come out. Thinking about it now, I suppose that managing it was just my way of dealing with the anxiety triggered by my mother's premature death the best I could. I guess it turned out okay.'

I smiled when I saw Eric's body relax into the chair.

'Yes, now it seems strange that managing my anxiety felt like a weakness to me, like an illegal trick I had to hide from other people.'

Eric paused. 'Wow. Now I am thinking of the enormous energy I invested over all of these years into managing my anxiety, hiding the fact that I am managing it and outperforming everyone else. And all in order to prove how normal and well-adjusted I am.

'So, perhaps there is something else here... what if I gave myself permission to not be special, to not always excel, and to not always be well-adjusted. To be okay with how I am. But if I allow that, am I not just three feet from the coffin?' He chuckled. 'What do you think?'

I squinted at my notes and grinned. 'Interesting. As you were talking, I scribbled, "it's okay to be special" – even though what you said was "it's okay to not be special". But perhaps this mental Freudian slip is actually pointing to something helpful here. Perhaps you have been trying so hard to prove something that is a given anyway. You are special. Because of your drive, because of your fears, because you are asking yourself all of these big questions. But you didn't want to be *this* kind of special, you wanted to be *that* kind of special. And you invested a lot of effort to make everyone see that you are *that* kind of special.'

'That is funny.' Eric laughed. 'You are right. I like that. I don't have to be *that* kind of special because *I am* already *this* kind of special. But why do you think I fought so hard to be recognised as the right kind of special in the eyes of others?'

'I actually think what you are describing is something many people struggle with. Remember the idea of the dragons we run from? We want to be recognised as special because it gives us meaning and significance. To feel meaningful and significant is important to us. Connected to this need is the fear of non-existence, of the master dragon. We know that we exist, but we also know that we have not existed and will not exist. This brings up the question how any of this, how our individual life, even matters. A part of us is aware that the world will continue to spin and the universe will continue to exist and that *I* am probably of no more relevance to this universal dance than a grain of sand at the bottom of the sea. For a few people, discovering their cosmic irrelevance is incredibly freeing, even funny. For most people, being confronted with this makes them feel afraid or terrified. They prefer not to think about it, and they never understand why being significant, being special, is so important to them.'

Eric looked stunned. 'I think that is exactly right! As you were speaking, I realised that my panic attacks were always about this fear, the fear of *not being*. I had to manage my panic attacks because I didn't trust myself to handle the fear of not being. I thought that if I allowed this fear to come through, it would kill me, or drive me insane. What occurs to me now is that the possibility of not being is what makes *being* so amazing! We don't exist, then we exist, then we cease to exist. Without not being, being doesn't mean anything.' He closed his eyes and smiled.

About a year after our conversation about panic attacks, life, death, and the universe, I ran into Eric at a business event. When I asked how he had been doing and, specifically, how his panic attacks had developed, he paused and looked surprised. 'I have been doing really, really well. And you know, it's funny you should ask about the panic attacks. I haven't had one since we spoke that time. I guess I just stopped running from my dragon and stopped being afraid of being afraid. And I had a lot more fun being my kind of special!'

The chapter in a nutshell

We feel fear whenever we suspect that one of our core needs is threatened.

There is a connection between our needs and our fears:
- Need: love/belonging—Fear: abandonment, being alone
- Need: autonomous self-expression—Fear: engulfment
- Need: predictability/safety—Fear: loss of control
- Need: growth/stimulation—Fear: stagnation
- Need: meaning and significance—Fear: non-existence

We treat our fears as if they were dragons that we need to run from or defeat.

On the self-realisation compass, our biggest growth opportunity may lie directly opposite to us. We can choose to leave our comfort zone and our familiar dragon behind. If we embrace the gifts of our opposite pole and discover strengths in us that may be most unlike us, our options in life will increase.

Our dragons are fuelled by F.E.A.R. = False Expectations Appearing Real. Our false expectations are often unconscious.

In order to avoid feeling the fear of non-existence (the master dragon), we create anxiety buffers that supply us with meaning and significance (eg nationality, religion, attempting to be powerful and/ or famous). The more strongly we are attached to these buffers, the more we distance ourselves from others who do not share our beliefs or association.

Dancing with the master dragon (looking at it, sharing it with others), creates connection and deepens compassion.

ENDNOTE

1. In the 1920s, the psychologist Fritz Riemann developed a framework for looking at four central fears that served as the foundation for the model presented in this chapter. Again, as with all models, this is not 'the truth', it is simply a model that can guide us in our exploration.

REFERENCES

Becker, E. (1971). *The Birth and Death of Meaning: An Interdisciplinary Perspective on the Problem of Man* (2 ed.). Free Press.

Riemann, F. (1971). *Grundformen der Angst / Eine tiefenpsychologische Studie* (6. Auflage / 1971 ed.). Ernst Reinhardt Verlag München/Basel.

Rosenblatt, A., Greenberg, J., Solomon, S., Pyszczynski, T., & Lyon, D. (1989). *Evidence for terror management theory: I. The effects of mortality salience on reactions to those who violate or uphold cultural values.* J Pers Soc Psychol, 57(4), 681-690.

Taylor, J. B. (2009). *My Stroke of Insight.* London: Hodder and Stoughton Ltd.

FURTHER RESOURCES

Download a PDF of the 'Dragon Chart' here:
https://tinyurl.com/YourPetDragon

Bolte Taylor, Jill (2008). TED talk: My Powerful Stroke of Insight.
https://tinyurl.com/strokeofinsight

What was once called the
OBJECTIVE WORLD
is a sort of Rorschach inkblot,
into which each culture,
each system of science &
religion, each type of personality,
reads a meaning only remotely
from the shape and colour derived
of the blot itself

– LEWIS MUMFORD

CHAPTER 7

The Butt-Naked Emperor

'Am I crazy? Seriously, I don't get what happened. When I spoke to my mother over the phone last night, she said some things I supposedly said to her during our last Thanksgiving dinner that simply aren't true. I was so baffled by how she recounted the events of that night that I was at a complete loss for words. I have often felt that she had a slightly slanted view of events, but this time around, she literally made stuff up that I had supposedly said. Either that, or I am really going crazy!' Michael shrugged his shoulders helplessly, as he was telling me about yesterday's phone conversation with his mother.

Anyone who has ever been in a relationship with another person will have had the often puzzling – and sometimes painful – realisation of how our own perception of reality doesn't necessarily match the other person's perception of reality. If we want to have more joy in our relationships, and in life in general, it is helpful to understand a few fundamentals about how we create reality and how this leads to our particular experience of other people – and of life.

The biology of beliefs

Not surprisingly, the human brain is an incredibly complex organ, and the neuroscience that explains what powers our experience is well beyond the scope of this book. Nonetheless, I will share a few basic facts about the brain in the hope that they may help us understand a little better how the brain creates reality.

For our purposes, we will focus on three structures of the brain: the brain stem, the limbic system, and the neocortex. The lowest part of the brain is the brain stem, also called the reptilian brain. It is responsible for our automatic nervous functions (such as breathing and skin temperature) as well as for our instinctual behaviours. The limbic system, a set of interconnected brain structures, is thought to have a central role in our emotions and motivation, particularly those related to survival, and is therefore sometimes referred to as *the feeling brain*. The brain's final layer is the neocortex, a 2-5 mm thick layer of cells that covers the surface of the brain (*cortex* comes from the Latin word for *bark*, like the bark of a tree). Our cortical structures are involved in higher brain functions such as conscious thought and language, spatial reasoning, and sensory perception.

The brain's development begins soon after conception, reaching around 90% of its adult volume by the age of six, but continues to undergo significant structural changes until the age of 21 years. Although the brain's plasticity (its capacity to re-wire) and ability for adaptation shortly after birth is unequalled at any later stage, more subtle processes of restructuring continue until we die. How our adult brain turns out is dependent on a nearly infinite number of variables.

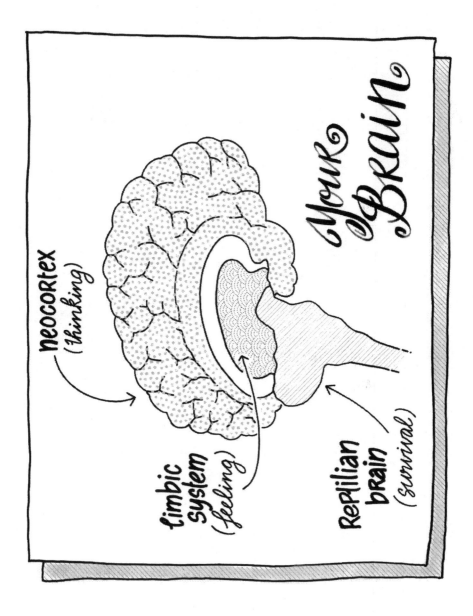

The two big factors determining brain development are *nature* (our biology) and *nurture* (our socio-cultural experience). Researchers continue to argue about the relative relevance of these influencing factors, but roughly speaking they each seem to account for about 50% of the variance. Although I would not dare to discard the influence of genetics on our development, for the sake of our exploration, we will focus on how our socio-cultural experience has shaped the person we are today.

At birth, humans are not able to communicate with language, and require years to develop an internal representation of *self*, which is necessary for conscious decision-making. But just because we don't have conscious awareness of our thought processes at very early developmental stages does not mean that the experiences we have during this period are unimportant. On the contrary; our experiences during these early months are essential to the formation of our neurological pathways, and are retained as emotions as well as body memories, safely stored away for future reference in our muscles and cells (there is more on the role of the body in 'Don't Panic'). Throughout our toddler stage, we deepen our emotional bonds with people close to us, experiment with relating to people in general, and learn to express ourselves emotionally. In interaction with our biology, the emotions and body-memories that we form during infancy constitute the foundational brickwork for the future: we develop core assumptions about how relationships work, about how we need to behave in order to survive and to have our physical and psychological needs met (see 'Needy Icebergs' for a deeper exploration of needs), and about which emotions are safe and desirable, and which aren't.

Fundamental to the transmission of information in the brain is a special type of cell called a *neuron*. Our neurons seem to be, to a large degree, responsible for making the human brain remarkably different from any other animal brain. A human brain weighs only 2% of the total mass of the body (which is relatively little) but consumes 25% of all energy used (which is relatively a lot). The human brain packs an estimated 86 billion neurons into a fairly compact-sized brain (some sources even speak about 100 billion neurons). This is possible because each individual human neuron is very small, particularly compared to the neurons that make up, for example, a rodent's brain.

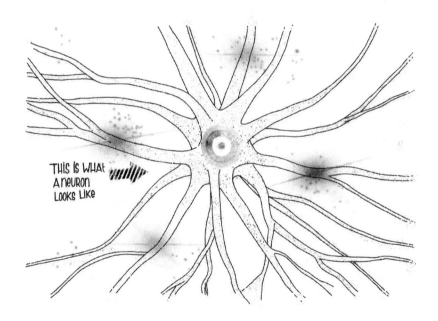

THIS is WHAT
A neuron
Looks Like

By way of comparison, if a rodent had a brain made up of 86 billion neurons, this brain would weigh 36 kg. A brain of this size would literally crush itself with its own weight. A human brain weighs a very manageable 1.2-1.5 kg. Of our 86 billion neurons, 16 billion are located in the cerebral cortex, our so-called thinking brain. Compared to other species, we have more neurons specialised for higher-brain functions; the size of our frontal-cortex is relatively large, and it continues to mature for a long time (until we are about 21 years old). Each neuron is capable of forming more than 1,000 connections with other neurons, which means an average adult brain has at least 60 trillion neural connections. Neurons are connected through fibres: dendrites (which cover only a short distance from the cell body) and axons (which can cover very long distances between neurons).

At their tips are growth knobs called *synapses* that serve as a point of connection. It is via the synapses that one neuron passes information, in the form of a chemical or electrical impulse, to another neuron.

By default, the human brain is equipped with an exceptional ability to think, make choices, and communicate. This begs the question of why, in everyday life, we seem to make relatively little of much that we have been given. Despite our innate ability for logical thinking and communication, we act irrationally, we argue, and we fight. All throughout history, humans have made decisions that have led to the deaths of thousands and thousands of people or that have even had the potential to endanger the survival of our species. Instead of investing in efforts to deepen our ability for self-awareness (to understand what is driving us) and to enhance our communication skills in order to avoid costly conflicts with others, most countries choose rather to invest a fortune in their arsenal of weapons.

The reason for this may be found in how we develop our brain, this 'hardware', during childhood and adolescence. By the time we are three years old, our brain has already reached approximately 80% of its adult size, but amazingly, has twice the number of synaptic connections as it will have by the time we reach adulthood. Over time, superfluous synaptic connections are eliminated, leaving us only with those synapses that we use frequently. In other words, the more often we 'practice' a specific mental experience (made of thoughts, feelings and behaviours), the more that experience is reinforced in our brain, making it more likely that we recreate this experience in the future. We effectively alter our own hardware by strengthening the connections associated with a particular experience and by deleting those connections that would favour another experience.

Thoughts, behaviours, and emotions that we engage in frequently create the equivalent of eight-lane motorways in our body and brain. Axons that transport information like electric wires between neurons are, much like wires, insulated in order to improve efficiency. In the brain, the insulating substance covering the axons is called myelin. There is now evidence that the more often a specific connection is used, the thicker the myelin coating becomes, thus enabling faster information transmission. In our motorway metaphor, this translates into having the smoothest surface tarmac, allowing information to be transported with great speed; thus a common, often-used response is processed much more rapidly than a new, unfamiliar response. Whenever we attempt to express a response that is different from our usual response (for example when we attempt to listen instead of getting defensive, or to try speak about our emotions instead of running away from the conversation), it can feel as if we are hacking a path through virgin jungle with a penknife. This is obviously a far less pleasant experience than the smooth ride on our eight-lane motorway.

This is why it is so much easier to fall back on what we have always done instead of choosing a different response. We are creatures of habit, and our brain has a preference for sticking with whatever we have already learned from our days playing in the sandpit; we think how we have always thought, we feel how we have always felt, and we do what we have always done. As a consequence we get the response from our environment we have always got, and produce the results we have always produced. Any new response (whether in thought or behaviour) is by definition not yet optimally supported by our physiology – which is why it can initially feel clumsy, uncomfortable, or even frightening. But there is hope for us creatures of habit. The connections among our 86 billion neurons are not fixed. They have a built-in capacity for reconfiguring themselves – when stimulated to do so – in new and creative ways. This means that it is possible to un-learn old patterns and create new ones at any time (in neuroscience this phenomenon is referred to as *use it or lose it*; or, *the cells that fire together, wire together*). The way we direct our attention plays a central part in this process of re-wiring.

The truth about reality

If neuroscience is pointing towards one truth about the reality of humans, it can be summarised as this: reality doesn't exist. To be more precise, the Reality (as in Reality with a capital *R*) of the physical world exists, but the reality we experience internally as human beings differs from person to person. As we will see, Reality and reality are two entirely different things. The Reality of the physical world can be measured and described through mathematical formulas, and its unfolding can be predicted through the laws of physics. And here is the crux: the objective language of maths we use to describe Reality doesn't *mean* anything in terms of how we experience *reality* in our day-to-day lives. Whatever happens 'out there' is void of an inherent message that would mean the same thing to all humans. The neuroscientist Jill Bolte Taylor, who experienced, survived, and eventually fully recovered from a massive stroke, summarised her post-stroke understanding like this: 'Reality is nothing but a turbulent sea of electromagnetism.' And she continues: 'And I must say, there was both freedom and challenge for me in recognizing that our perception of the external world, and our relationship to it, is a product of our neurological circuitry. For all those years of my life, I really had been a figment of my own imagination!' (2008). In effect, she is saying that nothing that happens out there means anything until it means something to someone.

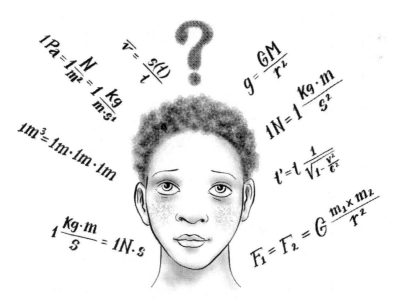

Our brain is physiologically incapable of mirroring Reality exactly as it exists outside of our body. The overwhelming amount of raw data our body is confronted with is immediately compressed, interpreted, and changed the moment it is perceived through our senses (sight, sound, touch, taste, smell). Our senses perceive only energetic pulsations or electrochemical data reflected or emitted from things outside the body. Only a commonly useful spectrum of those pulsations is then converted into electrical, acoustic, and electrochemical data to be further processed by the brain. Not only is the data reduced and filtered, but it is converted differently according to the sensory acuity and capacity of each unique individual. This means that data entering our system is divorced from objective reality in the moment of perception. The already skewed data continues to be distorted in a myriad of ways; not least by our subconscious cortical filtering systems that each put their own spin on the meaning of the incoming signals. Cultural and social norms, previous experiences, and personal judgements are all applied to the stream of information before we even so much as become conscious of what is happening. By the time we experience reality, it is impossible to know how much resemblance it still carries to the outside world. In the end, it is largely a futile exercise: it is impossible to separate precisely the moment of perception from the moment of interpretation. In this sense, when we mistake reality as Reality we are believing our own self-deception, our self-created illusion.

The artistic brain

The fact that our eyes appear to function like a camera lens and our brain like the hard drive of a camera recording actual events in real time, makes us want to reject the idea that reality is self-deception. But the brain is not a camera, it is a projector. Perhaps you followed the heated online discussion that erupted about the photo of a dress on the internet (Rogers, 2015). This simple picture divided the world into factions and led to hours of online debate, with perfectly civilised people insulting others who did not see the dress the way they themselves saw it. Some clearly saw a white dress with golden lace. Others saw a blue dress with black lace. And a third group saw a mix of the two, like a black dress with silver lace (I even heard of one person claiming to see an orange dress... don't ask!). The blue dress/ white dress debate was a global demonstration of how our brain fills in the blanks and 'sees' things that aren't there.

During my first year of studying psychology, we were presented with pictures of optical illusions as part of foundational research around human perception:

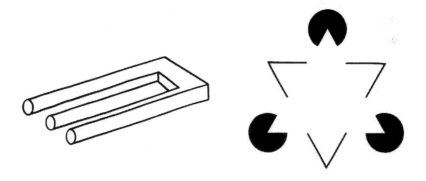

What we saw was not there, and in many cases could not possibly be there: a three-pronged object on the left and a white triangle overlaying some black dots and the outline of another triangle on the right. Uncomfortable with ambiguity and unanswered questions, our artistic brain fills in the blanks in the drawing and gives us an answer based on what it believes *should* be there. Just because I can see something does not mean it is real. When I first came across these optical illusions, I thought they were rather entertaining, but their deeper implications escaped me at the time. Only later did I begin to understand just how much these simple illusions reveal about human reality.

The fact that *what I see* is not the same as *what is out there* applies to all of human perception all of the time, not just to these simplified drawings (I could still swear the dress is white, even though the owner claims it is actually black!). In reality, life works like this:

Do you see the old woman? Do you see the young woman?

Do you see both? Two people look at something but what they perceive is not the same – and they are both right.

What we think is true is what we see and what we see is what we think is true. If this circular reasoning didn't have such profound consequences in our day-to-day lives, it would be merely amusing.

If you are still not convinced that what happens inside of you has no connection to what happens outside of you, consider this: if our internal experience were simply a recording of external occurrences, we should experience nothing once we are removed from the sensory stimulation of the outside world. How researchers try to simulate *nothing* is to contain a person in a sensory-deprivation tank. A person locked in a sensory-deprivation tank floats in salt water at body temperature, shielded from light, sound, smell, and touch. The senses receive virtually no input; therefore the person should experience nothing, right? On the contrary: deprived of sensory stimulation, we vividly witness the phenomenon of projected reality; after a certain amount of time in the sensory deprivation tank (usually anywhere from an hour to two hours) most people will begin to experience *things*. Some see the most vivid colours and images – even though their eyes are closed. Some notice smells – even though there is nothing to smell. Some might even hear sounds – even though there is nothing to hear. To the person in the tank, these experiences feel as real as anything else they have ever experienced (Kasten, 2011).

All evidence about reality and the human mind points in the same direction: the principles behind the process of reality creation outside of the tank are the same as inside the tank. Our brain is an artist who constantly creates hallucinations for our entertainment: stories (the thoughts in our head), music (what we hear), paintings or movies (what we see), perfumes (what we smell). Now, naturally, no matter how much we understand about this mirage we call reality – there is no way for us to escape it. But to live in the awareness that the reality we know is *always* an event inside of us opens entirely new ways of interacting with the world: we can experience ourselves as simultaneously being spectator and creator of the story we call reality.

The power of mind

Perhaps you agree with the previous arguments on a conceptual level. But I dare to predict that you probably think that this only applies to some things, while there are other things that are, in fact, real and that are therefore outside the realm of interpretation. As one of my clients said, 'I can see how this applies to emotions. I can be angry about something in my head that has no effect on you at all. But if I hit you in the face, you will experience pain like the next person. Pain is real.'

So, let's take pain as an example. Pain is real and measurable, right? Yes and no. What is true is that our body is hardwired to notice potentially harmful stimuli such as mechanical (pinching or crushing), chemical (acid), or thermal (hot or cold) sensations and respond automatically if the stimulus is strong enough. What we call pain, however, is a subjective and internal experience that is different for every person. The same intensity of an outside stimulus creates very different responses in different people. Each of us attaches a label to what the stimulus means. This means that even real physical pain is, to a large degree, a psychological creation. There are Yogis (practitioners of yoga and related meditative practices), who can push nails through their lips and apparently feel less discomfort than I do just thinking about pushing a nail through my own! The Yogis' nerves register pressure and hot and cold just like mine – but pressure/hot/cold in and of themselves have no inherent emotional or psychological implication. Without the involvement of our neocortex, there is only the autonomic and emotional response to stimuli as pleasurable – something to move towards, or painful – something to move away from. Naturally, our body will automatically try to remove itself from a painful stimulus, but everything beyond this reflex is the result of a more complex appraisal of what is happening and what it means. The human experience of pain is inseparable from thought and a Yogi who disconnects from the meaning of pain will not experience pain.

Now, you might still argue that Yogis have achieved mastery at directing their attention, something most people never accomplish in their lives. This is true; however, the relativity of pain is still true for everyone. The psychologist and game researcher Kelly McGonigal (2016) speaks about the ground-breaking progress made at the University of Washington to help patients suffering from severe burns. Burn wounds are considered to be among the most painful. The pain of burns is often barely manageable, even with strong opiates. The doctors and researchers at the University of Washington developed a creative, and unexpectedly successful, treatment. They created a 3D virtual reality (VR) environment that burn patients can enter by strapping on a headset. The immersive 3D reality is called 'Snow World' and allows patients to enter a cold world in which they can 'walk' through snow, build snowmen, explore ice caves, and marvel at winter landscapes. Patients who engage with this 3D environment while their wounds are being treated (which is one of the most horrifying and painful moments for most patients) experience a reduction in the pain experience of 30-50%. This is more than what can be achieved through opiates! Also, patients who receive traditional painkillers still report that they are thinking about their pain 100% of the time during treatment. In contrast, patients who are immersed in the virtual reality snow world report being aware of their pain only 8% of the time. These findings, besides obviously having massive implications for pain treatment, are also proof of the fundamental role of cognitive processes in our experience of physical pain.

When it comes to *psychological pain*, the story is much the same. Since no two human beings react exactly the same to events, it appears that the meaning we assign internally has an enormous influence over our experience. A person can be diagnosed as clinically depressed, based on the objective levels of neurotransmitters such as dopamine or serotonin in their blood, but not *feel* depressed. Conversely, a person can *feel* depressed without displaying the correlated physiological markers of depression. Some people who have experienced abuse during childhood end up severely emotionally impaired for the rest of their lives, while others leave adverse experiences behind them and proceed to live happily ever after. Even though psychological research has demonstrated correlations between childhood events and adult behaviour and psychology, there is no *causality* between event and outcome that is true for everyone. The mere fact that there are outliers (people who lie outside of the norm) – who experienced abuse and are unaffected by it – shows that anything is possible when it comes to the human psyche.

Over the last ten years or so, psychological research has dedicated more attention and resources to uncovering the magic influence of thought on psychological conditions as well as on the body. The placebo effect is a great example of this. In a nutshell, the placebo effect describes measurable changes in symptoms after patients have been given an imaginary treatment (for example sugar pills, described as a new and potent medication). The improvement experienced by patients on a placebo cure is, in some cases, as high as 72% (Brynie, 2009). The placebo effect works just the same the other way round: if I *believe* I have been exposed to a toxin producing unpleasant symptoms, I am more likely to experience symptoms ranging from intoxication to pain, all in accordance with whether and how strongly I believe the substance will adversely affect me. Today, most doctors recognise that the expectation of relief (or impediment) as a result of a treatment administered by a respected source will produce changes in our brain chemistry, which in return produce an improvement or decline in our healing processes. Our mind can prompt our body to tap into our natural capacity for well-being or *dis-ease* through thought: if I expect that something will happen (good or bad), it is more likely that it will happen.

The past is a creation of the present

In order to allow us to stay appropriately functional and to respond and act in socially acceptable ways, the brain selects bits of data it deems relevant and discards those it deems irrelevant. One way to assess relevance is to compare data to internal representations of past events, also known as memories. If, in the past, I have had experiences that were unpleasant for me, or that induced fear, my artistic brain might have chosen to paint these experiences in shades of grey to correspond to how I felt at the time. Now, instead of painting on a fresh canvas every time something new happens, the brain simply paints over existing areas of the old canvas. Unless I prompt my brain at some point to use a different set of paints, it usually sticks to the colours it has used previously. This inevitably leads to the most current version of my painting strongly resembling past versions of my painting; if my brain has only used grey paints, my painting is grey.

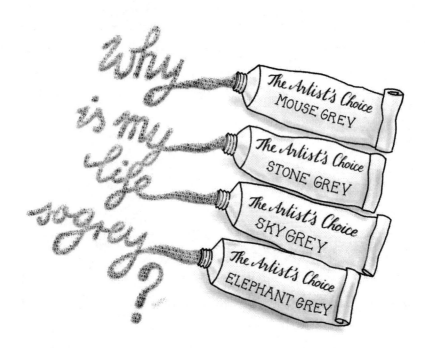

Staring at my grey painting understandably leads me to believe that Reality is grey, *because I can clearly see that it is grey.* I assume that I am painting what is happening right now, when I am in fact only making gradual adjustments to the existing image on my canvas. Very rarely do we perceive the landscape in front of us with fresh eyes, we merely reiterate what we already know. Our brain has tricked us into a feedback loop in which it is impossible to experience anything new because we keep staring at an image of the past. We don't remember original events – we only remember the last time we remembered them, and every time we remember them, we change them.

From an evolutionary perspective, recreating the world based on past experience serves a clear purpose. The amount of information received by our brain via our senses (touch, smell, vision, taste, hearing) is so large, that the fastest way of processing is to keep things as simple as possible: group data into chunks, compare it to memories, and act on the most likely hypothesis for the future. This process organises incoming data into manageable portions and brings personal meaning to the chaotic realm of the infinite complexity of Reality. Without this efficient data-selection process, our brain would freeze like a computer with too little processing capacity, leaving us incapable of understanding and interacting effectively with the world around us. To stick to the palette of colours we have used previously is nature's attempt to keep us functional. Unfortunately, as I explained at the beginning of this chapter, whatever we do over and over does have a tangible influence on the hardwiring of our brains. The more we repeat the same feelings and responses, the more we reinforce specific pathways and clusters of neurons, which in turn makes it more likely for us to experience the same feelings and responses in the future. Alternative pathways, which generate different responses, eventually wither away.

In one of our sessions, my client Matilda addressed her pattern of going into 'flight' mode whenever it was time to reach for something she wanted professionally, such as a promotion or an interesting project. She described how she turned away from an opportunity instead of towards it by distracting herself with irrelevant errands until the deadline had passed. When we explored the notion of really wanting something, to her surprise, Matilda recalled a situation she experienced as a five-year-old at a family gathering. While the adults were standing and talking, little Matilda had gotten on the tips of her toes, reaching for a plate full of cake on the dining room table. Her mother saw her going for the cake and, angered by what she judged as misbehaviour, yanked back Matilda's arm and yelled at her for being a bad girl. Matilda was frightened by her mom's anger and started to cry. Her tears made her mother even angrier, and she began to shake Matilda violently while threatening her that she would shake her until she would never dare to want anything ever again. After her mother had let go of her, Matilda had hidden behind a sofa for the rest of the event, not touching any of the food that was served.

Matilda hadn't thought of this event for a long time. When the memory came up, she noticed how the feelings she experienced today when wanting something were very similar to the cake incident when she was five. It seemed that Matilda had learned to hide and distract herself whenever there was something she wanted, because in the past, wanting hadn't been safe. In a sense, this had been a very intelligent reaction for a five-year-old. Matilda's brain had stored the survival pattern of flight, keeping her system in a constant state of alertness in order to get her out of harm's way if necessary. Unfortunately, as time had passed, the triggers that caused her to run and hide and pretend not to want anything, had become more generalised. Looking at her life, Matilda began to see how this strategy had affected all areas of her life over time. First, it wasn't safe to want cake, then sweets, and at some point it wasn't safe to want anything at all. She found herself reliably turning her back on just about anything that made her feel like *I want this*. Matilda was in fact stuck in a painting she had created as a terrified five-year-old.

We all have stories such as Matilda's in our own lives. Some are much worse, others are not this bad, but they still influence us. Our system (as in the intricate connection between our brain and the rest of our body) has a tendency to specifically retain memories about traumatic events. A trauma is hereby defined as any event that overwhelms our processing capacity. In more simple terms: if something was too much in the past, today our system tries to protect us from experiencing the same sense of too much again. In order to avoid experiencing the negative emotions connected to the original event, *any* event that so much as has the potential to remind us of these emotions is labelled and experienced as potentially dangerous. When this happens, we set into motion the response chain we established in order to deal with the initial situation. If this is successful (for example if running out of the room makes the fear subside), our system takes this as confirming evidence that what was in the room was dangerous, that fleeing works, and that we should use this strategy again in the future.

The obvious downside to our habit of projecting the emotions of the past onto events in the present is that we are stuck in a type of Groundhog Day illusion; outside of our brain, the past no longer exists. We only create an experience of the past through recreating and reliving emotions and memories. The more we conflate our recreated past states with the present, the more our life resembles a vicious circle in which we stumble from one unpleasantly familiar experience to the next. Most of us have no awareness of the fact that we created the painting we are looking at in the first place. We are therefore also oblivious to the fact that there are many more colours in our paintbox, which we *could* use to paint. We assume the paints that we once selected for ourselves (inspired by our family, our nation, life events) inadvertently doom us to use the same palette for eternity. When we discover that our reality is created from the inside out in every moment anew, we are only stuck with our grey paints as long as we believe that we are.

The butt-naked emperor

How our brain creates reality inside of us is nothing short of miraculous. Our brain has the astounding ability to create reality by transforming raw data into symbols or metaphors in the form of pictures, sounds, smells, sensations, and words. These symbols allow us to create meaning out of the shifting states of energy in this turbulent sea of electromagnetism (Reality) and enable us to interact with our environment. Given that we have to learn to navigate in a world we share with seven billion other humans, each constructing their own personal reality, social life would be pretty impossible if we didn't somehow jointly agree on some symbols or metaphors. In subgroups (families, tribes, or cultures), we decide on how to appropriately describe and relate to the world around us and define what is real

200

and what is not. In order to be considered sane within the context of our subgroup(s), we need to accept and apply the symbols and metaphors shared by the majority.

Most of us have a large enough overlap in our illusion with other people in our environment to feel validated in our perception of what is real and what is not. As helpful as this mechanism of a shared illusion is, it doesn't change that we are effectively playing 'The Emperor's New Clothes'. In the fairy tale, the emperor is talked into believing that the imaginary garments handed to him by two imposters can only be seen by those intelligent and cultivated enough to see them. As a result, the emperor himself, along with the rest of his court, endlessly praise the beautiful fabrics, the wonderful designs, and the flattering cut of his garments. Eventually, it is a little boy who states the obvious by pointing his finger at the emperor during a parade and crying out loud, 'He is naked!'

Just because a majority of people agree on something being true, that doesn't actually make it true. Nevertheless, our shared illusions are essential for obvious reasons; they allow us to interact constructively (most of the time) and without them it would be quite impossible to be in relationships, raise children, hold a job, and have friends. Without agreeing which illusions qualify as reality, our fragile construction of the social order might be so destabilised it could collapse. However, there is a difference between *consciously* living in a shared illusion and actually *believing* the illusion to be true.

Our shared delusions are specific to cultural frames of reference and can easily create misunderstandings and tension when we venture beyond familiar ground. Anyone who has ever travelled to a land far away has likely experienced how strange it feels when we are confronted with a group of people who happen to have an entirely different perspective about what is normal and maybe even about what is real. For example, behaviours that are considered distinctly ill-mannered in Europe and North America are judged rather differently in some Asian cultures. Not a few Western visitors have been taken aback by the sight of perfectly groomed Asians who hawk and spit on the floor, burp loudly during a tasty meal, or start to nap in the middle of a business meeting. In our Western-Hemisphere illusion, these behaviours are looked down upon. In their Eastern-Hemisphere illusion, these behaviours are a sign of status or enjoyment.

My brother-in-law provided an even more extreme example of culturally-grounded illusions clashing. During a journey through India, he was catapulted completely out of his comfort zone while walking in a poorer neighbourhood of Kolkata (or Calcutta, as most people will still know it). As he was making his way down a crowded street, he noticed a man crouching on the sidewalk. When he looked at him closer, he realised the man was openly defecating in the street. To make matters worse for my brother-in-law, the man looked up and smiled at him innocently. In our cultural frame of reference, not only is it unacceptable to defecate in public, but it would be considered outright crazy to smile at a stranger while doing so. In a country with an entirely different relationship to personal space and privacy and, in impoverished parts, very limited access to sanitary facilities, there are places where the same action is regarded as unavoidable and therefore normal.

If you caught yourself cringing while reading the description above, I congratulate you for having had a glimpse of the mechanisms of self-deception that we practice every day. We construct reality inside of us rooted in the illusions we share with others within our culture or peer group. As we saw in 'The Transformation Map', our individual experience is inseparable from our collective experience. For example, I am certain that my brother-in-law, given his European socialisation, will never forget that particular scene. If you would, however, ask any local Indian passing by who was present that day on the street, it is likely that they will not even remember seeing a defecating man. If the sight of a man having a poo in the middle of the street is not particularly strange, the information is not special enough to be retained as a memory. What we don't deem important is simply not represented internally, and what is not represented internally is not part of our reality.

Now, you might argue that the man indisputably had a poo in the middle of the street and that this is Reality whether you are Indian, German, or any other nationality. This may be true – but what does it matter? The fact of a man defecating in public itself is as meaningless as anything else you are not *thinking* about (or were not, until now): a particular satellite orbiting Earth, a leaf on a tree, a child stealing a lollipop in Brussels, your co-worker's cheating spouse, a pimple on the American President's nose. Things only matter once we relate to them internally by labelling them as good, pleasant, bad, ugly, beautiful, terrible, or wonderful. It becomes reality once it gets our attention.

This is of course the reason why any inter-communication (inter-cultural, inter-religious, inter-personal) is such a challenge for humanity. Every system, every person, couple, family, organisation, culture, religion, insists on its version of reality and strongly objects, ridicules, or sometimes even attempts to annihilate any other system that subscribes to a different reality. It is the unchangeable nature of the human condition to create our reality internally. But when we understand how our reality is a rather arbitrary creation, to a large part based on or even determined by cultural metaphors and symbols, we access our capacity to see that the emperor is actually butt-naked. Because if it is not inherently true, I should not literally believe everything I see! To discover that the concept *this is reality because I can see it!* is false can be confusing – but also incredibly liberating.

Inter-brain reality

The objective Reality of what surrounds us may be the same for every person – but because the meaning and internal representation of what is happening depends on personal context and memories, our *subjective* reality is vastly different. Our brain, the artist, allows us to see that which, according to our past experiences, is the most likely interpretation of reality. With the goal of reducing complexity, creating predictability, and maintaining a coherent worldview, our brain actively discards all information which does not fit with our (prefabricated) interpretation of ourselves, others, and the world that surrounds us.

I bring up the brain's inability to create an accurate internal representation of external events, because the drama between people could be summarised as *a paintbox misunderstanding*. Most of the time, we have sufficient overlap in our palette with the palette of people around us to validate our shared delusion and agree on the colour of the clothes the emperor is wearing. But sometimes, our painting is outright challenged by others and we experience a crisis. In our interactions with others we feel wronged, angered, puzzled, or saddened, when they unashamedly ignore *the facts* about the situation at hand. What is hard for us to grasp is the fact that although they might ignore *our* facts this does not mean that they ignore *the* facts. Based on the paints they have selected, their picture of reality is as accurate and their response as reasonable as our own. This leaves us stuck in a world full of conflict, angst, and confusion caused by each of us being fixated on the correctness of our own painting. We have a tendency to insist that our version of reality is right, even if it makes us unhappy or ill, or destroys relationships with people we claim to love.

The moment we perceive something, our brain begins to recreate what it already knows. We live our life as a self-fulfilling prophecy. This is especially true in relationships, where we act out dramas that have nothing to do with the person in front of us. Let's assume I was severely criticised or rejected by my parents when I was a child. My brain stays on high alert and picks up any signals of criticism or rejection from my environment, however faint, as a means of pre-emptively avoiding future damage. When I enter into a romantic relationship, my brain will skilfully remain oblivious to all the wonderful things my partner has to say about me while detecting and overemphasising even the slightest trace of disapproval. Every raised eyebrow, curled lip, or pitched question will be interpreted as a mortal attack, to which my brain responds with fight, flight, or freeze (learn more about the fight-flight-freeze reaction in the chapter 'Don't Panic'). If I employ this response pattern often enough, I am sure to create the very thing I am most afraid of: criticism and rejection. Eventually, I may succeed in driving away the person I was once so enamoured with, to be left once again with the bitter confirmation that women/men/pets/bosses/friends/politicians (take your pick) cannot be trusted.

In effect, I am creating a continuous loop that only factors in information confirming what I already know. In the process, I actively dismiss discrepant information (that could lead me to a different conclusion). The reality I know and the reality I see are the same thing: I only see what I know.

A few years ago, I coached a manager in a manufacturing plant. We spoke for a long time about how our thoughts create our feelings. As homework, I asked him to observe himself observing and notice the feelings following his thoughts. To make the connection between thoughts and feelings as transparent as possible, I instructed him to focus on two specific employees – one he liked because he thought of him as skilled and friendly and one he disliked for being lazy and unhelpful.

OBSERVER
CREATED
REALITY

Reality I know ⇄ *Reality I see*

When my client returned for our next session, he reported on the outcome of our little experiment. 'It's Monday morning 9am and I'm sitting at my desk. When I look outside the window facing the parking lot, I see two people walk towards the building. As luck would have it, they are the two employees I was supposed to focus on. At our plant we normally start the workday at 8am – so 9am is about an hour later than usual. I watch the "good" employee and think: he is unusually late but probably had something urgent to take care of this morning. I hope everything is okay. Then my eyes wander to the "bad" employee and I think: I can't believe he is late and doesn't even pretend to be in a hurry to get to work. Typical! I wonder what his excuse is going to be. At this very moment, I noticed my own thoughts and the feelings they created in me. My thoughts about the good employee resulted in genuine concern and a warm feeling, my thoughts about my bad employee in annoyance and anger. I actually had to laugh at myself when I realised this.

'Now, of course in both cases I have a history with these guys and whatever my issue is with my bad employee goes back much further than his coming to work late once. However, I do have to admit that at that very moment, they were doing exactly the same thing, and there was no way for me to know why they were late. But the story in my mind unfolded automatically and in a very biased way. It did make me wonder in how many instances in the past I saw something that could have meant anything and immediately created a feeling of frustration in me because of how I thought about it.'

Different people likely trigger different memories of past experiences in us. Whatever they are – what we are experiencing is not Reality but a creation in the present based on our interpretation of memories. So again, if all the paints in my paintbox are grey, I experience my entire world as grey, and I (rightfully) expect it to be grey in the future. If someone were to claim the world was orange, I would accuse him or her of lying, or being delusional – because any sane person can see clear as daylight that the world is grey. Thus, negotiating common ground in our inter-brain reality is tricky. Interacting constructively with others depends on our ability to: a) acknowledge that I see an old woman while you see a young woman, and: b) acknowledge that we are both right – given our particular frame of reference. Knowing that parallel realities exist with different levels of overlap at different times with different people will affect the way we interact with others. What was once 'clearly so' becomes less rigid and more fluid, more relative. Being aware of how our brain literally 'writes' ever changing versions of reality allows us to be less attached to our story and opens the door for new, more exciting, and happier stories to emerge.

Real-world example

While studying for my masters in psychology, I worked briefly as an assistant to Mrs Meier, a licensed psychologist and therapist. Mrs Meier was a woman in her early fifties who looked like a cover model for *The Trusted Therapist* magazine; she was well dressed, sported a distinguished bob of grey hair, and always carried reading glasses around her neck. But Mrs Meier did lack a skill that some would assume essential for a therapist: in her late teens she had suffered through a vicious ear infection, which had left her 90% deaf. Over the years, Mrs Meier had become masterful at hiding her disability: at school, at university, later from her colleagues, the insurance companies, and even from her patients.

I was flabbergasted to discover that none of her patients seemed to detect that she was deaf. As you can imagine, her ability to lip-read was quite developed, but because she alerted no one of her impediment, people did not make an effort to talk more slowly or pronounce their words more clearly when around her. Quite often, her lip-reading was amazingly sufficient to keep the conversation flowing, but sometimes she could not decipher in real time what was being said. For later reference, Mrs Meier had me transcribe the audio recordings of her therapy sessions, which she used to review her sessions and supplement her own notes in the patient's file.

I was fascinated by how Mrs Meier's clients didn't think to question her when she responded in ways that made no sense. While transcribing the therapy sessions, I witnessed countless misunderstandings, some of them rather hilarious. Mrs Meier's patients sometimes seemed confused by the randomness of her comments, but they never appeared to be fundamentally disturbed by them. Whenever there was a breakdown in the flow of communication between Mrs Meier and a patient, it was always the patients who assumed they must have made a mistake. They responded as if they had misunderstood something that Mrs Meier had implied, or as if what she had said was part of a skilful and paradoxical intervention intended to challenge their thinking. And in most cases, it did challenge their thinking. Even the most severe misunderstanding did not cause the session to stop. Mrs Meier never once acknowledged that she hadn't heard something and, eventually, the session carried on in a more or less logical flow. Since most of her patients returned on a regular basis, I assume they got value out of these interactions, even if the interaction often appeared nonsensical to the outside observer.

During this period as Mrs Meier's assistant, I understood something important about the human psyche. When we believe something *has* to make sense, we will make sure it does. Mrs Meier's patients were practically conducting a form of self-therapy, generating the meaning they needed out of her arbitrary responses and disjointed questions. They played 'The Emperor's New Clothes' and filled in the blanks of the conversation. We may laugh at the gullible patients of Mrs Meier that were oblivious to her condition – but in reality, all of us are doing the exact same thing all of the time. We interact with an internally created and fluid universe, logical only to us.

The chapter in a nutshell

The human brain has the highest number of neurons dedicated to higher brain functions (thought) than any other known species.

Thoughts, behaviours, and emotions that we employ frequently create the equivalent of eight-lane motorways in our body and brain. The more often we travel on such a motorway and practice a specific experience (made of thoughts, feelings and behaviours), the more likely we are to recreate this experience in the future.

Any time we attempt to display a response different from our usual response (for example: when we attempt to listen instead of getting defensive or try to speak about our emotions instead of running away from the conversation) it feels as if we have to fight our way through virgin jungle, hacking a path with a penknife. If practiced, new thoughts, emotions, and behaviours will create new eight-lane motorways over time.

Reality (as in the Reality of the external world) and reality (what we experience) are two entirely different things. External Reality is nothing but a 'turbulent sea of electromagnetism', void of inherent meaning. We create our personal reality internally, moment by moment through thought. All of our individual reality is self-deception, an internally created illusion. Even the experience of physical pain is a cognitive process.

The illusions we share with others are a version of 'The Emperor's New Clothes'. Just because I share an illusion with someone else, doesn't make it true. However, our shared illusions allow us to successfully interact with people around us.

What we consider 'real' depends on our shared cultural frame of reference, on what most people can agree upon. We often experience misunderstandings and tensions with those who do not share our frame of reference.

We live in an (optical) illusion. The past is a creation of the present. Our brain creates meaning based on our interpretation of past events (the colours in our paintbox).

Our mind can prompt our body to tap into our natural capacity for well-being (as well as our capacity for 'dis-ease') through thought: if I expect that something will happen (good or bad), it is more likely to happen.

Two people can look at the same thing and see something entirely different. They are both right, given their level of understanding.

Being aware how our brain literally 'writes' ever changing versions of reality allows us to be less attached to our story and opens the door for new stories to emerge.

REFERENCES

Taylor, J. B. (2009). *My Stroke of Insight*. London: Hodder and Stoughton Ltd.

McGonigal, J. (2016). *SuperBetter: The Power of Living Gamefully*. Penguin Books.

Brynie, F. H. (2009). *Brain Sense: The Science of the Senses and How We Process the World Around Us*. New York: Amacom Books.

Heifetz, R., and Linsky, M. (2002). *Leadership on the Line: Staying Alive Through the Dangers of Leading*. Boston: Harvard Business School Press.

Kasten, E. (2011). *Bilder im Dunkeln*. Gehirn und Geist. November 2011. (The same article on sensory deprivation was published by Spiegel Online under the title 'Wenn das Gehirn sich auf einen Trip macht').

Rogers, A. (2015). *The Science of Why No One Agrees on the Color of this Dress*. Wired Magazine. https://tinyurl.com/DressWired

Keefe, F. J., Huling, D. A., Coggins, M.J., Keefe, D. F., Rosenthal, Z. M., Herr, N. R., Hoffman, H.G. (2012) *Virtual reality for persistent pain: A new direction for behavioral pain management* Pain, Volume 153 - Issue 11

FURTHER RESOURCES

Online article: University of Washington, Snow World, a virtual reality for reducing pain in burn victims. https://tinyurl.com/VRPainReduction

Video: Soldiers Get Virtual Reality Therapy for Burn Pain. https://tinyurl.com/VRSoldiers

Shen, J. *Why Practice Actually Makes Perfect: How to Rewire Your Brain for Better Performance*. Bufferapp.com. https://tinyurl.com/PracticeRewiresBrain

Stiles, J., and Jernigan, TL (2010). *The Basics of Brain Development*. Neuropsychology Review.

Loftus, E. (2013). TED talk: How reliable is your memory? https://tinyurl.com/TEDFiction

Lotto, B. (2009). TED talk: Optical illusions show you how we see. https://tinyurl.com/TEDOptical

Dennet, D. (2003). TED talk: The illusion of Consciousness https://tinyurl.com/TEDConsciousness

DON'T PANIC!

— DOUGLAS ADAMS

CHAPTER 8

Don't Panic

'I froze, I simply froze. I could see everyone in the room staring at me, but I couldn't get myself to speak. It was absolutely awful. I actually prayed the ground would open up and swallow me. After what felt like an eternity, my boss got up and took over the presentation. He was kind enough to make a harmless joke while jumping to my rescue. He did a good job completing the presentation, but all I could think of was that I had just made a complete fool of myself in front of the top executives of our company and our CEO. I am so ashamed!' Glen was still visibly shaken when he recounted the fiasco of last week's presentation to the board. He was flabbergasted at his own blackout and was terrified that this experience might repeat itself on the next occasion.

When the brain dials 911

Imagine yourself in Glen's shoes: You have to give an important presentation before the twelve members of the top team of your organisation, including your CEO. Just as you begin to speak, you notice the CEO tapping his pen on the table, wrinkling his forehead, and clenching his jaw. Your eyes take in this visual information, which is then immediately processed by your brain. What happens internally is incredibly fast and complex, but we will try to understand some of what is unfolding inside of you.

The visual stimulation received through the optical nerve is routed to the thalamus, a walnut-shaped symmetrical structure located at the top of the so-called reptilian brain, which controls the body's vital functions. The thalamus can be thought of as a switchboard, directing sensory information to the appropriate cortical areas as well as to the amygdala. Before relaying the information, it does a rough assessment of the incoming sensory impulses by comparing them to any information from the past. If you had an encounter with an agitated older man with a clenched jaw that resulted in unpleasant emotional or physical consequences for you (eg being ridiculed, criticised, or beaten), your thalamus will flag the visual information about your CEO as a potential threat. The information about possible impending doom is dispatched to two places: the amygdala and the neocortex.

The amygdala (the Greek word for *almond*) consists of two almond-shaped structures, one in each half of the brain embedded within the limbic system. The limbic system is an important centre for emotions (sometimes referred to as *the feeling brain*) while the amygdala is a major, though far from the only, player when it comes to the detection of and response to threats. If the amygdala is damaged, a dampened response to a threat is often the consequence, while the *feeling* of fear remains intact because fear is a product of cognitive processes in the neocortex. When we are exposed to a threat, the neural activity in the amygdala is heightened and our internal panic button is pushed; we are kicked into our survival responses of fight, flight, or freeze.

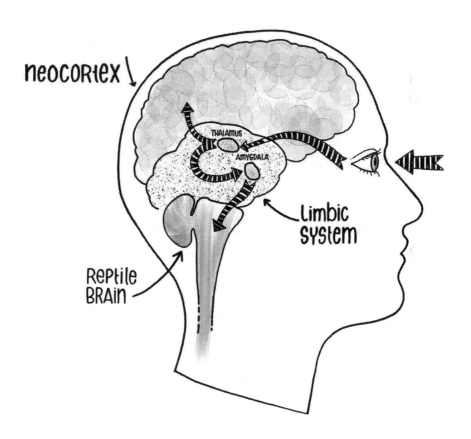

In case of actual or anticipated danger, our body tries to get away from or terminate the threat by engaging first in a fight or flight reaction. If neither fight nor flight is an option, we go into freeze mode in order to dampen the physical impact, numb us to the potentially painful stimulus, and save energy by reducing our bodily functions to the bare minimum.

Let's return to Glen's agitated CEO with the wrinkled forehead and the clenched jaw. In the chapter 'The Butt-Naked Emperor', we learned that in many ways, our present is a function of our past; when the red flag of *looks just like Dad before he got sarcastic and critical of me!* is raised, this prompts our amygdala to hit the panic button immediately. While this is happening, our neocortex also begins to process the data it receives from the thalamus. By comparing the current situation to past events, our neocortex can either confirm our suspicion or come to the conclusion that there is not enough overlap with *sarcastic dad* to justify a full-blown panic. If our neocortex decides that the CEO is unlikely to be upset with us and that he might actually just really need to go to the loo (which leads him to appear agitated, wrinkle his forehead, and clench his jaw), the de-escalation sequence is initiated. In this case, our neocortex signals *stand down: false alarm* to our amygdala. In turn, this prompts our amygdala to stop hitting the panic button, and the release of chemicals in our bloodstream is interrupted, making it possible for us to calm down. However, since the pathway leading directly to the amygdala (the thalamic pathway) is much faster than the pathway leading through the neocortex (the cortical pathway), our amygdala has already hit the panic button ten times before our neocortex has even had a chance to issue the *stand down* memo. By the time we come to our senses, the damage has already been done.

Our reactive survival response patterns are obviously quite useful in the face of genuine danger, such as when we step on a snake, the tail of a lion, or the ego of an angry drunk wielding a knife. Yet, under normal circumstances, our reactive amygdala-driven response is most often only marginally constructive – given how unlikely it is that our boss will really hit us in the face, that we will get fired for giving one bad presentation, that everyone will start laughing at us... or that there really is a monster under the bed. Thankfully, by the time we have grown up, most of us have learned to manage our amygdala-driven response in a more or less socially acceptable manner. Even if our amygdala has been triggered, we respond in a way that is not immediately identifiable as a survival response to the outside observer. Instead of tackling the CEO (fight response), running out of the conference room (flight response), or playing dead under the conference table (freeze response), we might respond in the modern, civilized way: defensively challenge the CEO to share his view (fight response), back down from our position while deferring to the strongest opinion in the room (flight response), or proceed to give our presentation in autopilot mode (freeze response). But often, even if our outside appearance may be calm, internally we are still experiencing a state of emergency.

Fear and the body

Many people have a somewhat neglectful relationship with their body and dismiss it as being little more than a transport vehicle for the brain. More often than not, we find numerous faults with our body. In the face of its imperfections, we either punish it with ignorance or try to beat it into submission through diets and exercise. Even doing sports on a regular basis doesn't necessarily mean that we comfortably inhabit every corner of our human shape. Very rarely do I come across someone who simply feels comfortable with their body and who has found some balance between loving attention to it on the one hand and quiet self-acceptance on the other. While the focus of this book is on shifting and expanding our thinking and feeling, it is our body which makes thoughts and feelings – and indeed our entire experience – possible in the first place. As embodied beings, our body is an essential part of the transformational process, and any true insight is one that happens on a physical as well as on a mental level.

Because bodywork, and learning to accept and love myself through my body, has been such an integral part of my own journey, I want to bring attention to our body as the essential partner in our journeys of transformation. Even if you are not going to hire a professional bodyworker, just paying more attention to your body is key to becoming more emotionally intelligent in order to feel more at peace, relaxed, and healthy.

From my teens to my mid-thirties, my body felt somewhat rigid, and I was never comfortable in my own skin. Most people would have described me as physically composed or serene – but some people, usually those familiar with bodywork, gave me the feedback that they experienced me as stiff. The more I learned to be aware of myself, the more I became aware of my own rigidity – and the more I felt as if I was locked in a corset that restricted my movement and sometimes made it hard to breathe. Over the years, I sought the support of different bodyworkers to change the relationship I had with myself. Eventually, a body therapist pointed out how some of my experiences as a child and teen had been traumatic and that in response, my body had retained behavioural patterns that contracted my muscles and restricted my movement. I had created these physical holding patterns, as she called them, with the intention of protecting myself from feeling or re-experiencing the same kind of trauma again. Thus my corset was actually a protective muscle-armour, which I had developed with the intention of keeping myself safe. Today, I have released most of the tension I held onto for many years, and on the rare occasion that it reappears, I have helpful strategies allowing me to reconnect with the flow of breath and movement.

The brain in the gut

Generally, an event, or a series of events, is classified as a trauma if it overwhelms our ability to process this event adequately. In trauma research, a distinction is made between a shock trauma and a developmental trauma. A shock trauma is a sudden, and often extreme, occurrence that immediately triggers our survival instincts – such as an explosion, an earthquake, someone shouting at us, or a fire. In contrast, a developmental trauma results from a series of events that triggers constant anxiety or fear over a period of time. For example, a developmental trauma can be caused by recurring abuse or even by constant criticism or humiliation. Physiologically, our body's response to such intense events, whether they are physical, emotional, or both, follows the same pattern. If an external stimulus is tagged as potentially threatening or harmful, our fight, flight, or freeze response is set in motion. The more often this chain of reactions is triggered, the more our body creates a so-called holding pattern, resulting in chronic tension or even pain.

It appears that a significant amount of information is retained in a part of our body called the *abdominal-pelvic-brain* or *gut brain*. The *abdominal-pelvic-brain* is an extensive network of neurons widely dispersed throughout the gut, spanning the area of our solar plexus down to our pelvic bone. The doctor and researcher Byron Robinson wrote about the abdominal-pelvic-brain in 1923. In the last twenty years there has been an increase in research about the connection between our neocortex and our gut brain, alluding to the possibility that future psychiatry may have to take into consideration the treatment of our gut brain as well as the brain we carry in our skull (Hadhazy, 2010).

Top-down and bottom-up

Our amygdala response can be triggered through different channels. The *top-down* response is initiated when our cortical brain interprets a stimulus (something we see, hear, feel, or even something we remember) as threatening. The *bottom-up* response is triggered when an instinctive reaction by our gut brain sends a stress signal upwards to the amygdala (for example, when we are exposed to a sudden and startling stimulus like a loud noise or the loss of balance).

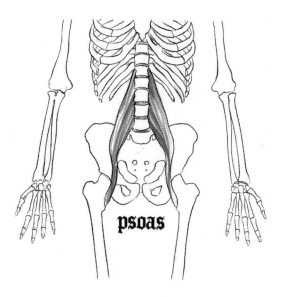

psoas

Some of the nerves in our gut brain belong to the vagus nerve, a bundle of nerves that run through our upper body and neck into our brain. The vagus nerve in our lower body is embedded in a big muscle called the psoas muscle. The psoas connects our upper thighbones with the lower part of our spine.

When the psoas muscle contracts fully, it pulls us into a foetal position in the attempt to protect our internal organs from anticipated harm. From within the psoas, the vagus nerve measures the degree of tension and sends this feedback to the amygdala. As long as the vagus nerve continues to detect a significant degree of tension in the psoas, it signals to the amygdala that the threat has not yet passed.

One of the consequences of unresolved trauma is the tension held in our body, particularly in the gut brain and the psoas muscle. If this tension is not released, our gut keeps signalling the brain that we are not yet safe. In other words, if our gut isn't fully relaxed and there is residual tension, our system is kept in a constant state of alert. As a result, our amygdala also fails to relax, and we continually have heightened levels of adrenalin and noradrenalin rushing through our system – leading to irritability, anxiety, irrational behaviour, numbness, or even flashbacks.

Fear vs F.E.A.R.

Fear is useful for the protection of the physical body but not when it becomes the dominant driver of human behaviour. Unless we live in a war-torn country, experience a natural disaster, or face violence, an amygdala response is not required to ensure our safety. If we are lucky enough to live under relatively safe environmental conditions, our amygdala is generally not triggered by actual danger, but rather by the fear that somehow *I am under attack*. This happens when something is judged as an attack because of our brains overlaying what has been emotionally painful in the past onto what is happening in the present. This process of projecting negative images of the past over the present results in a skewed assessment of the situation, panic, and disproportional emotional responses.

No one enjoys panic, because panic means loss of control. In an attempt to avoid the unpleasant experience of being overwhelmed by panic, we have developed fears that serve no other purpose than to alert us ahead of time to anything that could potentially result in a loss of control. This intricate system of tripwires is now triggered at the slightest hint of threat. For some people, this tripwire alarm system develops a life of its own, and the alarm system virtually self-replicates. Before they know what's happening, they are trapped in an internal prison of alarm systems, each as impenetrable as the hedge of thorns around Sleeping Beauty. Life itself has turned into the enemy because danger and attack are suspected at every turn.

When we are afraid, we literally cannot think straight because those areas in our brain dedicated to higher functions are deprived of oxygen. Living in fear physiologically impedes our ability to learn and develop. The neuroscientist Gerald Hüther (2012) describes the effect of fear in a beautiful article on his website as follows: 'Fear triggers a chain reaction in the brain that impairs our ability to learn new things, destabilises what we have already learned, and pushes us to regress to old and rather rudimentary behavioural strategies.' Fear keeps us chained to a set of responses that were only meant to resolve an immediate threat to our physiological integrity, not to be a long-term solution for issues that we create through our thinking!

When it comes to fear, we are mainly dealing with F.E.A.R.: **F**alse **E**xpectations **A**ppearing **R**eal. These false expectations are some of the dragons we hide from, run from, or feel we need to defeat. Many things we shield ourselves from are highly unlikely to happen – and even if there is the possibility that they might, the price some of us pay for mistaking F.E.A.R. for fear can be the equivalent of burying ourselves alive.

If you are afraid of getting hit by a falling flowerpot and you never leave the house, you might actually avoid getting hit by a falling flowerpot, but you also effectively prevent yourself from living life, period. If you don't let anyone close to you for the fear of being hurt, you condemn yourself to a life of isolation. Moreover, we are driven not only by avoiding the thing we are afraid of, but by the associated fear that if this thing happens (whatever we happen to be afraid of), we will not able to deal with it.

Moving with and beyond fear

For human beings, emotions are unavoidable – the ones we find pleasant as well as the ones we label as undesirable, such as fear, pain, sadness, or anger. The problem doesn't lie in the emotions themselves, but in our response to them. Fear, pain, and anger are facts of life. On occasion we will be afraid and we will feel pain – but prolonged suffering is not the logical consequence. Suffering is the result of the story we create around fear and pain, the meaning we assign to these emotions and our unwillingness to experience them. Emotions like anger or sadness or fear may not feel pleasant, but they do not destroy us.

In fact, fears have the potential to guide us towards areas where we are not yet fully conscious, so that we can feel more alive (see

226

'Dance With Dragons' for more information about how to use your fears as a guide). Engaging our emotions instead of running from them can turn a vicious circle of fear avoidance into a circle of virtuosity in which we experience being alive. Allowing fear and pain to pass through us without judgement is the pre-requisite for experiencing other human qualities to the fullest as well: love, self-efficacy, gratitude, creativity, ecstasy, friendship, wisdom, humour.

Traumatic experiences that override our processing abilities are a part of human reality. One might even go so far as to argue that human evolution takes place not *in spite of* such events, but *because of* our innate resilience to even the most challenging of times. Each physically and emotionally intense event, if processed appropriately, allows us to reach another level of psychological, emotional, and spiritual maturity. Significant growth or transformation is quite often preceded by deeply painful experiences, which confront us with some of our deepest fears. But every painful experience contains a point of choice that challenges us to move on, thus moving higher on our *ladder of learning* (for an explanation of the ladder of learning see 'The Tale of the Hot Potato'). If we don't insist on staying stuck, life will eventually carry us along, and past fears and pains will fade away. Being aware that fear and pain are simply part of being alive, and that they will ebb and flow as anything else in life, can help us not to stay mired in them for longer than we need.

Sit with it

Meditation is becoming increasingly popular as a way of reducing anxiety and stress while improving physical and mental health – not least because of the impressive results demonstrated by a large body of meditation research. There is an incredibly wide range of schools of thought and religious practice in which meditation techniques are grounded and that each differ in their approach and intended outcome. Meditation techniques vary from eyes-closed varieties, with or without mantras, to open-eyed versions, and even incorporating different forms of movement. The intended results range from strengthening the capability of mind and body, to self-balance, to a spiritual experience of states of oneness, or connecting the meditator to a divine presence as defined by the relevant cultural or religious context.

The measurable changes that meditation produces therefore also differ quite substantially and can produce rather contradictory results. For example, Yogi Masters, while in a meditative state, show no reaction to external stimuli; when their hand is placed in ice water, their EEG displays no change. At the same time, Japanese Zen monks, who practice a form of highly *concentrated* mindfulness, show no sign of habituation to a repetitive sound played throughout their meditation; every time the sound is played, the monk's brain responds as if they hear it for the very first time. In contrast, the brains of subjects not trained in this particular practice of directing attention eventually get used to recurring sounds, ignoring them as background noise. Given the incredible diversity of meditative practices and traditions, it is impossible to describe meditation as a particular process. Different forms of meditation may be suited for achieving specific results, which is supported by the great range of effects that studies on meditation have documented to date.

For the sake of simplicity, I will name some general benefits associated with both concentrated forms of meditation (training a single-pointed focus) as well as *mindfulness* meditations (training a form of non-judgemental awareness that allows any external or internal signal to pass through) (Haupt & Fell 2010). To meditate regularly has the power to change our brains and our physical and mental health. The impressive list of positive measurable effects of meditation includes: increased ability to focus, lower blood pressure, a strengthened immune system, more empathy, increased feelings of happiness, stress-reduction, increased emotional and behavioural self-regulation, improved ability to resolve conflict, less rumination, and lower levels of anxiety.

People meditating regularly often report progress in stepping out of the hamster wheel of thoughts and feelings and becoming more capable of looking at their own iceberg with a sense of detachment. This balcony perspective enables them to view their situation with less drama, notice which parts of them are feeling what, get unstuck quicker, and develop more creative solutions by tapping into Mind (see 'This Too Shall Pass' for an explanation of Mind). If you would like to understand the degree to which you are currently mindful, the Five Facet Mindfulness Questionnaire allows you to rate your capacity to: 1) act with awareness, 2) observe/notice, 3) describe, 4) be non-judging of inner experience, and 5) be non-reactive to inner experience.

Generally speaking, meditation 'slows down' the brain, so that in successful meditations the brain activity decreases measurably from the busy beta waves to the calmer alpha waves (experienced meditators can decrease their brainwave activity even further, while remaining fully conscious at the same time). The state of relaxation meditation can bring about in the brain is therefore as much subjectively pleasant as it is objectively beneficial to our health.

Despite a number of promising studies and a surge of mindfulness training, which has been adopted by companies for some years now, many people still do not have easy access to meditation. The major complaints about the meditation process are about experiencing an uncontainable flood of thoughts (monkey brain), or an inner restlessness that makes it difficult to 'relax into the moment', and the often near-impossibility of being able to 'think nothing at all'.

The neuroscientist Lester G. Fehmi (2008) tried to figure out how he could reliably (and in the shortest possible time) induce the brain to achieve the health-promoting and relaxing alpha wave state. In his studies, he measured the effect of different forms of meditation and relaxation. To his frustration, the objective measurement results confirmed the subjective experiences of the test subjects: none of the methods investigated reliably put all the test subjects into an alpha state.

It was more or less by chance that Fehmi stumbled across a key to the alpha state, which gave a large number of his test subjects immediate access to this state.

When he began to instruct the test subjects to direct their attention to the spaces between objects that are mostly neglected in our everyday perception, ie the 'nothingness' that lies between objects, alpha waves appeared in the EEGs (electroencephalogram, used to measure brain activity) of the subjects within a very short time. Focusing on 'spaces in between' or 'nothing' in his meditation instructions literally translates as something like, 'Can you imagine the space between your eyes, or the space between your fingers?'

Based on his findings, Fehmi developed a series of exercises, which he called *Open Focus*. The aim here is to increase physical well-being and relaxation through the special, open form of attention orientation. You can test for yourself whether the Open Focus method is more accessible for you than traditional forms of meditation and whether, with regular use, you benefit from better sleep, less fear and worry, and more inner calm, and even better health. Fehmi's book, *The Open Focus Brain - Harnessing the Power of Attention to Heal Body and Mind*, includes a CD with two guided meditations, and on his website you can buy different Open Focus meditations.

As with anything, meditation is not a one-size-fits-all solution. I find that some people take to meditation almost immediately and are struck by just how much calmer and more centred they feel, while still others need to practice for some months before feeling any difference, and some never experience it as relaxing or otherwise beneficial. It seems that quite a few people choose to meditate because they assume it makes them a more spiritual person. Many of the meditative practices popular today are rooted in cultures and religious and philosophical traditions in which meditation is one of a multitude of practices applied to promote a spiritual awakening. This takes an entire way of life, made up of complex and interconnected rituals, life conditions, and cultural history, and reduces it to a single practice in the search for enlightenment. Using meditation as a 'spiritual sport' and mixing it with whatever personal belief system we happen to be invested in is no shortcut to personal transformation.

I often find that the more feverishly people are invested in creating it, the further they tend to drift from that which they are seeking. There is a difference between the act of *meditating* and a *meditative state of mind*. I have been around people who spend a not insignificant portion of their day meditating, but who are hardly close to a meditative state of mind during the rest of their day. To me being in a meditative state of mind means to allow for thoughts and feelings to flow through without needing to manipulate or fix them, to have less on our mind, to pause more often before reacting, to feel a deep connection with other people and nature, and to generally live life from the awareness that *my reality is my creation*. This state is accessible to anyone without meditating. That being said, even if there is no causal relationship between meditation and being a more spiritual person, this doesn't minimise the aforementioned potential health benefits of meditation, nor the possibility that meditating might help one to be in a meditative state of mind more often!

As they say, there is a lid for every pot, and you will have to test it in order to judge for yourself. If you want to experience how meditation affects you personally because you think that meditation could be 'your lid', I encourage you to select and stay with a practice for a few months, before moving on to the next approach. See if you can find joy in the process, without getting hooked on what the outcome has to be. I personally practiced a closed-eye mantra meditation daily for five years and today I enjoy the calmness Open Focus meditation brings to my mind. When my personal objective shifted to finding more *aliveness* in my body, I turned to approaches engaging my body in a more active way through movement.

232

Shake it

In the late 1970s Dr David Berceli, a trauma relief worker, made an important observation in a bomb shelter. As the mortar shells were hitting the area surrounding the shelter, he observed how, following every loud explosion, the people in the shelter instinctively moved their upper body into a curled position, sometimes even into a full foetal position. As we learned above, the muscle responsible for this movement is the psoas muscle, which pulls our body into a foetal position in order to protect our internal organs. Once the immediate danger had passed, the children in the shelter began to tremble and shake – whereas none of the adults did.

Berceli began to witness this pattern all around the world – shortly after a 'traumatic" event, children were trembling and shaking but adults were not. He began to realise that the children's response might be the body's natural attempt to heal the system by releasing additional tension stored in the psoas through tremors. It seemed that adults across cultures had learned to suppress shaking as a sign of weakness. He began to wonder if we had hereby rid our body of a natural mechanism that allows us to process and release the physical and psychological aftermath of traumatic events. Berceli was finding evidence of the important role of the psoas muscle in our reaction to 'traumatic' events and its connection with the fight/flight/freeze response triggered by the amygdala. He began to search for exercises that would assist our body in letting go, thereby unlearning the harmful pattern of suppressing involuntary tremors. Ultimately, he selected a set of seven simple exercises that are known as the *Trauma Releasing Exercises (TRE)* (Berceli, 2008).

Today, Berceli travels across the world teaching this simple seven-step process to others – sometimes hundreds of people simultaneously – who have endured a 'traumatic' event. I was surprised by just how enjoyable and relaxing I find the involuntary movement triggered by the exercises. I trained in TRE in order to teach these exercises to clients who feel tense and rigid or who suffer from lower back pain. I value the TRE especially because they don't necessarily require the support of a trained therapist. The exercises are easy to learn and can be done by my clients in the privacy of their own home.

In addition to TRE, I have personal experience with a number of other body-centred processes, two of which I would also like to touch upon briefly.

Dance with it

Another approach to feeling and experiencing ourselves from the inside out is the 5Rhythms dance, as developed by Gabrielle Roth. The approach is based on the idea that we move in five distinct rhythms: flowing, staccato, chaos, lyrical, and stillness. Through dance, we experience and express these human rhythms in a playful manner, while engaging our right brain in the process. There are dance studios all over the world offering 5Rhythms classes. Even though dancing in a group has a wonderful and unique quality to it, you can experience the process at home. Gabrielle has recorded an album called *Endless Wave*, available on iTunes, in which she guides you gently through the experience of 5Rhythms.

Stop it

For me, the Grinberg Method has also been valuable in supporting me in letting go of rigidity in my body and encouraging fluidity. The physical holding patterns we have developed as a response to painful experiences in the past are based on the hope that by being (moving and thinking) a certain way, we will avoid similar painful experiences in the future. In reality we are limiting our body's ability to move spontaneously, to experience the full range of human emotions, and to respond appropriately to any given situation. The Grinberg Method focuses on helping people experience their body by allowing emotions and movement to flow freely. Avi Grinberg created the method with the intention of helping people to tap into their ability to learn a new way of being while stopping old and unhelpful patterns – thereby increasing our capacity to experience well-being. To do so, a combination of touch, breath, and movement exercises are used to help us become aware of and stop our automatic reactions. However, it is necessary to be instructed by a trained Grinberg practitioner. You can find a list of trained Grinberg practitioners on their website.

Play with it

Recent studies have demonstrated the positive effect that playing the computer game Tetris (a visually demanding pattern-matching computer game) can have on preventing or stopping flashbacks (re-living an experience in your mind) as well as limiting cravings for potentially harmful substances such as drugs, alcohol, and high-caloric foods (Holmes et al., 2009, 2010; Skorka-Brown et al., 2015). The sooner after a traumatising event a person plays a round of Tetris, the more the likelihood of post-traumatic stress is reduced. Patients who suffer from cravings for drugs, alcohol, or food report a significant decrease in cravings after playing Tetris for only three minutes. Computer games such as Tetris or Candy Crush require constant visual processing, which seems to block other cognitive processes such as replaying a trauma in your head or fantasising about food. Another study showed that playing the casual video game Bejeweled (played for one month three times a week for 30 minutes) increased mood and decreased stress (Russoniello et al., 2009). In effect, visually captivating computer games can take your mind off your problem. The next time you feel anxious, re-live a trauma, or are trapped by a craving, try playing a game for a few minutes instead.

If you are experiencing anxiety, fear, or anger on a regular basis, it is probable that you are trapped within a painting from the past. One of the objectives of this book is to help you not believe everything you think (and see) and learn how to keep your amygdala at a safe distance from the panic button. The next chapter will dive deeper into the principles behind F.E.A.R. and deepen our understanding of reality.

The chapter in a nutshell

Overlaying memories of adverse past events over present events can trigger our amygdala-driven response of fight/flight/freeze. If we live in conditions under which our physical safety is ensured, our amygdala is not triggered by actual life-threatening danger but because of a generalised fear *that my psychological safety is under attack.*

Once our amygdala has triggered our fight/flight/freeze response, blood is re-directed to our extremities and away from our brain. These reactive survival responses are useful in the face of genuine danger – but they are often disproportional and unhelpful in the context of our daily social interactions.

When our survival responses have been activated by a perceived threat, we literally cannot think straight because those areas in our brain dedicated to higher functions are deprived of oxygen.

Our body stores memories in the form of physical holding patterns – with the intention of protecting ourselves from feeling or re-experiencing the same kind of trauma/hurt again.

Memories of past events can be perceived as a threat, especially if we labelled the past event as 'traumatic'. An event, or a series of events, is classified as a trauma if it overwhelms our ability to process this event adequately. Trauma research distinguishes between shock trauma and developmental trauma. A shock trauma is a sudden, and often extreme, occurrence that immediately triggers our survival instincts. A developmental trauma results from a series of events over a period of time that causes us to maintain a constant level of anxiety or fear.

Fear keeps us chained to a set of responses that were only meant to resolve an immediate threat to our physiological integrity, not as a long-term solution for issues that we create through our thinking. Upon closer investigation fear is mostly F.E.A.R. = False Expectations Appearing Real.

In addition to the brain in our skull, we have a second brain in our gut: the abdominal-pelvic brain. Our gut brain is an extensive network of neurons widely dispersed throughout the abdomen, spanning the area of our solar plexus down to our pelvic bone. One of the consequences of unresolved trauma is the tension held in our body, particularly in the gut brain and the psoas muscle. If this tension is not released, our gut keeps signalling our amygdala that we are not yet safe (which in turn prompts the amygdala to trigger our fight/flight/freeze response).

Fear, pain, and anger are facts of life. On occasion we will be afraid and we will feel pain – but prolonged suffering is not the inevitable consequence. Suffering is the story we create around fear and pain, the meaning we assign to these emotions and our unwillingness to experience them. Emotions like anger or sadness or fear may not feel pleasant, but they do not destroy us.

There are practices that can help to calm body and mind:

Meditation can be a powerful practice to increase mindfulness (as in our ability to be present to and not judge our experience) in daily life and reduce tension and anxiety.

Open Focus meditation can help us enter an alpha brainwave state of unfocused, open or expanded attention that we need in order to regenerate and relax.

Movement, touch, and tremoring (shaking) can release residual tension in the psoas muscle and help our body and our brain to relax and feel safe.

Playing a visually demanding casual video game can take your mind off unpleasant or traumatic memories, decrease cravings for unhealthy substances, decrease stress, and improve your mood.

ENDNOTE

1.   I am putting 'traumatic' in quotations because there is not a class of events that is 'traumatic' per se. What ends up being 'traumatic' is dependent on the complex interaction of perception and mental processing.

REFERENCES

Robinson, B. (1907). *The Abdominal and Pelvic Brain*. Hammond, Indiana: Frank S. Betz.

Hadhazy, A. (2010). *Think Twice: How the Gut's 'Second Brain' Influences Mood and Well-Being*. Scientific American. https://tinyurl.com/GutSecondBrain

Hüther, G. (2012). *Biologie der Angst. Wie aus Streß Gefühle werden (Sammlung Vandenhoeck) (12., Auflage ed.)*. Vandenhoeck & Ruprecht.

Fell J., Axmacher N., Haupt S. (2010). *From alpha to gamma: electrophysiological correlates of meditation-related states of consciousness*. Med Hypotheses Journal.

Fehmi, L.G. (2008). *The Open Focus Brain. Harnessing the Power of Attention to Heal Body and Mind*. Trumpeter.

Berceli, D. (2008). *The Revolutionary Trauma Release Process: Transcend Your Toughest Times*. Namaste Publishing.

Holmes E.A., James E.L., Coode-Bate T. & Deeprose C. (2009). *Can playing the computer game "Tetris" reduce the build-up of flashbacks for trauma? A proposal from cognitive science*. PLoS One 4: e4153.

Holmes E.A., James E.L., Kilford E.J. & Deeprose C. (2010). *Key steps in developing a cognitive vaccine against traumatic flashbacks: visuospatial Tetris versus verbal Pub Quiz.* PLoS One 5: e13706.

Skorka-Brown J., Andrade J., Whalley B. & May J. (2015). *Playing Tetris decreases drug and other cravings in real world settings.* Addict Behav 51: 165-170.

Russoniello C.V., O'Brien K. & Parks J.M. (2009). *The Effectiveness of Casual Video Games in Improving Mood and Decreasing Stress.* Journal of Cyber Therapy & Rehabilitation 53-66.

FURTHER RESOURCES

Damasio, A. (2011) TED talk: The quest to understand consciousness.
https://tinyurl.com/TEDQuest

Website: Information about the Grinberg-method
www.grinbergmethod.com

Website: Information about the 5 rhythms dance as developed by Gabrielle Roth
www.5rhythms.com

Online article: The Amygdala is Not the Brain's Fear Center
https://tinyurl.com/AmygdalaNot

Online article: This is Your Brain On Meditation
https://tinyurl.com/YourBrainMeditation

Online article: The Abdominal Brain and Enteric Nervous System
https://tinyurl.com/AbdominalBrain

Lester G. Fehmi's website. Here you can download free articles about Open
Focus and buy different Open Focus meditations. www.openfocus.com

TRUTH
IS A MATTER
OF THE
IMAGINATION

~UrsulaKLeGuin

CHAPTER 9

This Too Shall Pass

'I am afraid I will hurt my kids,' Laura cried and covered her face with her hands.

'Why are you afraid you will hurt your kids?'

'Because I have this recurring thought, it just keeps coming back. When I come home from work, I am exhausted. Lately, things with Larry haven't been great. And then the twins, Justin and Marie, they fight until one of them is crying. Justin drives me crazy, he is really stubborn and when he doesn't get what he wants, he gets violent. Yesterday, he kept hitting Marie over the head with his toy shovel, for crying out loud! I just don't know what to do with him and then I get angry and what I really want to do is take the shovel from his hand and smack him with it. Or worse. I can't believe I am telling you this, I don't think I am a bad mom, and I really don't want to hurt them! But these thoughts keep coming and they really freak me out.' Laura looked at me with desperation, wringing the handkerchief in her hands.

The tragic misunderstanding

When we feel frustrated, unhappy, depressed or angry, it is a normal human impulse to look for an explanation (or, more likely, to look for *the* reason) for our misery. We assume that isolating this reason will a) make us feel better because at the very least we now know *why* we feel bad and b) allow us to take the appropriate action to fix it. We are therefore quick to attribute our unhappiness to our children's fighting, our husband's silence, our mother's constant nagging, our boss's shouting, or to our own limitless psychological or physical imperfections.

Whether we locate the source inside or outside of ourselves, we narrow an incredibly complex internal process down to *one* circumstance that, in our mind, has a causal relationship to our feeling. The more strongly we believe the circumstance we have identified to be the source of our feeling, thinking, and of our actions, the more we are compelled to fix or correct this circumstance. We invest endless amounts of energy, time, and money to make things right, to optimise ourselves, to fix the people in our life and improve our circumstances, hoping to be rewarded with happiness and peace of mind. We scramble to become smarter, more educated, thinner, prettier, stronger, more devout, calmer, richer, and more successful; we try to acquire status, power, and material possessions. Not only do we push ourselves relentlessly, but we also drive our husbands or wives, children, siblings, or co-workers, hoping that *their* positive change and subsequent success in life will make *us* happy.

We have been raised by our family, our peer group, and to a large extent by the media (advertising, news, pop-culture, social media),

244

to believe that happiness is a destination that will surely be reached once we have succeeded either in *eliminating* **it** (replace it with any random reason for unhappiness) or in *creating* **it** (replace it with any random prerequisite of your choice). We have also been taught to believe that it is impossible for us to be happy if we somehow fail to create *it*. Worse still, these imaginary 'conditions of happiness' have become so deeply ingrained in our subconscious that we are completely unaware of the programming that runs our life. Driven by this hidden programme, we find ourselves forced to secure and preserve our must-have assets: our body, education, abilities, money, success, our handsome partner, our cute and talented children, or successful friends. As long as it is a perceived pre-requisite for happiness, we need to create more of *it* in order to continue to feel safe and accomplished – or at least to create enough in order to maintain the Status Quo. Any sight of our assets disappearing or dwindling (something that invariably happens, at least to our physical appearance) causes great anxiety.

One of my clients is an investment professional in Asia. Over the course of his career, Paul has created more wealth than most people can imagine. He is even so lucky as to be in a wonderful and loving marriage with two kids who bring him joy. Paul decided to work with me because he felt misaligned with the values of his company and struggled to find a deeper meaning in his work. While talking about his longing to do something more meaningful with his life, he kept justifying his need to stay at the company just a bit longer in order to create financial security for his family. After listening to versions of this story for some months, I pointed out that he was running after a moving target. 'Financial security' is not a thing, not a place that exists outside of a person's head. What constitutes financial security to me would likely give Paul nightmares of living under bridge, collecting bottles, and keeping all of his possessions in a shopping cart. In Paul's world, there is always someone who makes more money, who is more financially secure than he is. The image of being a dog running in circles after a toy rabbit made him laugh, and our conversation moved away from discussing how to create 'financial security' to exploring the longing that had brought him to work with me in the first place.

I suspect that even if Paul's reality feels like a far cry from your own, you too will have experienced periods in your life during which everything appeared to be going reasonably well from the outside, but you still didn't feel good on the inside. You had a job and a relationship, you and your family were in good health – yet you still felt unhappy. At the same time, it is likely that you experienced moments of happiness even during the direst of circumstances, while your work situation was terrible or a beloved family member was gravely ill. There are many people who, for all intents and purposes, *should* be happy yet are miserable, and many people who *should* be miserable who are okay.

From these observations we can deduce at the very least that circumstances apparently matter less than we have been taught to believe. Therefore, investing all of our attention, energy, and money into bettering our circumstances in order to be happy means entering a rat race that we are bound to lose. The tragic misunderstanding we have been taught to believe is this: my happiness depends on my ability to create the right circumstances. The right circumstances will lead me to have nice feelings. When I have nice feelings, I will have nice thoughts and will be happy. But it doesn't work that way. Happiness is not a stage to be conquered but a state to be cherished.

As you know from the chapter 'The Tale of the Hot Potato' my wish to understand the phenomenon of happiness led me to the quest of finding the truth behind this tragic misunderstanding.

Everything I have shared in this book became for me an important piece of the happiness puzzle I had begun to put together: The four quadrants of the Transformation Map made me realise the interconnectedness between my individual experience and the collectives I am a part of as well as the importance of those elements that are more intangible, such as mindset and culture. The idea presented by Voice Dialogue – of 'I' being a combination of different inner selves or facets of my personality – allowed me to understand and accept my own perceived incongruities and to be kinder to myself. Discovering the values and needs driving the observable behaviour of my different selves allowed me to pay more attention to needs I had previous neglected and thus feel more balanced. Understanding the connection between my needs and my fears led me to discover the dragons I had created in my mind and had been running from all my life. Learning about how my brain creates reality opened my eyes to the relativity of reality and made me more accepting of other people's realities. However, it wasn't until I came upon the insights I am sharing in this chapter that all the pieces fell into place and I started feeling as if I had finally 'arrived'.

We are spiritual beings having a human experience

Along this path towards deepening my own understanding of human nature and happiness, I stumbled across a famous quote by the French priest and philosopher Pierre Teilhard de Chardin (2007):

We are not human beings having a spiritual experience; we are spiritual beings having a human experience.

— Pierre Teilhard de Chardin

At first, this quote startled me. Now, I am not religious. I personally don't happen to believe there is a God who overlooks and guides my every step. Unsurprisingly, the notion of being a 'spiritual being' felt somewhat alien to me. But even as an atheist, I believe in the existence of *something* intangible connecting me not only to my fellow human beings but to all of nature and to the larger cosmos. Rephrasing the quote in my own words, I would say that humans are an immaterial energy, temporarily materialised in a physical form (see how the neuroscientist Jill Bolte Taylor described her stroke experience in the chapter 'The Butt-Naked Emperor'). The intangible spiritual connection I sensed to something greater made me curious enough to make me want to explore what it means to be 'a spiritual being having a human experience'. The more I began to understand about human nature, the simpler the answer to my happiness question appeared: if I am in fact a spiritual being, I can't possibly be broken and therefore don't need to be fixed in order to be happy. What if all it takes *is to look* inside – but *not meddle* with my inside (or with the outside world for that matter)? What if the key to my well-being is understanding that my well-being can't be compromised unless I think it so?

If the thoughts I have shared so far feel vague, esoteric, or too simplistic for your liking, I ask you to bear with me for a bit longer and carry on reading. Whatever your particular belief system is, whether you consider yourself to be religious, agnostic, or atheist – I ask you to treat this chapter as a thought experiment. Allow the possibility that the principles I share on the following pages *could* be true, or, at the very least, that they can be useful. While you read, notice with curiosity any changes or feelings in your body. Understanding doesn't just happen in our mind. When you are done with this chapter, sit with it for a while. Perhaps even re-read it for a second time to allow an even deeper, post-intellectual understanding to emerge.

The principle of Thought

You have probably heard the term *stream of consciousness* or *stream of thought*, which serves a metaphorical description of the constant flow of thoughts and inner monologue produced by our brain. Just as a stream of water flows whether we pay attention to it or not, our brain produces thoughts and inner dialogue, whether we pay attention or not. Our thoughts only become visible to us after we have materialised them through attention. As we bring our awareness to the stream, we don't just see water but notice a variety of objects drifting in it: big fish, little fish, grey fish, colourful fish, old tins, plastic bags, leaves, abandoned tyres, broken toys, and driftwood and other flotsam.

 **thoughts**

When we were children we were most likely equally fascinated by any and all of these objects; a dirty old sock was as fascinating as a colourful fish, a piece of wood as mesmerising as an old tyre. Our childlike attention was held captive by one object until another, more interesting, item floated by. Growing up, we observed and eventually began to emulate the judgements that our parents (and other important care-givers) held towards the objects in the stream. We quickly learned that some fish are apparently more preferable than others, that old tins and socks are bad, but that leaves are okay, that driftwood and old tyres are dangerous, and that the occasional flower drifting past is precious and worth collecting.

The more we ourselves began to judge the things drifting past and to sort them into 'good' or 'bad', the more stressful being in the stream became; we now needed to navigate our attention constantly in order to get closer to the good things and keep our distance from the bad ones. We learned to distinguish between 'good thoughts' (which are positive, happy, confident, pro-active, loving, or creative) and 'bad thoughts' (which are unhappy, insecure, angry, sad, vengeful, scared, jealous, lonely, and disappointed).

By the time we have grown up, labelling, judging, and avoiding flotsam occupies most of our waking day, and life can feel like a joyless and at times terrifying struggle; the bad stuff seems to be everywhere! We are less and less able to freely shift our attention from one thought floating by to the next, because we have become increasingly occupied with what the thought means and how to control it. Judging, managing, or manipulating our thoughts has turned into a full-time job!

But there is hope: our childlike ability to experience thoughts without having to assign a deeper meaning to them isn't lost. We can return to a state of mind where a thought is just a thought – not the truth, not our destiny, and not a statement about our character. Knowing this, we can invest significantly less energy in avoiding the 'bad' ones or trying to figure out how to make the 'good' ones stay. Thoughts are like driftwood: they come, they go, and sometimes they get stuck – but the force of the stream will eventually pull them free and make room for new thoughts to appear.

We live in the feeling of our thinking

For a long time, I subscribed to a commonly shared belief: I thought that I had sad thoughts *because* I felt sad. It was a major revelation when I discovered that I had the order wrong; I feel sad because I have sad thoughts. This is not to discard the importance of emotions but only to say that without a label, we simply wouldn't know what we feel because without a cognitive label there is only pure experience.

Let's assume that you hear your partner shout loudly. How you *feel* about her shouting is determined by what you *think* about her shouting. You will feel differently depending on whether you think she shouted way too loud or just a little too loud, whether you take her shouting personally ('she shouted at me') or impersonally ('she shouted because she was angry with something/someone else'), whether you were having nice thoughts about her right before she shouted, or whether you were thinking she was insufferable, whether you believe she was only excited when she shouted or believe she was angry, whether you think she was rightly or wrongly angry, and whether you were feeling content or unhappy right before she shouted. If you have fearful thoughts about her shouting, you will feel fear. If you have angry thoughts, you will feel anger. If you have no judgement about her shouting aside from *that was loud!* you will feel no emotion, or you might even be curious about what is going to happen next. What it boils down to is the fact that your reality in this moment depends entirely on how you create it through your thoughts in the moment.

There is no predetermined outcome for my personal experience of hearing someone shout because shouting doesn't mean anything until it means something to me. Thinking and feeling are two sides of the same coin. Emotions come into existence through thought. As described in the chapter 'The Butt-Naked Emperor', the process of creating emotions through thought is mainly automated and subconscious; thinking happens within us, without our conscious participation. We do have the capacity to observe small parts of the stream of consciousness, yet even to those parts, we hardly pay attention. If we find ourselves stuck in a reality that continuously feels bad, the best way out might be to uncover the origin of these feelings. We are not thinking *about* reality. What we think about is *creating* our reality. We feel what we (quite often subconsciously) think.

Without thought, our reality would be pure experience; cells growing and dying, neurons firing, energy shifting states. This would most likely be beautiful but it would also render us incapable of staying alive, having relationships, raising children, holding a job. It would be a short life. Through our capacity of thought we label and categorise pure experience, creating emotions and subsequently creating a reality we can navigate. The true power of thought unfolds wherever we don't see it as thought (which is nearly all of the time). Thoughts are like contact lenses; if we are wearing blue-coloured contacts, everything we perceive is tinted blue. To us it doesn't appear as if the world is tinted blue, because what we see is all we know, and we can't compare it to a world that isn't blue. It is this inability to realise that everything is actually thought that is the source of our problems.

A few years ago, I had a big argument with my brother about a situation in which I felt he had broken an agreement. At the beginning of our argument I was slightly annoyed, yet generously willing to consider that he might have misunderstood our agreement. Instead of accepting my graceful peace offering (which, in my mind, consisted of allowing the possibility that *he* had misunderstood something) my brother flat-out refused to take any responsibility for what he had done. Needless to say, I began to feel somewhat less forgiving and became rather pissed off with him instead. The more he refused to admit his evident wrongdoing, the angrier I became. The angrier I became, the more I was convinced that I was right.

What makes our reality seem so real is the attached emotion. If I *feel* it, it must be real *because* I feel it – since I obviously wouldn't feel it if it wasn't real! Our logic comes full circle. When we feel something strongly, we are misled into believing that it must be true when in fact we are simply feeling the intensity of our own thinking. My feeling angry with my brother meant nothing else than that I was thinking angry thoughts laden with judgement about his thoughtlessness, lack of care, selfishness, and ignorance.

As long as I am stuck in the causality of this outside-in understanding of the world (I am angry because he was inconsiderate), I am at the mercy of all kinds of things I cannot control: my negative feelings about my brother, my partner, children, or mother-in-law; my worries about money, my job, or the lousy mood of my boss; the anger of my colleague, the ranting of my dad, the decisions of my president, the economy, the weather, or the Pope.

The incredible power of our thoughts was demonstrated yet again by a study conducted at Harvard (Jamieson, Nock, & Mendes, 2012). Interested in the connection between stress and heart disease, the researchers demonstrated that the detrimental health effects of stress experienced after a stress-inducing situation on the heart depended on how people interpreted their bodily changes. If they thought sweaty palms and a higher heart rate were bad for their health, they felt anxious and the blood vessels in their heart constricted. However, those test subjects who were led to understand that their body was actually attempting to help them during the extreme situation by raising their general state of alertness and by pumping more blood to their brain, experienced not only subjectively less stress, but their heart vessels stayed relaxed. *On a physiological level, there is no difference between anxiety and excitement.* Our beliefs about what is happening in our body, and why, not only determine our emotional state but also our physiological reality.

The entire self-referential process of *living in the feeling of our thinking* is much like sitting in a mirrored room. The mirrors inside our head endlessly reflect any changes in our energetic state, any sensation, emotion, or thought. As humans we are bound to sit in this mirrored room and sit in the reflected thoughts and feelings about our past, present, and future. Even if that doesn't sound very comforting, it is not a reason to despair. In fact, what I argue is that *knowing* I am sitting in a mirrored room vs believing that what I perceive in this room is reality, has a profound impact on how life appears to me.

The past is an invention of the present

Building on the idea of the mirrored room, it is not only present life that happens through me, but the past as well. In 'The Transformation Map' I shared the story of my client Andreas who, in his seventies, was able to see his upbringing during and after World War II in a new light. When Andreas discovered how much of his experience was a collective phenomenon common to many children of the war, he was suddenly able to view his parents' desperate struggle to make ends meet with more compassion. The stories he discovered of other children of the war, which were so remarkably similar to his own experience, had prompted Andreas to stop taking the details of his early years so personally.

You might argue that Andreas really *did* get valuable new information about his upbringing and that true facts would naturally affect anyone's interpretation of the past. But who is the judge of what constitutes a 'true fact'? Theoretically, there has been factual information on the effect of wars on family dynamics for decades. Yet, until that particular moment, Andreas did not hear or seek information allowing him to put his experience into perspective. Even if he had been made aware of how many families shared his family's trauma, such knowledge would not have been guaranteed to change the resentment he harboured towards his parents or stop his own self-destructive behaviour. Andreas's experience changed because, in a moment of insight, he was receptive for new thinking to emerge, and this new thinking created a new emotional reality for him. Our personal past and how it happened exists only in our own mind. The past is gone, and the past we experience now is a creation of the present. When our thinking about the past changes, our memories change, and so do our feelings about the past. The transformation of our childhood happens *inside* of us, in the same place where we have kept any stories of heartbreak or trauma alive. It only takes one new thought to enter our room of mirrors to create a different reality.

I write these words with deep compassion: for Andreas, for you, and for myself. My own process of waking up to the fact that the hot potato was a myth (see the chapter 'The Tale of The Hot Potato') evolved over 15 years and many different layers of insight. I started my journey battling dark feelings, which seemingly came out of nowhere to hijack me without warning. Through therapy I learned how strongly my inexplicable feelings of despair seemed to be connected to my family's past. Without my awareness, my family's traumatic journey had impacted me deeply. However, the discovery that I had inherited most of my miserable beliefs about life and myself was not enough to allow me to let go of them. On the contrary, I felt cheated by life, unable to breathe under the crushing weight of all the hot potatoes piled up on me. I was angry with my family for having burdened me with their drama and for having let me down with their inability to deal with their own lives. Frustrated, I carried on with my quest for answers and a way out.

When I was introduced to the idea of the hot potato being a creation of my own mind in the present, I was confused. After all, I had just managed to discover the hot potato and how deeply it had affected all aspects of my life. And now they claimed the hot potato existed only in my head?!? First, I found this notion offensive. Then I got angry with myself; had I unnecessarily made myself suffer all these years? Thoughts such as *I should have known this* or *See, there is no need to suffer! Then stop being such a wimp and feel better already!* made me feel guilty, insecure, and overwhelmed. Although one part of me immediately embraced the idea of *I live in the feeling of my thinking*, most other parts were at a loss as to how to use this truth to turn my life around.

Looking back, being angry with myself for not having seen that the past is *my* creation in the present, was like being angry with my two-year-old self for not knowing how to tie her shoelaces. Before I learned how to tie shoelaces, I was simply not able to do it. When my level of understanding of the mechanics of tying shoelaces finally matured, I integrated this ability into my skillset and have been able to do it ever since. As this concept dawned on me, I stopped being angry with myself. I saw how, unbeknownst to me, my subconscious had written a script for my life based on other people's stories about their lives. Trapped in my room of mirrors, I lived in the feeling of my thinking about these stories until new thinking emerged. Having empathy for myself made it easier to integrate my new awareness. Everyone, including me, is doing the best they can – given their current level of thinking.

Fighting windmills

At the very start of this chapter I recounted my conversation with Laura, the distressed mother who was plagued by the thought that she might hurt her children. During our discussion, I shared one of my own recurring thoughts with Laura. I live in Berlin, a city with a subway. When I stand on the platform waiting for the train to arrive, I sometimes have the slightly strange thought of jumping in front of the approaching train. This thought is not accompanied by sad or hopeless feelings, it seems to be more a curious *I wonder what would happen, if...* exploration, but when it first appeared, I didn't know if I should feel worried about it.

I ask Laura if she had ever had a thought like that.

'Sure, I suppose so. Everyone has, haven't they?'

'I don't know about everyone, but it seems that a lot of people I spoke to about this have. Now, you said you've had this thought before too. Have you ever jumped?'

Laura laughs. 'No, of course not!'

'Why not?' I enquired.

'Well, I guess because it would be crazy. Because I don't want to kill myself.'

'So, even though you have had the thought that you *could* jump, you didn't because you don't actually want to kill yourself?'

Laura tilted her head and looked at me expectantly. 'Yeah, I suppose that's right.'

'So why do you believe that *thinking* you could hurt your children can *make* you hurt them – even though you know you do not actually want to hurt them?'

Laura went quiet, rubbing her finger over her nose. 'I don't know. I guess I am afraid that having these thoughts means something terrible. Like a curse, opening a door that should never be opened. I was afraid that thinking it would inevitably lead me to do the unspeakable. But the more I tried not to think of it, the more often I did – and then I really got scared. And I couldn't tell anyone, because of what that says about me as a mother. They would take my children away from me. And everything would fall apart and it would be my fault.'

After a deep sigh, Laura chuckled.

'Why are you laughing?'

Laura exhaled deeply. 'When I listen to myself, I sound truly crazy. Like I am the worst mother on the planet.'

'Do you think you are the worst mother on the planet?'

'No, no, I don't! I think I am a pretty good mom, for the most part anyway. I don't *want* to hurt my children. So far, when I get angry, I just go to another room and scream into a pillow or something.'

'Laura, you may have already noticed that thoughts come and go. Some of our thoughts are sensible, some are kind, some of them crazy, and some even violent. They don't actually *have to* mean anything. When I saw that thinking *what if I jumped* in front of the train didn't mean I *have to* jump, the thought was no scarier than thinking that I need to buy some tomatoes for dinner.'

She nodded. 'Yeah, I think I understand now. I guess you are saying that the thought cannot *make* me hurt my children. That a thought has no power unless I believe I need to act on it. If the thought comes, it doesn't have to mean that I will hurt my children. I don't choose to act on it; it will pass, and a new thought will appear.'

We get annoyed or worried about some of our recurring thoughts, because we think we are obliged to follow them, learn how to stop them, or make ourselves think the opposite. We don't have to treat our thoughts (or feelings) as a call to action and we don't have to believe everything we think. Put more bluntly; perhaps we really shouldn't believe anything we think. After changing what she believed her thoughts had to mean, Laura was surprised to notice that the thought about hurting her children came up less and less and eventually, the thought of hurting her children ceased to re-appear entirely.

Taking what we see and think of as a call to action, we often behave like Don Quixote, the tragic self-proclaimed knight in the novels of Miguel de Cervantes. Don Quixote, mesmerised by ancient stories of heroic acts of knighthood, sets out on a personal crusade to achieve fame and revive chivalry. On his journey, he fights the infamous windmills, convinced that they are evil giants, and confronts a herd of goats that he believes to be a hostile army. Only on his deathbed does Don Quixote deeply regret the years he wasted battling the fantasies in his head. To see windmills as just windmills instead of as giants makes for a more fearless life.

I don't have to think that

I recently had a small bite to eat in a restaurant in London. Having travelled in the US extensively, I have become used to tipping religiously and always get confused about different tipping rules in other countries. As the waiter charged my credit card, I told him to add two pounds as a tip. He replied that he could only charge the credit card with the exact amount of the check, but that I was of course welcome to leave a tip in cash. As I put two one-pound coins into the little bowl in which he had brought the check, I saw that '12% gratuity included' was printed on the receipt.

I stalled and noticed how anger flared up in me as one of my selves called out, 'He is screwing you over. I can't believe he didn't tell you that the tip is already included. He did this on purpose, because you are a foreigner, and he probably figured you don't know any better! Take the money out of the bowl and walk away.' As soon as I thought that, I noticed another emotion: embarrassment. Another part of me exclaimed, 'How stupid will you look if you claw the two pound coins from the bowl? What will people think of you? Have you no self-respect?' Slightly amused by the intensity with which my two parts battled over the two-pound tip, suddenly it occurred to me: I don't have to think that. Any of it. With this insight, I relaxed, and from the quietness, another line of thinking emerged: I realised that whatever the waiter earned per hour, it would likely not be very much and therefore my two-pound tip on top of the included gratuity would probably be more than welcome. My anger instantly softened and so did my embarrassment.

When the waiter returned to my table, he pointed at the bowl and asked, 'Can I take this away?'

I smiled at him and said from the bottom of my heart, 'With pleasure!'

This too shall pass

According to Jewish folk wisdom, King Solomon once lost a chess game to his most trusted advisor, Benaiah Ben Yehoyada. Being a bit of a sore loser, King Solomon decided to teach Benaiah a humbling lesson by assigning him an impossible task: to find him a ring with the power to make a happy man sad and a sad man happy. Benaiah is given half a year to produce this magical ring. He searches in every corner of the kingdom, but to no avail. Just as he returns to face the king and admit defeat, Benaiah stumbles into a small and dusty workshop tucked away in a little alley not far from the castle. After one look at the inside of the dusty little store, Benaiah disappointedly turns to walk away. It is impossible that this goldsmith will have what not even the most famous goldsmiths in the kingdom have ever even heard of.

In this moment, the owner, an old and rather frail-looking man, approaches him and asks how he might be of service. Benaiah sighs and shares his quest for a ring that possesses the power to make a sad man happy and a happy man sad. The old goldsmith nods and says he might have just what Benaiah is looking for. Stunned, Benaiah waits patiently as the old man rummages in the back of his store. After a short while the goldsmith returns and hands him an unassuming gold ring. Inspecting the ring, Benaiah discovers an engraved sentence on the inside. As Benaiah reads the sentence his face lights up. He pays the old goldsmith handsomely for the ring and hurries back to the castle. King Solomon watches him approach, looking forward to Benaiah's admission of his inevitable failure. With a knowing smile Benaiah hands Solomon the gold ring. Solomon frowns, turns the ring in his fingers, and finally detects the engraving. He reads: 'This too shall pass'. And Solomon, in his wisdom, sees that this ring contains the truth. Life is impermanent and everything will pass.

THE ONE AND ONLY RING

This too shall pass

Because of our obsession with wanting happiness but not sadness we fail to witness what thoughts and their accompanying feelings do naturally – they pass. There is no need to be so scared of our experience. To put it in the words of my client Barbara: 'What now happens more and more is that I feel a certain way and then

I suddenly remember that this state, this depression, is only here now, only true in this moment. When I remember that this feeling of sadness or the dark thoughts I have are not permanent, they most often begin to lose their grip on me. In the past, feeling *down* turned into feeling *terrible* because of all the doomsday thoughts I had *about* feeling down.

'My problem was not actually feeling low-spirited. My problem was getting in the self-blame-cycle of, "OMG – I should be beyond this darkness after all these years. Why do I feel down now? Is this starting again? Was this period of being happy and full of energy only make-believe? Who did I think I was fooling with my good mood this past week? *This* is how I *really* am." When I thought *that*, feeling low-spirited turned into feeling depressed,' Barbara said.

She continued, 'The other day, I noticed I felt down and thought of the story of King Solomon you had shared with me. *This too shall pass.* And you know what? It actually does pass! In a way, it now appears so astonishingly simple. Or at least it does sometimes. Of course, the moment I think, *It's so simple!* another part of me loudly exclaims, *Oh no, it's not! I'll show you how simple it is when you lie in bed depressed!* But what I seem to manage more often lately is, instead of getting all panicked about *that* thought, to go back to: *This too shall pass.* And then it is simple again.'

Arguing with the weather

One year in June, my wife and I travelled to one of our most favourite cities in the world, San Francisco. I generally love this city: the beautiful architecture, the quality and diversity of the many restaurants, and the inspiring kindness and creativity of the people we know there. Yet, as much as I love the place, there was one thing I had a lot of negative thoughts about: San Francisco weather. As we walked across the city it seemed to change every five minutes, and in the course of an hour I would go from feeling too hot in a tank top to wishing I had brought my puffer jacket to shield me from the freezing wind. According to my wife, I kept commenting on my experience non-stop: 'I wish it wasn't so hot!', 'Ah, now it's perfect!', 'Oh no, I wish the wind would stop', 'I wish the fog wasn't so cold', 'Can you believe it – now it's raining!'. After listening to me being irritable for most of the day, my wife eventually brought to my attention that I hadn't exactly been a role model of living in the present: instead of surrendering to the flow of the day and the San Francisco climate, my attention was entirely occupied with arguing with the weather.

Today, I can't help but smile about my 'weather-upset' because it is such a perfect metaphor for what we often do in life; we get lost in thoughts about what or who to blame for our unhappiness. By the time we are done with all that, we have successfully missed anything that could have been enjoyable about our day.

I have had more than one client who has come to me with the agenda of, 'I want to change my self-limiting beliefs and my negative thinking', because they had pinpointed those as the source of their suffering. They proudly recount how many limiting beliefs or negative thoughts they have traced back to their origins in their unhappy past and list the self-affirming messages they have crafted to replace the negative ones. Unfortunately, after a few hours, days or, rarely, a few weeks, their familiar anxiety or anger takes hold of them yet again. Since they believe their lack of disciplined positive thinking to be the root of all evil, they not only suffer from their 'bad' thoughts but additionally from the severe criticism they inflict on themselves every time they slip into a negative thought. The ability to control their thoughts has turned into yet another pre-condition for living the right life. They seek my help, assuming that I can teach them the right method to once-and-for-all replace their bad thoughts with good thoughts.

Even amongst the most diligent self-improvers I have yet to find anyone who hasn't complained that trying to control reality through thought-control is frustratingly unstable. Thoughts are, after all, as evanescent as San Francisco's weather; they are constantly in flux. The bottom line is that most people's attempts to secure everlasting happiness by uprooting every single limiting belief or negative thought they have about the world or themselves have proven about as successful as trying to catch sunshine in a jar. I do not want to discard the potential beneficial effects of focusing on the positive. Nonetheless, when we become obsessed with positive thinking and continuously force it upon ourselves, we are no different than a pit bull who wants to play but cannot let go of the rag doll ('Think positively! Grrr! You have to think positive thoughts! Grrr! You cannot allow negative thoughts!'). It is unlikely that biting down harder will create more lightness or playfulness. Instead of forcing ourselves to think a certain way, which is incredibly energy-consuming and usually provides just short-lived pain relief, we can simply acknowledge that thoughts, like clouds, will dissolve naturally and the sun will re-appear.

The Three Principles

By now, we have extensively explored the concept of thought as the source of all pleasure and pain in our lives. According to the late philosopher Sydney Banks (1998), Thought is only one of three spiritual principles explaining how we create reality as human beings. The other two principles are *Mind* and *Consciousness*.

In very simple terms,
- *Mind* is the spark of life, the creative organising force that propels evolution.
- *Consciousness* is our capacity to know that there is life. Only because of consciousness do we know that we are alive and do we have the ability to experience being alive.
- *Thought* is the creative principle; through thought we create, label, and express the experience of being alive.

In other words: We are *alive*, we have *consciousness* of being alive, and we *think*, thereby creating reality as we know it. Sydney Banks further differentiated between the *individual* and the *collective*, assuming that each of us has an individual mind, individual consciousness, and individual thought, which are embedded in a larger whole: collective Mind, Consciousness, and Thought. To better distinguish between the collective and the individual, I will spell the collective Mind, Consciousness, and Thought with a capital letter. To Sydney Banks, the Three Principles describe what is driving 'the human experience of spiritual beings'. In the following pages, we will explore the two remaining principles of Mind and Consciousness.

To me personally, the discovery of Sydney Banks's work and the *Three Principles* created a major shift in my thinking and feeling. With every layer that deepened my understanding of *Mind, Consciousness,* and *Thought* I felt more supported by life instead of feeling I had to struggle against it. Moments of mental and emotional clarity became more common. I began to move without fear or effort from one situation and one decision to the next. In short, I felt well. For years, I had believed that such a degree of well-being was either a rare talent, bestowed on the lucky few, a happy accident, or a tonne of hard work. Today, happiness is a frequent guest in my life – and when it is not, I don't worry so much about it, knowing that this too shall pass.

At this point, the notion of *Three Principles* being the 'foundation of our reality' may appear to be a rather abstract concept of little practical value. I will share my understanding of them to the best of my abilities, in the hope that they appear more practical by the end of this chapter and perhaps even create a similar shift in feeling for you. That being said, please approach the following sections with the attitude of 'what if?' For the sake of simplicity, I have decided to treat these ideas as matter-of-fact in many places in this chapter and not repeatedly point to their only being concepts. I don't know if they are true. Ultimately, even the principles of *Mind, Consciousness,* and *Thought* are a projection invented by humans – and I trust that you will come to your own conclusions as to how much the *Three Principles,* and the observations that follow from them, resonate with you.

The principle of Mind

When attempting to understand Mind, it is helpful to remember that we are trying to put something into words that is intangible and, essentially, unverifiable. The idea of Mind cannot be validated other than through personal experience. However, given that the properties assigned to Mind are based on subjective accounts and anecdotal evidence, it is all the more striking that humans across ages, cultures, and religious beliefs describe encounters with 'the intangible' in surprisingly similar terms. If nothing else, treat the principle of Mind as a hypothesis. In essence, Sydney Banks proposes a pantheistic worldview in which Mind is a form of god that is the same as cosmos or nature. Mind is the creation principle, the source of life, awareness, and consciousness. Mind is simultaneously the source of all life, the field within which all life unfolds, and the destination to which all life returns. Mind is like a limitless ocean birthing and holding the collective experience of life, a place beyond time in which we were never born and never die, where there is no beginning and no end, no judgement. To Mind, nothing is beautiful or ugly, right or wrong, happy or sad, good or evil, and no experience is better or worse than the next; it just is.

Given my own atheist disposition, I understand Mind as the ever changing field of energy we are all part of. Mind is life; it is all-encompassing, interconnected, impersonal, and strives for development and expansion. This field of energy produces energy spikes, which materialise as transient, conscious, and physical identities. One of these energy spikes is I, Nadjeschda. After a brief period of embodiment as my current physical form on this planet, my biological matter dissolves back into the grand pool of energy, waiting to be recycled into a star or perhaps into yet another being. Mind simply *is* and our individual mind is a facet of the collective Mind.

Most of us are unaware of this connection and go through life like a wave looking for the ocean, rather oblivious to the fact that *we are* the ocean. We look for connection, seeking to belong, having forgotten that we could not be disconnected if we tried.

It is *within* this universe of the collective that our individual mind, consciousness, and thought come into existence. People who develop more awareness of this inseparable connection to Mind (or whatever their preferred word for it may be) report how it enables them to access insight and wisdom, appearing to expand far beyond their individual knowledge.

Of course, on a day-to-day basis, we experience life through our individual mind. Yet, when I think of my individual mind as suspended in the timeless sphere of Mind I feel inner peace and a deep sense of connection.

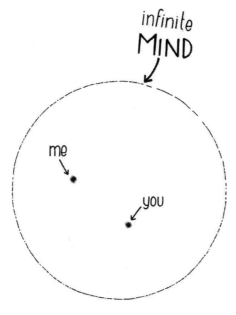

When the interconnectedness of everything is no longer just an esoteric concept but a visceral experience, we seem to interact with life differently. I like to believe that innate to this experience of connectedness is the intelligence and ethics of what it takes to preserve and further life instead of destroying it. If you see life as one organism, as one Mind, any form of cruelty inflicted by one part of the organism towards another is exposed as nonsensical. Given the impartial nature of Mind you could of course argue that to Mind it is all the same because there is no 'good' or 'bad' experience, and neither pain nor death is anything more than yet another energetic state. Still, I find it comforting that people who drop into the feeling of this connection come out of the experience kinder, more empathic, and more peaceful. It gives me hope that connectedness could be a kind of vaccine against some of the less pleasant human traits such as greed or violence.

Living suspended in this connection, or as some Three Principles practitioners call it, *living from Mind,* allows us to connect to what Eastern philosophy calls the Buddha within: our essential nature that is serene, sacred, and full of infinite love and wisdom. When I speak to people about their personal experience of living from Mind, they describe blissful moments of clarity and expansiveness, moments in which they simultaneously feel love and detachment, and in which they know intuitively and with great clarity what to do next. We appear to access this state of clarity, inner guidedness, or flow more frequently if we allow ourselves to relax in the notion of Mind as our origin – our past, present, and future.

The principle of Consciousness

The next principle is consciousness. Because humans are conscious, we are aware of being alive and can experience ourselves as living beings. To describe how our consciousness works, let us return to the metaphor of 'a stream of thought'. At any given time, there are thousands of streams of thought running through us simultaneously since most of our thinking happens unconsciously, outside of our awareness, and without our active participation.

Imagine consciousness as an entity with the ability to soar high enough to observe the entire planet from afar but also to hover just barely above the ground or even dive deep into the stream. Consciousness allows us to not only to *conceive* of the streams of thought, but it is our consciousness that materialises individual thoughts. Observation is creation. Without the focused awareness of consciousness the content of our multiple streams of Thought would remain undifferentiated and unknown to us.

Even without our interference, our consciousness fluctuates between being highly focused or unfocused, attached or detached, clear or foggy. In the stream, there are moments when our consciousness is stuck, pre-occupied with a particular object, as well as moments when it is violently whipped along by the current. The more it struggles to regain control the more the resulting mud storm clouds our vision. The moment our consciousness calms, the mud settles and clarity returns. Yet although we have a varying ability to direct our consciousness, most of the time we are not the ones guiding it. In a sense, consciousness has us, not we it. Skilful meditators describe the experience of being in pure consciousness as a state free of judgement, dissociated from thoughts, and liberated from labels such as good or bad or right or wrong. But even for them, as soon as thought returns, they are back to living in the feeling of their thinking like any other mortal.

Along with the discovery of the Three Principles of Mind, Consciousness, and Thought, Syd Banks made a few observations that came directly out of his experience of living from Mind. I will attempt to summarise some of them because they resonate with many who have since embarked on their journey of deepening their understanding of the Three Principles.

Well-being is our nature

Let me tell you about Otto. He is a white Spitz belonging to friends of ours who converted an old castle in the countryside into a small hotel. Otto looks like a canine top-model; his long legs and perfect white fluffy fur make for a distinctly regal appearance. Like any dog, Otto loves being outside and gracefully deems my wife and me to be acceptable walking companions. Having grown up in the countryside, Otto is not accustomed to walking on a leash. For the most part there doesn't seem to be a need for a leash either, since he behaves rather well – that is until he smells a rabbit or a deer. On these occasions there is no stopping him. Like a white flash, he disappears into the forest and when he re-emerges, he looks more like a bear than a Spitz; his white fur is covered in mud and he smells like game – a fact that seems to give him tremendous enjoyment.

The first time my wife and I took him for a walk, we were horrified when Otto raced into the forest, ignoring any of our pleas to stay with us. When he re-emerged from the woods, he was caked in mud and branches and reeking of boar. Upon returning what now looked like 'Otto the Beast' to his home, we begged our friends to let us give him a bath. Unperturbed, they shrugged their shoulders and assured us that he would be back to his old self in no time. Looking at the sullied creature besides us, we were highly dubious, to say the least. But low and behold, when we saw Otto again a few hours later, he looked as if he had never set a paw in a forest ever. It turned out that Otto indeed has self-cleaning fur – if you let him be, dry mud just falls right off and after a while, he returns to his natural and beautiful self. There is nothing to do. Nature takes care of it.

OTTO - the self-cleaning dog

Otto was born with fluffy white self-cleaning fur. *What if* we too were born with the equivalent of self-cleaning 'fur' – if we were born *well* and with the ability to always find our way back to well-being? What if well-being is not a distant destination to be reached but an original state to be remembered? When I speak of well-being, I refer to our ability to flow with disorder and to respond flexibly to what any moment brings. The less we trust in our ability to deal with unpredictable change and chaos, the more we try to control life: to control our thinking, our body, other people, or our circumstances. These attempts at control are futile because life itself is chaos. When we realise that each of us is one beautiful and unique expression of life and therefore *designed* to dance with chaos, chaos ceases to be quite so scary. In this sense, well-being simply describes our ability to dance with life, to dance with chaos. This is arguably less energy-consuming than feeling stressed, unhappy, or depressed. Perhaps we are designed for well-being because it is the most energy-efficient way to be in the world.

Symptoms (mental, emotional, or physical) that seemingly remove us from well-being are simply a misled attempt to self-heal and re-establish balance. As long as we believe that well-being is something alien to us, something we need to create, we look for solutions in the wrong place. Being afraid of our own chaotic experience makes us want to forcibly establish the right constellation of circumstances in the external world to create structure and safety. If our attempts fail, we might even try to lull our fear and pain with medication, alcohol, or other drugs. Any of these strategies can result in momentary relief, but they are neither a reliable nor a lasting source of well-being. We look for relief everywhere, but rarely in the one place where it resides: inside of our own body and mind. Just as Otto's fur is meant to be white and fluffy, we are meant to dance and be well. That's not to say that Otto's fur doesn't sometimes get muddy, or that we don't feel disconnected from well-being at times; it just means that we will return to that state, because nature designed us to be well.

There is nothing to do; don't push the river

Many years ago, one of my mentors gave me a quote to ponder:

> Don't push the river.
> It flows by itself.
>
> PROVERB

It took me a while to understand what this saying was supposed to mean. Today, I read it with the Three Principles in mind: trying to manipulate our thinking is about as sensible as trying to catch a wave in a bucket – or push a river. Our consciousness and thoughts unfold, and in a sense we are simply invited along for the ride. Sometimes we can consciously choose to give energy and passion to a thought, or to drop it. However, most of our thinking happens unconsciously, and it is rather tedious to drag every thought into the light, investigate its quality, and consciously decide to follow it or discard it. That's not really how life works. Even if I actually managed to correct my thinking every time I catch myself having a bad thought, thoughts will continue to come and go whenever I don't will them into a specific direction.

Instead of having to dissect my every thought, it might be enough just to recognise myself as the artist of the experience I have. To the extent that I am unconscious of creating reality through my thinking, I will experience things happening to me (unpleasant as well as pleasant) that are caused by a power outside of myself. Events in my life will appear arbitrary. Knowing that I am the creator of my reality allows me to see the quality of my thinking as a mirror of my current consciousness. Life appears to me as it does, until my consciousness shifts and life begins to appear differently. From this understanding, doing less might sometimes equal doing more.

Instead of acting from a *low state of mind* where my consciousness is pre-occupied with angry, fearful, or sad thoughts, it might be wiser to simply wait until life appears differently. Even big upsets will subside; the onslaught of thoughts will wane, and my consciousness will return to clarity. In other words: instead of acting when I am most emotional, I can suspend action until I enter a higher state of mind. In a higher state of mind, I am present to the moment and to the deeper wisdom arising from Mind.

Living from Mind is therefore not something I have to figure out how to do, not a state to be reached, nothing I have to master or surrender to. Living from Mind is merely something I can realise is happening all the time, because Mind is me and I am it.

The sun always shines

When I first began studying the Three Principles, I had a conversation with my wife in which she challenged me by saying, 'OK, let's assume that everything I experience is made of thought. But if we are all doomed to be trapped in this "room of mirrors" forever and nobody has the choice to step out of it because of the way the human brain functions – then what is the practical *relevance* of this? What you are effectively saying is that when I am trapped in an unhappy thought, I am trapped in an unhappy thought until I am somehow not trapped in my unhappy thought anymore. But if and when I stop being trapped is not up to me, and I can't speed up the process. If I don't have the power to do anything about it, then I don't understand how knowing that *it is all thought* changes anything in my daily life.' I didn't have an immediate response for her. I only knew that for me personally, truly understanding that thought created reality had been the missing piece of my puzzle – but I was at a loss to describe why this made such a big difference.

Then I remembered an interaction I once had with Leo, the five-year-old son of friends of mine. Leo had developed a new habit: he was scared of the sunset. In his mind, the sun setting was forever the end of light and every evening he became terrified as night approached. One night, he shared his worry with me, and we started speaking about how the Earth circles around the sun and how darkness comes when we are on the part of the Earth facing away from the sun. When we are rotating towards the sun, it appears as if the sun rises. Looking at the model I had built on the fly with a tennis ball and a basketball, Leo replied thoughtfully, 'So, the light really always shines. We just can't see it when we are facing the other direction?'

'Yes, that's right, the sun always shines, just not always where we can see it.'

'So, like, when I turn around and I can't see you anymore but you are really still there?'

'Yes, exactly. And when the world has finished turning once around its own axis, we can see the sunlight again.'

Leo was very pleased with the discovery that tomorrow the sun would surely rise again. And from that moment he stopped being terrified by the sun setting.

Knowing about the Earth's rotation will not change the fact that night is inevitable. Likewise, knowing our experience is created through thought will not change the fact that there will be dark thoughts and subsequent feelings of sadness, fear, or anger. But knowing that even if I can't see them, feelings of joy and creative thoughts are still there has relieved the terror of momentarily not having them in my field of vision.

The Three Principles have triggered two essential insights for me. My first insight is that neither darkness nor light is permanent – they are both temporary guests in my consciousness. From a peaceful state of mind, I can observe them come and go, appreciating the unexpected beauty in the full spectrum of light. My second insight is the discovery of Mind. Again, for me Mind isn't God, it is life, but depending on your interpretation of the concept, those might be used interchangeably. The wisdom and clarity of Mind is always available to me because it is part of me and I am part of it. I might not always know how to unlock it, but I find my way more often than I used to.

Real-world example

Claudia was furious. 'I just can't understand why John is doing this. He knows exactly how important this is to me, but when I want to talk about it, he just shuts me out, he stonewalls. I could strangle him. He clearly doesn't give a damn about what I feel or want. I can't understand how someone with his talents can waste them away by ruminating and getting lost in the internet every day. He has all these really promising projects he could get engaged with and all these people lining up to do business with him – but he never follows up on anything because he says he wants to focus on writing his stupid book – which he obviously doesn't ever get around to writing because he sits there and ruminates. He is effectively playing roulette with our savings by behaving this way. Our savings are dwindling because I am the only one making money. What is going to happen with the kids' education if he continues to behave like this?' Claudia stared at a point somewhere behind my head.

'Do you remember when we talked about how thought creates our feeling?' I asked.

She looks at me with squinted eyes. 'Yes...'

'Let's assume it is true: whatever you are thinking creates what you are feeling. How would that change your view of what you are experiencing right now?'

Claudia glared at me, clearly not happy with my challenge. 'Well, I guess it would mean that I feel furious because I have a bunch of unpleasant thoughts about him. But – come on! Of course I have unpleasant thoughts about him and of course I am unhappy when he acts like that. I tell you what I think: I think if John actually cared about us, he would behave differently!'

'Okay, I get that you really think that. And how does it make you feel when you think the reason for him doing what he does is that he doesn't care about you?'

Claudia didn't reply but bit her lower lip.

'Why are you biting your lower lip?'

'Because I want to keep myself from saying that, sometimes, I really find you annoying!' She chuckled. 'Well, let's see... if I think that the reason for him ruminating is that he doesn't care, that makes me feel awful. So, if I follow your logic, I am making myself feel awful. And I have been doing it for a while.' Claudia went quiet. 'I find this somewhere between hilarious and infuriating.'

'What do you find hilarious and what infuriating?'

'That I am apparently *doing* this feeling to myself.' She breathed in deeply and sat up with her back straight. 'So, are you saying that it is all in my head?'

'Claudia, I am not saying this to make you wrong. But where else could it ever be than in your head? There is no other place than *in your head* when it comes to your reality.'

She shrugged her shoulders. 'Okay, okay, I get that. I guess. Does that mean that John isn't ruminating? That I am just imagining all of this?'

'It doesn't really matter what John is doing or not doing, because the anger you feel is created by thought. Your thoughts. That's all it means. You have the right to think what you think and feel what you feel. You can leave him, if that is what you want to do. Or you can decide to stick around. We can feel really miserable when we see our loved ones do things that we don't agree with. But sometimes we feel miserable even when they do everything right, when they actually behave the way we want them to.'

'Whenever we get caught in our insecure thinking about them, we feel as if they are the last person on the planet we want to be with because they are the reason for all our suffering. When we happen to get caught in happy thoughts, we feel like we won the lottery by having them in our life. Because our thinking is in flux, we feel differently about our partner at different moments in time. This doesn't mean that you can't or shouldn't leave him and perhaps you will. It just means that whatever you happen to think about him right now is creating how you feel about it. So, potentially, even though that might seem far-fetched, you are only one thought away from loving John.'

Claudia looked at me quizzically. 'Hmmm, I don't know. What you said about the ability to be unhappy even if John does what I want resonates. Before he quit his job to write his book, he actually did what I wanted him to do professionally – but I can't say that I was particularly happy during that stage of our relationship for reasons that had nothing to do with his career choices. So, fair enough, I see how I can be unhappy even if he does what I want him to do. A while ago you said something to me that stuck in my head: "And you don't have to think that". Does that mean I don't have to think those things about John if they don't make me happy?'

Now it was my time to smile. 'Yes, that is exactly what that means. If it doesn't make us happy – we don't *have* to think that. We can. We might. And we probably will. But the key is that we don't have to. Part of the "don't have to" is that we don't have to take our thoughts so seriously. Again, this doesn't mean we shouldn't take them seriously; it just opens the space of possibility for a new thought to occur. You may remember that I also said, "And this too shall pass". In other words, even if we think thoughts which make us unhappy, they are only flotsam drifting by; most of them will pass.'

Claudia looked equally puzzled as she looked relieved. 'I am not entirely sure what just happened, but somehow, I feel lighter. I suppose that John's not writing isn't actually a life-threatening problem. Even though it is not easy with just one salary, we have pulled it off so far, and we probably will for a while longer. I just wish for him to get unstuck.

'I think I will talk to him again and see how he feels about it. Perhaps we can come to some kind of agreement as to how long we will continue like this before he actively looks for a job again.'

A few weeks after our session, Claudia summarised her progress and the difference it had made to her. What Claudia had experienced during the session was the freeing moment when a new thought disrupts an old story. She described it as the realisation that 'I can leave John if I want to. I don't have to make up a horrible story about his behaviour to justify my decision. And suddenly I knew that I didn't want to leave him but that I needed a plan we both agreed on.' A new thought feels like opening a window in a smoke-filled room; fresh air pours in and we can breathe freely. During one of our subsequent conversations, Claudia said something that has become one of my favourite quotes: 'Anything I could ever want is within me. Therefore, it is always within reach.'

The chapter in a nutshell

Due to a tragic misunderstanding we have come to believe that happiness can be created by manipulating circumstances. However, circumstances, no matter how dazzling, do not create lasting happiness.

Happiness is not a stage to be conquered; it is a state to be cherished.

We are not human beings having a spiritual experience; we are spiritual beings having a human experience.

Thought: There are multiple streams of thought that flow whether we pay attention to them or not. When we bring our attention to a stream, we materialise thoughts. We differentiate between 'good' and 'bad' thoughts. This separation requires us to get closer to the good ones and keep the bad ones at bay. When we realise that any thought is just a thought, it loses power over us and we have to invest less energy in avoiding it.

We live in the feeling of our thinking. More intense feelings don't make us more right – they merely point at the fact that we have more intense thoughts.

We sit in a mirrored room where every thought is reflected back at us.

The past is an invention of the present. It is created by my thinking in the moment. When we treat everything we see and think as a call to action, we end up battling windmills because we think they are giants.

I don't have to think that, and I don't need to argue with the weather.

This too shall pass.

Mind is the spark of life, the creative organising force that propels evolution.

Consciousness is our capacity to know that there is life. Only because of consciousness do we know that we are alive and do we have the ability to experience being alive.

Thought is the creative principle; through thought we create, label, and express the experience of being alive.

I am not a wave looking for the ocean, I am the ocean. Our individual mind is a facet of the collective Mind.

Consciousness allows us not only to *conceive* of the streams of thought but it is our consciousness that *materialises* individual thoughts. Well-being is our nature, our ability to flow with disorder and to respond flexibly to what is in any moment. It is not a distant destination to reach but our original state.

There is nothing to do. Don't push the river. Life appears to me as it does until my consciousness shifts and life begins to appear differently.

The sun always shines, even when you can't see it.

REFERENCES

Banks, S. (1998). *Missing Link, The: Reflections on Philosophy and Spirit*. Lone Pine.

Chardin, P. T. D. (2007). *Le Phénomène humain*. Seuil.

Jamieson, J. P., Nock, M. K., & Mendes, W. B. (2012). *Mind over matter: reappraising arousal improves cardiovascular and cognitive responses to stress*. J Exp Psychol Gen, 141(3), 417-422.

Human freedom involves
our capacity to pause,
to choose the one response
toward which we wish
to throw our weight.

— Rollo May

CHAPTER 10

Push P.A.U.S.E

Life imitating art

In the chapter 'The Butt-Naked Emperor' we explored how our individual reality is actually a painting created by our brain. Organised as it is, our brain stores every piece of art in an internal art vault. Instead of creating a new painting for every new experience, our brain simply pulls an old painting from the vault and applies new layers of paint on top of old layers. There is a classic Jewish joke I love: A mother gives her son two sweaters for his birthday, a green one and a red one. The next morning, her son arrives at breakfast wearing the green sweater. With a raised eyebrow she sourly comments, 'So you didn't like the red one?'

Clearly, the son in the joke didn't stand a chance, since had he worn the red sweater the result would have been just the same. The truth is that we often act no more rationally than the Jewish mother in the joke. Triggered by who knows what (a look, a sentence, a raised eyebrow, a delay in reaction), we pull a painting from our memory vault with the inspiring title of *I Am Not Appreciated, Never Have*

Been, Never Will Be. Instead of looking at what is in front of us right at this moment, we stare at the amalgamation of every moment of our life in which we felt underappreciated. Fully immersed in this reality, we then take out our paintbrush and add another layer of rejection or insult on top of the old memories. The more often we return to the same painting, the more layers of paint we add over time, which not only makes the painting feel more real but also increases the likelihood that we will refer to it again and again. If we interact with the same painting often enough, the painting will become our life.

This is what we call 'life imitating art'!

By pointing out how we are caught in a self-referential loop, I don't mean to diminish the impact a particular event can have on us. Nonetheless, however painful a situation may have felt at the moment of its occurrence, this past no longer exists, except as a painting in our vault. The event is gone, and the people involved in this past situation do not actually live in our brain. Whatever mood or emotion we experience when thinking of this situation, whatever angry dialogue we may hear in our head, or heart-breaking scenery we see in our minds eye – we are witnessing our artistic brain at work. If we feel terrified, we feel terrified because our brain keeps pulling terrifying pictures from the vault, adding more gruesome layers to them. Past events continue to shape us because of the attention and meaning we give them – consciously or unconsciously.

Luckily, some of our paintings also carry promising titles such as: *Life Is Good, In the End Everything Turns Out Well, I Can Do This* or *I Really Deserve This.* Moments during which we look at those paintings make us happy and content with the life we are living. The moment we pull a painting from the vault with a title such as *Nobody Loves Me, Nothing Will Ever Be Okay, I Am Not Good Enough*, or *Life Is Unfair*, our mood sinks and our life can turn into one big mountain of discontent in the blink of an eye. Sometimes, the internal replacement of the picture we are looking at happens so fast, we haven't got the faintest idea how we went from *Life Is Good* and *Nothing Will Ever Be Okay* in less than thirty seconds. Often, the sudden change of artwork can be attributed to an upset – a conscious or unconscious disruption. So, let's investigate what upsets are and how we can interact with them without letting them hijack us.

The nature of upsets

When I asked my clients for examples of upsets which triggered change in their lives, these are some of the examples they gave me:

- getting fired from a job
- finding out their spouse was having an affair
- having an affair
- being overlooked for a promotion
- a big fight with their father
- feedback they received from colleagues
- being immobilised by an accident
- seeing poverty in a third world country
- being lied to by a friend
- haggling over inheritance with a sibling
- a friend or family member falling ill or dying

Most of you will probably agree that at least some of these situations would be upsetting or distressing to you as well. But that's exactly it. The fact that to *some* of you, *some* of these situations would be upsetting *some* of the time is our first opening for a change of perspective. To someone struggling with obsessive-compulsive disorder, it is upsetting if someone messes with the order of pens on their desk. To someone who survived a war, fireworks exploding on New Year's Eve can be re-traumatising. If I was diagnosed with a terminal illness it might feel devastating to me, while a Buddhist monk might calmly surrender to another stage of life unfolding.

If I can see a messed-up haircut just as a messed-up haircut, it is a minor upset. If I see a messed-up haircut as further evidence of people mistreating me, or of generally being disrespectful or careless towards me, it has the potential to be a major upset. Anything or nothing can be an upset and the depth and length of the upset is determined by the meaning we assign to it in the moment – which picture we pulled from our memory vault – and possibly also whether or not there is a full moon, or how hungry I am, or who was elected as president. If what qualifies as an upset is so different to different people – then what is an upset?

Generally speaking, we experience something as upsetting when life is not how we think it *should* be. The difference between a small and a big upset depends on: a) how big the disparity is between what we experience vs what we believe we should experience, and b) how deeply we have got lost in contemplating one of our more challenging art-pieces that we pulled from the vault. Now, this doesn't mean that we shouldn't get upset. It merely describes why we do get upset.

Just 'stop it'

The ingenious comedian Bob Newhart gave a disarmingly simple answer about how to move beyond our troubles in his iconic sketch 'Stop it!'. In this hilarious skit, Newhart plays the psychiatrist Dr Spitzer, who delivers a very unique kind of therapy. In the beginning of the session Dr Spitzer promises a distressed patient suffering from claustrophobia that his therapy will not last longer than five minutes because he will give her two words that have the power to solve all of her issues instantly. To her dismay, the patient quickly discovers that these two magic words are: 'Stop it!'. Every time she begins to speak about another one of her problems (being afraid of driving, making herself throw up, having issues with her mother, or having dysfunctional relationships with men, Dr Spitzer just yells, 'STOP IT!'

Dr Spitzer has no interest in exploring his patient's childhood, the alignment of the stars, or destiny as the root cause of her negative emotions and self-sabotaging behaviours. Because in the here and now, today, it is nobody else but herself who chooses to push the replay button on the things that make her miserable. From his perspective, the solution is deceivingly simple: if she *stops it*, a problem-free life filled with positive emotions is readily available to her.

This admittedly rather simplified approach to change does contain some deep wisdom. If we did indeed 'stop it', we would be free from our problems. If we stopped nagging, self-criticising, overeating, drinking, or watching TV – we would suffer fewer upsets, have happier relationships, like ourselves better, have a healthy weight, a clear head, and be more active. However, for many of us 'stopping it' is sadly easier said than done. Most likely, we have heard the message of 'just stop it' either from others in our lives or from an internal voice within us who keeps repeating the same thing. Every time we haven't managed to stop it, we feel we have failed on a grand scale.

Unwittingly, our shame and disappointment are often deepened by the messages we receive from self-help gurus and well-meaning friends. It has become a popular idea that we have the power to move beyond any upset or obstacle, if we only *think* positively and *want* it enough. There are drones of semi-enlightened people who offer plenty of advice as to how we should let go of our past and what we *have* to do to create exactly the life we want. It is the spiritual equivalent of the rags-to-riches story. According to this story, if you haven't yet overcome X (an unhappy childhood, eating disorder, abusive relationship, an addiction, etc) and created Y (a happy relationship, wealth, emotional stability, success, etc), you didn't want it enough – or you would have long emerged as the victorious master of your own destiny!

To hear that we are each the masters of our destiny can feel more than just a tad condescending. People who preach this blatantly ignore just how deeply our lives are affected by the interaction of our genes, our upbringing, and the socioeconomic conditions in which we live (Hughes et al., 2016). At the same time, there is also mounting evidence for our ability to flourish despite, and sometimes even because of, adverse circumstances, which researchers call post-traumatic growth (Joseph et al., 2008; Russo-Netzer & Moran, 2016). As humans, we are incredibly resilient and capable of change. An unhappy childhood does not sentence us to an unhappy life, and our genetic predispositions do not inevitably doom us to become alcoholic, fat, or depressed. How then do we integrate these two seemingly contradicting truths about life?

The wisdom to know the difference

When life appears to us as an endless stream of disappointments and upsets, we have got stuck with a crummy painting indeed. Looking at this painting over and over again strengthens the perspective of our 'inner victim', the part of us that feels wronged, forgotten, or abused by life. We can recognise our own victim voice because it often sounds like this: 'this is not how it should be...' or 'and this reminds me of the other terrible time when...' or 'of course this would happen to me again'. Victim-land is not a happy place. Not surprisingly, the mission of most self-help books is therefore to help us overthrow our victim self or wrestle it to the ground so that we can 'own' our experience, and start being the creator of the life we want.

As we saw in the chapter 'The Transformation Map', our individual experience is embedded in an endless number of collectives, each with their own requirements, rules, and limitations. Our individual circumstances vary greatly, and I wouldn't dare to presume how the slogan 'Be the master of your own destiny! Use your upsets as a starting point for personal growth!' resonates to a woman forced into prostitution, a young man born in a slum, or a single mom who has to feed four children. I am not saying that taking ownership and practicing positive thinking doesn't hold the potential to empower anyone, but I am also aware of just how insulting this position can be to people living in conditions different from my own. I agree that being in 'creator mode' is generally a happier place and offers more choices than 'victim mode'. Yet, feeling like a victim is a deeply human experience, which we neither can nor should have to eradicate. I have yet to meet someone who hasn't felt hopeless, disempowered, and victimised by life on occasion. In a conversation with a friend about this, he reminded me of the Serenity Prayer which is used in twelve-step programmes all over the world:

God, grant me the serenity to accept the things I cannot change, the courage to change the things I can, and the wisdom to know the difference.

This notion of 'the wisdom to know the difference' hints at a perspective that is neither our inner victim nor our inner creator. This third perspective is one from which I am an attentive witness to life unfolding. There is a time to move beyond, to act and create (engage the creator), a time to surrender and let go (surrender to the victim), and a time to be present and observe (stay present as the observer). Creator, victim, and witness form a trinity of important human states of being.

Feeling like a victim is as natural an experience as being a creator or being a witness. So don't be a jerk; be kind to yourself when you feel upset. If you have the courage and consciousness to embrace the part of you that feels like a victim, you will have more empathy for the part in others that feels like a victim. And empathy is the best way to connect with another person deeply enough to inspire them to shift their perspective. When our internal vantage point shifts, so does our experience of life. Therefore, the goal is perhaps not to weed out our inner victim and 'stop it!' with force, but rather to enjoy the fluidity of our different states: to experience being a victim, a creator, and a witness – fully and uncensored.

From victim to creator

Sometimes, a client of mine arrives at a session feeling upset by something that occurred in their life. At this point I often tell them the story of the 'beast on the beach': Imagine that you are wandering down a beautiful tropical beach with your best friend. In the distance, you notice a creature lying in your path. The closer you get, the bigger the thing appears to be. As you approach, you can see that the beast is huge, ugly, and menacing beyond belief. You are transfixed by this apparition, incapable of seeing anything but the beast blocking your way. You can't see the palm trees, the tranquil turquoise sea, the shells on the beach, you can't feel the gentle breeze or hear the birds in the distance. All you see is IT. You grab your friend's arm and begin to babble about all the gory details you notice about this monster: the scaly skin, the fiery eyes, the sharp claws, the giant teeth. Unfazed, your friend grabs a bucket some child left behind on the beach, fills it with water from the sea, and empties the bucket over the beast. To your amazement, it just melts away. You laugh because you realise that your scary beast was merely sculpted from sand.

Obviously, the beast is a metaphor for the upset or crisis we face. It is our mind that creates beasts out of sand. These beasts appear solid until someone pours a bucket of water over them. The water, in this case, is a metaphor for awareness. There is infinite power in awareness: it can help us experience a different reality. Think of a situation where something appeared like a huge problem to you, scared you, or made you angry – until you received additional information that changed the picture. To see something new or different instantly changes the shape of the sand beast in your head.

It happens all the time, but we are mostly too busy to notice how a thing reconfigures itself from moment to moment.

When we are stuck with an upsetting story we react from fear. With the intention of protecting ourselves from the upset, we revert to fear-driven responses; we are contemptuous, we are critical, we react by walling off, or by being defensive. All of these responses are variations of the fight, flight or freeze response we explored in 'Don't Panic'. Yet even a *moment* of awareness can be enough to make us see that our beast is made of sand, and can turn fear to laughter. Awareness brings choice, allowing us to connect with the creative energy within that is powered by love. From this place, we are able to access our innate ability for personal accountability, authenticity, acceptance and co-creation.

We all will, at times, find ourselves below the line, caught up in parts of us that think and feel like a victim, that react from fear because they feel surrounded by beasts. And this is okay: there is nothing to be gained if we violently push away the self that feels like a victim because it is scared by a beast made of sand. Telling this part to shut up or shaming it is about as productive as shaking a crying child in order to calm it down. Instead, tune in and listen, use the witness perspective, and you may discover how treating your own vulnerability with attention and love has the power to change your reality.

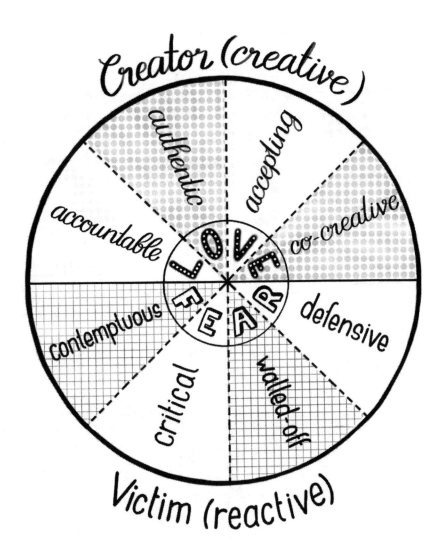

Push P.A.U.S.E.

Despite the bad reputation of upsets many of us will attest that major and often ultimately positive changes were set in motion by an upsetting event. So long as life is drifting along nicely, we usually don't feel it necessary to question the deeper meaning of life and our purpose, or leave our boyfriend, or quit our job, or stop talking to our parents, or start talking to our parents (!), or take a sabbatical and travel the world. Often, it is an upset that catapults us out of our comfort zone and forces us to pause, to reflect on who we are and why we do what we do – and sometimes prompts us to find the courage for real change. I therefore don't think we should try to avoid getting upset but rather embrace our upsets and learn from them as much as we can. When an upset appears my advice therefore is, 'Stay curious. Look deeper. Wait.'

Initially, most of my clients feel rather lost with all of this. Quite often, they will say something along the lines of, 'Okay, I kind of get that my upsets are all in my thinking. But knowing that I am causing my own upset doesn't make me feel any better. If anything, it makes me feel worse. So please tell me, what I can *do* when I feel upset!'

I have created a simple practice that may speed up the emergence of a new thought and can function much like a bucket of water emptied over a beast made of sand. I call the practice P.A.U.S.E.

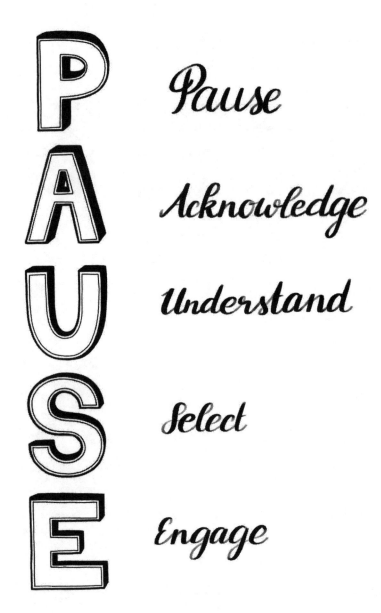

P Pause

A Acknowledge

U Understand

S Select

E Engage

'P' for pause

Literally. Slow down. Follow your in-breath and out-breath. Breathing interrupts the amygdala-driven response and supplies the brain with more oxygen (which you need in order to think). Try to count ten in- and out-breaths (it's harder than it sounds) or breathe in for the count of three and out to the count of six.

'A' for acknowledge

The guiding questions are a) *What do I feel right now?* The range of human emotions is actually quite limited – we spoke about them in 'Needy Icebergs' and b) *Where do I feel it?* Emotions are a physiological event because they unfold in our bodies. Notice what is going on in your body. Be kind to yourself. For example, you could say to yourself: *I feel angry and I feel this anger in my throat and shoulders. Even though I feel angry, I accept myself. It is OK to feel angry. This anger too will pass.*

'U' for understand

Questions have the power to bring even your subconscious thinking to your awareness and help you to pinpoint the thought that makes you most upset. Asking yourself questions also helps you to understand who in you, which part of you, is triggered (see 'Look Who's Talking' for an explanation of different selves). If you understand *who in you* is upset, you can explore the situation from this specific perspective, which can help you to develop more self-compassion while increasing clarity.

For example: Let's say you had a fight with a friend. You might notice a part of you is angry with your friend and feels like the Hulk screaming, 'MUST SMASH!' Another part of you might feel saddened or even ashamed by the things you said to your friend. Yet another part may even have empathy for your friend and wishes for both of you to find a solution. Simultaneously, you can hear your inner critic disapprovingly commenting on every aspect of your response. Generally speaking, you can understand your *thinking*, you can understand *your selves* and you can use empathy to understand *the other*. Depending on the depth of your upset and how much time you want to dedicate to this exploration, you can turn to the detailed questions in the workbook in order to understand your upset on a deeper level.

'S' for select

There is always more than one way in which we can respond. Be clear on what you can affect and what you can't affect. If in doubt, err on the side of optimism – we have a tendency to underestimate or deny our capacity to change things!

- What can I influence right now?
- What is my positive intention?
- What outcome do I want to produce?
- What options do I have to get there?
- Who could help me?

'E' for engage

In the end, the only thing that counts is the actions we choose. It is impossible not to engage with the world around us, because even choosing to do nothing is a choice that affects your environment.

- How will I move forward?
- Who will I engage with?
- Whose support will I ask for?
- What is my very next step?

Our upsets bring us repeatedly to a point of choice. We can choose to ignore the underlying theme or we can choose to pay attention. If we P.A.U.S.E. and tune in with compassion, it becomes much easier to see how to shift from a reactive to a creative energy.

To P.A.U.S.E. can help us to interrupt our reactive autopilot mode in which we are driven by automatic patterns rooted in negative paintings of past experiences. P.A.U.S.E. is *not* meant to be a prescription of what to do, but rather a description of what you probably do intuitively, even unconsciously, when you move from a reactive space into a creative space. To P.A.U.S.E. leads us to engage in the present with presence. When we calm down and interrupt our amygdala-driven response (see the chapter 'Don't Panic'), it is easier to remember that we are only ever feeling our thinking. Subsequently, we can choose our actions more consciously. The ability to graduate from brain *owners* to brain *users* is part of our DNA. We can shift from victim to witness to creator any time.

Don't panic if you forget what each letter in P.A.U.S.E. stands for. Even if the only thing you remember is to pause, you will greatly enhance your likelihood of becoming more present to what is and to the potential of all that could be.

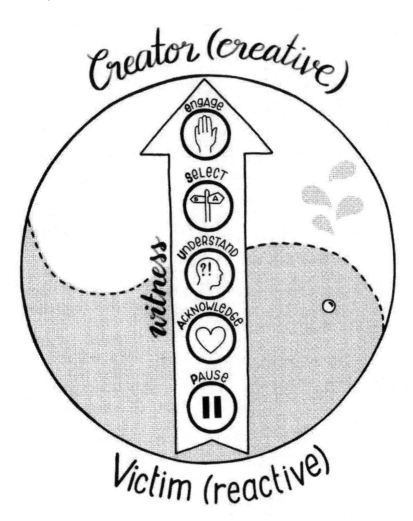

From upset to setup

When I first started out as a coach in 2001, Liz, a colleague I had met through a coaching association, proposed that we join forces. I was very flattered by her proposal. Liz was a vibrant woman, and I was in awe of her energy and determination to be successful. After agreeing on a target group and the content of the programme we wanted to deliver, we decided on the different tasks each of us needed to complete in order to get our endeavour on the road.

After a very brief honeymoon phase, my initial excitement about our joint venture faded quickly. I noticed that, with increasing frequency, Liz didn't deliver the results she had promised, and her excuses started piling up. I began to feel let down and abandoned. Pretty soon I found her demeanour so unprofessional that I began to question her credentials as a coach. I felt validated when I discovered she hadn't completed a single training course for any of the areas she had claimed to be an expert in.

In the light of this discovery, everything that had attracted me to Liz in the beginning now angered me and fuelled my distrust. Liz's poise suddenly appeared flat and superficial, and when I observed her interacting with a group, her friendliness seemed hollow and fake. Her wide range of interests was unsubstantiated by real knowledge, and her boundless energy appeared not to be much more than a show, covering up her unwillingness or inability to do any real work. The closer I looked, the more faults I found. I began to collect evidence in my mind leading me to the only possible conclusion: she was an imposter and I could no longer continue to work with her. Abhorring conflict, I did not address any of my frustrations directly with Liz.

Instead, I waited until I had collected enough 'evidence' to present her with a bulletproof case of her ineptness. To my horror, Liz did not respond gracefully to my well-laid-out case. Instead of saying, 'Mea culpa, you are so right, I will fix this ASAP,' she replied, 'You are the most terrible person I ever met! How could you do this to me? I thought you were my friend but it turns out you are ugly and you are mean.' We parted, both seething with self-righteous anger and a sense of having endured a terrible injustice at the hands of the other.

Even years after our blow-up, I found myself unable to put the situation with Liz behind me. This upset was like an infection in my system I couldn't shake. The price I paid for this festering wound was high; my well-being suffered (marked by many sleepless nights and sudden bursts of anger or crying), and I was caught in endless mental enactments of conversations we never had and which were doomed to stay unresolved. I am fairly certain that Liz in her mind imagined how she could cause me the same pain and humiliation I had inflicted on her. I would rather have hidden in a dumpster than actually confront her ever again. Because of the constant fear of accidentally running into her, I even avoided certain parts of the city.

Years later, I encountered Voice Dialogue as a process and used it to explore the upset with Liz. During my session, I made a surprising and deeply unpleasant discovery: I had been unaware that parts of me had re-created very similar unhealthy relationship patterns with many people over the course of my life. I discovered a self attracted to people with big ideas and big charisma, feeling they had much more to offer than I could ever dream of. More importantly though, I discovered a self so mortally afraid of conflict and separation that it successfully kept me from ever speaking about my feelings or frustration with the person concerned. This second self waited patiently in the background, collecting evidence that would eventually leave me no other choice but to sever the relationship with the person I had once worshipped – thereby arguably creating the very thing it was so afraid of: conflict and separation. Seeing these selves in action made me understand how little my upset had to do with Liz and how much it had to do with selves re-enacting my past. Through witnessing what I had created with Liz and others in my life, I (slightly reluctantly) moved from being the victim to being the creator.

From the position of creator, I suddenly had choices. I decided it was time to make peace once and for all. I wrote Liz an email and asked her to meet for coffee. From her response I could tell how surprised she was but also how nervous she still felt about seeing me. When we met in person, I got down to business quickly: I apologised to Liz – for having withheld my feelings and frustrations from her, for setting her up for failure, for not taking any responsibility for our breakdown, and pushing all the blame on her. Liz was stunned, to say the least. As she listened to my apology, she cried. Like me, our upset had affected her deeply, and like me she had carried it around like a rock around her neck for all these years. She was incredibly grateful that I acknowledged the pain I had caused her.

To my surprise, Liz then apologised for some of the things she felt she had done wrong, and even shared with me how our upset had triggered her to further her education and add some credentials to her CV, enrolling in a psychology course at university. Overall, our meeting was liberating and allowed us both to finally let go of the negative energetic bond which had tied us together for so many years. Today, when I see Liz on the street, I no longer feel like ducking into a side alley! I wish her well and know we are both free to continue with our lives.

Owning my part of the breakdown with Liz was not easy, mainly because I suddenly understood how, by being the victim, I had turned myself into the perpetrator. There is nothing more dangerous than a victim feeling entitled to take self-righteous revenge! This was not the end of the painful discoveries about my relationship patterns. The closer I looked, the more examples I found where I had willingly settled for being the victim. In some ways, being a victim had proven to be a rather comfortable position: for one, it got me a lot of sympathy from others, especially since my inner perfectionist made sure that my victim stories were waterproof and heart-breaking. It also freed me from taking any real responsibility because as a victim my hands were bound.

Uncovering the connecting principle between different upsets I had created in my life required me to not only move beyond denial but also beyond shame. Using the model of different selves and exploring their perspectives made it much easier – I could own up to my patterns while still feeling compassion for my selves. Eventually, I was able to see responsibility not as a burden but as a gift. Accepting that I was the creator of my reality freed me to choose my response, and I began to embrace life with curiosity; I had left my own prison cell behind. Had I discovered my ability to push P.A.U.S.E. earlier, I might have been able to save myself – and people in my life – many years of pain. At the very least, pushing P.A.U.S.E. would have shortened my cycle of insight and healing considerably. But, as I said before, it takes as long as it takes. Today, I find myself hardly ever creating an upset, and on the rare occasion when I do, I trust my ability to – eventually – use the upset as a set-up for my continued transformation.

The chapter in a nutshell

My brain is an artist who is painting my reality. My paintings do not *resemble* my life. My paintings *are* my life.

What I experience in the moment is the painting my brain creates. Instead of creating new paintings for every experience, my brain pulls out old paintings (memories) and paints on top of them.

The more emotional layers I add to a painting, the more real it feels and the more likely I am to refer back to it as proof for the validity of my reality.

I experience something as upsetting whenever life is not how I think it *should* be. The difference between a small and a big upset depends on: a) how big the disparity is between what I experience vs what I believe I should experience, and b) how deeply I have got lost in contemplating one of the more challenging art-pieces pulled from my vault.

Major changes are often triggered by an upset. I have the ability (innate resilience) to thrive not only despite but even because of the adverse circumstances I experience (post-traumatic growth).

I can just 'Stop it!' and choose not to engage with an upset.

It can help me to know the difference between what I can and can't change.

There are three fundamental perspectives from which I can experience life: Victim. Creator. Witness. If I allow myself to experience all three, I practice self-acceptance and lay the foundation for empathy with others.

Push P.A.U.S.E.

- Pause: breathe and pause.
- Acknowledge: How do I feel? Where do I feel it in my body?
- Understand: Option 1: Understand my thinking. Option 2: Understand my selves. Option 3: Understand the other.
- Select: What options do I have? What can I influence?
- Engage: What will I do? What is my first step?

To P.A.U.S.E. allows us to discover how every upset is a set-up for personal growth.

REFERENCES

Hughes K., Lowey H., Quigg Z. & Bellis M.A. (2016). *Relationships between adverse childhood experiences and adult mental well-being: Results from an English national household survey.* BMC Public Health 16: 222.

Joseph, S., Linley, PA (2008). *Trauma, Recovery, and Growth: Positive Psychological Perspectives on Posttraumatic Stress.*

Russo-Netzer P. & Moran G. (2016). *Positive Growth From Adversity and Beyond: Insights Gained From Cross-Examination of Clinical and Nonclinical Samples.* Am J Orthopsychiatry.

FURTHER RESOURCES

Download PDFs of the following graphics:

P.A.U.S.E
https://tinyurl.com/PAUSE-Chart

Creator/Victim/Witness
https://tinyurl.com/CreatorVictimWitness

Creator/Victim (Love vs. Fear)
https://tinyurl.com/LoveVsFear

Watch the wonderful Bob Newhart sketch 'Stop It!' here:
https://tinyurl.com/StopItSketch

LIFE CAN ONLY
BE UNDERSTOOD
BACKWARDS;
BUT IT MUST
BE LIVED
FORWARDS.

— Søren Kierkegaard

CHAPTER 11

Grow Like a Lobster

One of my mentors once told me, 'Every transformation starts with a lie'. What he meant to say was that anything holding the potential to rock our world is bound to be so radically different from our current thinking that it feels utterly untrue at first. If you have made it through all the chapters of this book, you will hopefully have challenged your understanding of yourself, your relationships, and reality. I have literally thrown a bagful of seeds at you. Some seeds have taken firm hold in your consciousness and are already in the process of developing their potential. Others will have fallen through the cracks, lying idle somewhere in your subconscious. Naturally, if you continue to water the green offshoots of your understanding (bringing your conscious attention to them), new ideas might grow a bit more quickly, but even the seeds in the cracks will grow over time.

I decided to dedicate this last chapter to some of the most common questions, objections, and concerns brought up by my clients. Each of the following segments is prompted by a question one of my clients asked me and the thoughts that I shared with them in response. Hopefully, these last reflections will allow some of the dust stirred up by the previous chapters to settle!

Riding the waves

'What if something truly bad happens?'

Sometimes, we are confronted with events that feel beyond our capacity to deal with: a partner who cheats on us, the loss of our job, the loss of our savings, our house burning to the ground, or our child dying. The somewhat disempowering truth is that the big events in life are hardly affected by our attempts to control our experience; the same holds true for political situations, illness, wars, accidents, or natural disasters. In this respect, life as we know it is much like a sine wave, constantly fluctuating up and down. We are just along for the ride.

Since we can't force the wave to go up, we should simply observe whether our wave is currently up or down. To have awareness of the status of the wave might not sound like much – but it is more than you may think. Firstly, awareness enables us to know the difference between what we can and what we can't change. If we have awareness of being at a low point of our wave, we can decide to relax and wait for the next up that will invariably happen at some point. The cycles may be long and deep, but they are not eternal. We can investigate the nature of our wave by applying P.A.U.S.E. or we can potentially even jump waves; while the wave we are riding right now might be down, another wave can be up. There also isn't an absolute measure of 'terribleness'. Even if we feel something is *truly bad*, it is still something we create inside of us. *Truly bad* is made of thought just like the rest of our reality, and therefore its appearance is constantly altered by every new thought that comes along. It is not solid, even if it appears to be so at times – especially when the pain we feel is crippling.

How many times have you looked back at a very challenging time in your life and marvelled at the wonderful thing that happened despite it – or even grew out of the challenge? A dear friend of mine lost her eight-year-old daughter overnight due to an undiagnosed illness. Losing a child is one of the most painful experiences most people can imagine. When it happened, my friend felt as if she was also losing her mind from the pain of her loss. For a long time, she, her husband, and her two boys were holding on for dear life. A few years after her daughter's death, when the pain had subsided somewhat, she gave birth to another wonderful daughter. The death of her first-born was a harrowing experience, and she still misses her presence on a daily basis. Yet today she looks at her cheeky, vibrant daughter fully aware that this girl would have never existed if it hadn't been for the death of her first daughter. Clearly, my friend didn't create this experience in order to learn something from it or to give birth to her second daughter. But she did learn a lot from this experience, and she did give birth to her second daughter. Who is to say what *truly bad* is? Life is mind-boggling. Not only do pain and happiness exist simultaneously, but we are often only able to see the benefits that came from a deeply painful event with hindsight.

Fear, sadness, or grief happen – but often we are stuck in these states longer than we need to be, because we somehow believe they are the appropriate response. There is a part in many of us which feels it is improper to get over a *truly bad* event too quickly – or even to get over it at all. According to this part, we should be devastated if we are diagnosed with a terminal illness; we should never recover from the death of a child; we should be furious when our partner cheats on us. We fear that to enjoy life, or to laugh during times of grief and hardship, somehow negates the depth of our love, devalues the regret for what we have lost, or minimises the vastness of our fear, anger, or sadness. No experience ever negates another. Even during moments of sadness, we have the capacity for happiness. There is no limit to the layers of experience. We unnecessarily prolong our suffering when we get stuck in a *should* instead of allowing life to be what it is in this moment and remaining open to its being something else the next moment. All feelings are true – for as long as they last.

If you are currently stuck in a place of *truly bad*, I suggest that you make the observation window of your sine wave either larger or smaller. To enlarge your observation window, 'zoom out' of the current moment and see the ebb and flow of your wave over a longer time period. From a very high balcony, you may notice that regularly, after every low, there follows an upswing. To minimise your observation window, zoom in. If life feels terrible right now, don't look at your whole life. Look at a week. If the week still feels terrible, look at a day. If the day still feels terrible, look at an hour. There is bound to be some variation when you pay attention to details. Despite feeling sad or miserable, you may have laughed hysterically at a video of an overweight cat treading water for weight loss (see references), felt happy because an old friend called, or felt accomplished because you completed a project. If you make your observation window small enough, you can notice that there is variation within any section of your sine wave. Let go of truly bad and catch life as it changes in big and in small ways.

On creating

'If I create my world from the inside out – do I create everything?'

As I wrote this book, my mother was dying. She had lived with bone marrow cancer for over ten years, and after three stem cell treatments and countless chemotherapies, she had exhausted all of her options. There was nothing medicine could do for her. Her illness and her death tapped into a well of deep sadness within me. My mom received her terminal diagnosis during a time when one of my spiritual mentors challenged me to see the entirety of my life as a personal creation. My mentor insisted that we create all of our experiences, including illness, in order to learn something or become aware of something. Confronted with my mother's illness, this philosophy felt rather cynical to me. My mother had been a poster child for a conscious and balanced life. She took responsibility for her emotions and throughout her life sought professional help if and when necessary. She was an artist and her profession was deeply fulfilling to her. She followed a healthy lifestyle; she ate well, exercised regularly, was never overweight, never smoked, and didn't allow stress to run her. I could not, for the life of me, understand how and for what purpose she might have created this illness in herself.

I *do* believe that illnesses also have a psychosomatic component and that we can use an illness to learn about ourselves – but I don't believe that we produce them in order to learn. I do believe that we create our experience – but not because we are responsible for everything that happens, but rather because we create our individual reality through thought. We live in the feeling of our thinking. You could say it is the difference between seeing myself as a creator with a small 'c' instead of a Creator with a capital 'C'. If I insist that everything is under my control (from happiness to financial wealth, to perfect health, to the ideal parking spot) I am megalomaniacal. Instead, to know that I create my own experience within my mind might allow me to create something other than suffering.

Throughout the last year of my mom's life, we spent a lot of time together as a family. We talked, cuddled, napped, cried, went for walks, and organised all of the bureaucratic details her death would entail. Despite the sadness and the pain that I felt witnessing her suffering, I dare to say that the last year of her life was one of the most beautiful and intense years in my life and in hers – because we made it so.

Make sure the cat knows

'Why does nobody seem to notice how much I have changed?'

The client of mine who asked this question told me a joke to illustrate his point: a man is admitted to a psychiatric hospital for believing that he is a mouse. After many months of intense therapy, his doctors finally declare him healed of his delusion. On the day of his release, he meets the head psychiatrist, Dr Finkel, for one last conversation. Dr Finkel greets him, 'Mr Mueller! Today is a big day! It is time to go back to the real world. I would like to ask you a final question to make sure we are making the right decision. If you could please tell me if you are a man or a mouse...'

Mr Mueller responds, 'Dr Finkel! Don't be silly! Of course I am a man, not a mouse!'

Dr Finkel is very pleased with the verve behind this response, shakes Mr Mueller's hand and wishes him well.

After a few minutes, Mr Mueller bursts back into the room, panting and sweating, while looking nervously over his shoulder. He cries, 'One question, Dr Finkel: does the cat know?'

My client told me the joke because he felt he had indeed changed through coaching, but he was unsure if his environment had picked up on the changes. And he was right – they probably hadn't. People have the timesaving but somewhat inflexible habit of putting others in boxes. Once we have someone labelled, we are unlikely to notice them changing, unless we are specifically prompted to do so.

For other people to notice your change, it could be helpful to ask them for feedback first. If you do ask others to give you feedback, tell them what you plan to do with it and ask them to pay attention to how you change. Agree on a second conversation with them a couple of months in the future. Compare notes and listen to what they have noticed. Gathering feedback from others can be achieved in different ways:

- a formal process like a 360° assessment (the way other people see you is contrasted with your own self-assessment),
- a semi-formal way in which you actively invite people to give you feedback, or
- unsolicited feedback; as everyone does, you receive continuous feedback anyway – simply because of being alive! You can choose to use it or ignore it.

If the thought of asking someone for feedback feels uncomfortable, it might be because at least two of our selves would rather avoid hearing about our imperfections: our inner narcissist is insulted every time anyone sees us as less than perfect, and our insecure inner child fears that people could be right in their judgement. Because they fear that the outcome will be either enraging or soul-crushing, both of them have limited interest in hearing another person's opinion. This is a shame, because uncovering our blind spots is a shortcut for our self-development, and others seem to see our blind spots much more easily than we do ourselves.

A number of years ago, I underwent the process of a 360° assessment. Based on my rather positive experience with previous feedback tools, I expected to hear a fair amount of praise regarding my strengths, accented with a few areas of improvement. I was drawn to an assessment called The Leadership Circle. I found it especially useful because it measures behaviours and mindsets, not personality traits, as many other psychological assessments do. At the time I didn't know that this particular assessment had the reputation of being spot on when it came to highlighting creative strengths as well as being utterly merciless in revealing reactive tendencies. When I received my feedback, there were a number of aspects to how people perceived me which made me happy; they saw me as a person with outstanding people skills, caring for others while remaining deeply invested in my personal learning.

But the assessment also revealed some reactive tendencies that came as an unexpected blow. The first was my tendency to please, driven by my insatiable need to belong. The second was my arrogance, which created an emotional distance between others and myself. It wasn't that I didn't have any awareness about these less admirable aspects of myself, but a part of me had hoped that I had been more successful at hiding them from others. At first the feedback made me feel defensive, then angry, then hurt. After being confronted with my shadow so clearly, I was eventually able to let go of the shame of seeing a side of my character revealed that I would rather have continued to ignore.

In the long run, the feedback turned out to be an enormous gift. I went on a quest to understand the subconscious assumptions leading me to behave this way. With time, it became clearer how the pieces of my puzzle fit together. As a girl, I hadn't felt safe speaking my mind and had instead developed the ability to anticipate what others wanted from me. Pleasing others had become my ticket to feeling loved and to belonging. Later in life, pleasing was a strategy to gain a degree of control over life. If I volunteered to do something, I at least had control over when and how it was done. When pleasing wasn't enough to keep me safe, arrogance was my last defence.

As much as I could develop compassion for the survival strategy of the girl I had once been, as a grown-up I was fully responsible for the outcomes I produced. To be in alignment with my values but also in order to be more effective as a coach, I had to learn to be honest and authentic with people around me – even at the risk of rejection. Uncovering my pattern made me realise how a lifetime of pleasing had actually produced the opposite effect to what I had intended: pleasing others had made it impossible for them to see the *real me*, and pushing them away with snarky remarks whenever I felt threatened did not make them more sympathetic. People around me *couldn't* love me – they didn't know who I was! The results of the 360° feedback brought me to a point of choice, and I chose to work on myself. A few years later, I retook the assessment and was delighted to see how I had managed to shift in the perception of others; my pleasing score had gone down dramatically, and my courageous authenticity had risen so much that being distant and arrogant was no longer a relevant self-defence strategy.

Going through a structured feedback process may be neither your wish nor practical – but that doesn't mean you can't receive feedback. One of the simplest forms of feedback is to ask people to answer three questions about you:

- What should I stop doing?
- What should I start doing?
- What should I continue doing?

Instruct them to be specific (in writing, preferably), ie to give you examples that tie their feedback to specific behaviours. What you receive is a gift that will likely be insightful and guide you to a deeper understanding of yourself, your qualities, and your survival strategies. If you discover a behaviour you would like to change, you can take yourself through the iceberg exploration, as outlined in 'Needy Icebergs', or push P.A.U.S.E. to explore the underlying logic of your behaviour. Whichever path you choose, do make sure the cat knows, by recruiting some allies to witness your change!

Three kinds of business

'My partner is really unhappy. How can I make him see he needs to change?'

We all know people who don't seem to make the slightest effort to change. They might be unhappy and have serious health issues but instead of taking decisive action, seeking support, or changing their lifestyle, they wallow in their misery like a hippopotamus in the mud. Any suggestion, invitation, or well-meaning nudge is rebuffed. From where we are sitting, it appears not only that they don't invest anything into being happier or healthier, but also as if they make an extra effort to stay in a place of misery, as if to prove a point.

To witness this may feel aggravating or saddening, especially if you happen to care about this person. It might be hard to accept that they, just as you and I, are taking care of their own iceberg to the best of their ability. They do what they think they have to, given their current level of thinking. At some point in their life they may have learned to believe that...

- change is hard work and I can't do it, or:
- deep down, I don't deserve to be happy, or:
- life will pull me back one way or the other, or:
- sooner or later I will self-sabotage my own progress anyway, or:
- being happy would be disloyal (to someone important in their life who also isn't or wasn't happy).

There are always reasons for seemingly irrational and self-harming behaviours, even if we don't understand them. Sometimes, people who are stuck with unhappiness unconsciously believe that by staying unhappy they can punish the person they deem to be responsible for their misery – as if screaming, 'See! This is what you turned me into! And this is what you get!'

As hard as this might be to accept, there is little we can do for others – but there are things we can do for ourselves. In her book *Loving What Is*, Byron Katie (Katie & Mitchell, 2003) concluded that there are three kinds of business:

1. My business.
2. Your business.
3. God's business (being the atheist I am, I prefer just to call it 'life's business').

The only business in which we can hope to affect anything at all is our own business. Meddling with the latter two is a sure-fire path to unhappiness. I am responsible for *my* business. The rest is not my business.

To go back to the question in the beginning of *how can I make them see that they need to change?* The answer is *you can't*. This also means that you have no obligation to stay or to be of continuous support to someone else – because it is not your business (let's be reasonable: this excludes young children – though it may not exclude your parents or siblings). You can certainly choose to be there, but you don't have to be. And you can choose the way in which you want to be there for them. Even if another person is doing the best they can, you have the right to conclude that it is not enough for you.

Four choices

'What about situations in which I really don't have a choice?'

You might be aware of three fundamental choices we have in dealing with any situation: we can love it (as in learn to accept it fully), change it, or leave it. After looking at my own life and that of many of my clients, I realised that whoever thought of this simple but true choice-summary failed to mention the fourth, most popular of choices: we can suffer it.

A client of mine has a college-age son living at home who has a habit of leaving his dirty dishes around the house. We talked through her four choices in responding to his behaviour.

1. Loving It: She can make peace with what is, and relax into the reality she experiences instead of fighting it. The anger she feels when she sees a dirty dish is an upset she is creating by arguing reality should be different from what she perceives it to be. What if she stopped fighting her reality and just picked up the damn dish and stuck it in the dishwasher?

2. Changing It: She can take action to better the situation according to her desires. Sometimes honest disclosure from the heart, delivered without blame, can actually lead another person to change. She could reveal something about her own iceberg to her son and explain why the dirty dishes that he leaves around the house are annoying her. She could also tell him what consequences will follow if he doesn't put away his dishes. The challenge is for her to be specific and ask her son to behave differently without expecting him to like it, agree with her, or approve of her.

3. Leaving It: If she knows that she doesn't want to deal with this situation any longer, she can ask her son to move out and find his own place – without blaming him for the decision she has made.

4. Suffering It: She can huff and puff, complain, and nag at him until he grudgingly cleans up his dishes, or until she cleans them up herself, feeling disrespected and put-upon while doing so. (She acknowledged that this had been her strategy for the past year.)

During an upset, we may not see any options, but this doesn't mean that there aren't any. Not doing anything but feeling bad about it already means we are exercising our choice to suffer it! We may avoid more proactive action based on some F.E.A.R. (False Expectations Appearing Real) of what might happen if we upset the status quo. However, if we don't move beyond 'suffering it', we will never know if we might not have created a more positive result had we chosen one of the other three options.

About forgiveness

'How can I ever forgive him?'

My client Petra shared with me that her father had beaten her when she was a child. Petra resented her father deeply for this and had not talked to him for almost 20 years. When I shared the Three Principles with her and the idea that her reality was created from the inside out, Petra was furious at first, because she felt I was somehow blaming her for creating her anger. For me, there was nothing wrong with Petra's anger. I have deep compassion for the little girl she once was who endured this impossible situation. I would never criticise her for being angry with her father or tell her to let go of her anger. Children should not be subjected to abuse. People who have experienced abuse have the right to be heard and to have their perpetrators brought to justice (sadly, I don't believe that the kind of justice we exercise is very effective in preventing future abuse, but that's another discussion). But for Petra, the past she re-created in the present was limiting her capacity for happiness.

I shared the principles of Mind, Consciousness, and Thought to explain to her how her thinking created the emotions she suffered. After continuing our conversation Petra began to see how her thoughts had trapped her for years and that her father, as well, had been trapped in his own thinking. Humans choose to hurt others as a strategy to relieve their own despair, helplessness, rage, sadness, or emptiness. In their search to cure their feelings they make tragic decisions, sometimes of horrific proportions. People beat children as the result of poor thinking. In the short term, hurting someone else may actually relieve tension, but in the long run, it is hardly suited to make anyone feel better about their life. Petra's father did not know that his feelings had nothing to do with Petra. He couldn't see that nothing he could do to her would lastingly resolve his frustration, his feelings of being overwhelmed or helpless. By changing her understanding, Petra also changed her feelings. Instead of being consumed by her anger, she felt compassion – for the girl she had been, the woman she had become, and the desperate man her father had been.

Forgiveness requires compassion. Forgiveness does not mean that we have to agree, forget, or not insist on legal consequences. It means acknowledging that we all do what we think necessary in order to protect our iceberg. To carry anger, guilt, and shame is like walking around with a millstone tied around our necks; we are so busy carrying the stone that we have little energy for anything else. Lewis B. Smedes spoke about forgiveness as follows:

> To forgive is to set a prisoner free and discover the prisoner was you.
> — LEWIS B. SMEDES

Powers of 10

'When I look at the state of the world, I wonder if anything I do even matters?'

I sometimes have this image of humanity being a giant ant colony. From a micro-perspective, if you zoomed in on one individual ant and followed it, you would witness the ant constantly being confronted with decisions of paramount importance. Do I carry the grain to the left or to the right around the rock? Do I get help for this piece of meat or do I dissect it and take a small part of it by myself? Do I drink now or later? Do I fight this moth or do I wait for backup? However, if you zoomed out and took the macro-perspective, you would see the entire ant trail, driven by a logic and purpose well beyond the comprehension of one little ant. The choices the ant makes are, from a macro-perspective, of no relevance; they will neither substantially alter the trajectory of the ant trail nor the construction of the nest. She is merely one ant amongst millions called to serve life to the best of her abilities. When she dies, another ant will take her place. Yet, at the same time, this little ant is of vital significance to the balance of life on this planet. She is a small cog that keeps the wheels of evolution turning, and her movements and cycles are in complete harmony with life unfolding.

What if we human beings are no different? Imagine if an alien were to observe our species from space over a few thousand years – it would appear that humanity is oblivious to being swept along by life's pulse. From the alien's macro-perspective, an individual's choices don't matter. Whether I write a book, or finish my degree, or work as dentist, or have a child, or don't have a child, or choose to climb

Mount Everest – humanity's course will remain unaffected by most of these choices. In the end, I will die and life will continue without me. This is true even for those who affect the fate of generations on this planet – eventually even they die, humanity regroups, and life continues. Yet if the alien zoomed in on the micro-perspective, and observed just one human being, it would be fascinated by the richness and depth of this individual life. The laughter, the heartbreak, the love, the anger, the beautiful things that are created, and the ripple effect set in motion by each choice this individual makes. On the micro-level our existence is meaningful beyond measure, because we affect the course of every life we interact with.

Charles and Ray Eames made a breath-taking movie in the 1970s called *Powers of 10*, which illustrates the relative size of things in the universe and the effect of adding another zero (Eames, 1977). The film allows us to experience our position in the universe from a completely novel perspective. The journey begins by observing a couple on a picnic blanket, zooms all the way out into the universe, and then back into the DNA of a cell. To me, the micro-view combined with the macro-view creates a deep sense of wonder and a gratitude for simultaneously being irrelevant and magnificent.

Making progress

'How do I even know I am really making progress?'

Change doesn't always arrive with a big bang. Actually, most of the time it doesn't. It creeps up on us. Before we know it, we have stopped doing things that we used to do all of the time, and started doing things we never used to do. Here are ten observations I have made about spotting illusive change:

1. There is less judgement of self and others. The voice in your head judging yourself and/or others speaks with less vitriol and less frequency. Or, if you do hear it, you recognise that it is not the voice of God – it's just a voice.

2. Instead of trying to be, you are. You notice you are more loving, more accepting, and happier more often without quite knowing how you got there.

3. You feel more. Transformation doesn't mean being happy all the time. It means being fully present, connected to what is. Emotions aren't permanent; the moment we truly get their impermanence, we become less afraid of our experience, and instead enjoy the ebb and flow of life.

4. Life feels lighter. You might feel bogged down less often by external events and more calm, even in the face of adversity. Life just seems lighter because you know a new thought is just around the corner.

5. There is less conflict. When you begin to be more self-aware, you project less of your own stuff onto your environment. You try less to change your circumstances or the people around you, you enjoy yourself more, and the pushback you receive from others subsides.

6. You push less and achieve more. What you do and how you do it is less dictated by your inner driver moving you forward with force and instead comes from pure joy in creation.

7. There is more clarity. You simply know what you want and what needs to happen next. You do things without having to put them on a to-do list, because it is apparent when they need to get done.

8. There is more gratitude. For many, gratitude seems to be an outcome of a more conscious life. Feeling gratitude is wonderful, and it can take different forms: a very quiet feeling or a loud one you would like to shout from the rooftops.

9. There is more laughter and joy. Knowing that reality is made of thought makes it a somewhat less serious affair, and we see the humour that life offers aplenty. When we stop taking ourselves quite so seriously, even someone else laughing about us is not as offensive as it used to be.

10. You worry less. The question of how bad this situation is compared to others in your life or trying to understand why you think this one appears to be worse than others ceases to be so interesting, because deep down you know that this too shall pass.

THE ONE AND
ONLY RING

This too shall pass

Not all of these changes may apply in your particular case, but some of them may sound familiar. Watch out for good stuff happening!

Grow like a lobster

There is a charming talk by Rabbi Dr Abraham Twerski on YouTube in which he offers an amusing perspective on personal growth, using the growth process of a lobster as an analogy. Apparently, a lobster can only grow if it sheds its rigid shell numerous times during its lifetime. It is likely that right before the lobster hides under a rock or in a cave to shed its old shell and grow a new one, there is some physical discomfort. Rabbi Twerski argues that if lobsters had doctors, they would never grow. If the lobster complained to a doctor about its discomfort, the doctor would prescribe painkillers or anti-depressants and the lobster would continue to live stuck in a shell that is too small. As humans, we are afraid of feelings such as anger, fear, or sadness and have become intolerant of discomfort.

We want 'bad feelings' to disappear as quickly as possible so that we can get back to feeling happy as soon as possible. If we weren't afraid of our 'bad' feelings, we might discover that they are just growing pains and that our new shell is in the making. Using the new and fresh thinking that arises when we get out of our own way, we can determine if this happens to be a time to roll up our sleeves and do something or a time to lean back and let life be.

Thus I say: Grow like a lobster. Stick with the discomfort until you shed the old shell – for you will grow a new one that fits like a glove. Here are a few last reflections that might help with shedding the old and growing the new:

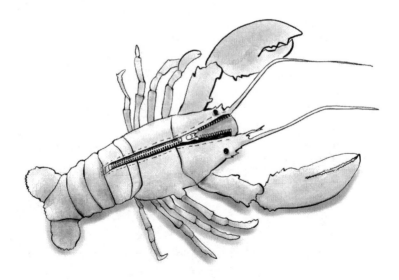

1.   Stay with It: As far as I am aware, committing to becoming more aware has paid off for everyone who hasn't given up. Change may be gradual rather than revolutionary. For some people, the

penny drops once and with fanfare, and that's that – the world is never the same again. For others, the penny might have to drop numerous times before the world finally appears different. It takes as long as it takes. Just stay with it.

2. Follow Rule #6: Benjamin Zander, famous conductor of the Boston Philharmonic, inspirational teacher and world-renowned speaker, came up with this small, but powerful rule. At the beginning of his talks he always mentions how important rule #6 is – without explaining what it is. Invariably, someone in the audience asks a question about this mysterious rule #6, to which he replies, 'Oh, rule #6 is very simple and very important: Don't take yourself so goddamn seriously'. I couldn't agree more. People on a quest for a better version of themselves can have a slightly unhealthy penchant for navel-gazing (myself included). If things get too heavy, do remember to apply rule #6!

3. Find Your Community: You are not an island. You share the world with other people who are affected by you and by whom you are affected. Enlist people who are excited to support your growth – or even better yet, who are eager to grow with you. Invest in loving people and people who love you. Don't walk alone.

That's all for now.
With love,

REFERENCES

Eames, Charles and Ray (1977). *The Power of Ten* (video):
https://tinyurl.com/Po10eames

Katie B. & S. Mitchell (2003). *Loving What Is: Four Questions That Can Change Your Life.* Three Rivers Press.

FURTHER RESOURCES

The Leadership Circle. An assessment tool that measures behaviours and driving mindsets. More info here:
www.leadershipcircle.com

Watch a video of a cat in a treadmill:
https://tinyurl.com/waterfatcat

Rabbi Dr Abraham Twerski on growing like a lobster (video):
https://tinyurl.com/TwerskiLobster

Acknowledgments

I dedicate this book to all the people who make my life worth living and who inspired me to write and finish this book:

To my soulmate, wife and business partner **Olga Taranczewski** for bringing joy to each and every day, for being my sounding board and most supportive critic.

To my mother **Theresia Hebenstreit** for being my friend and role model and introducing me to the benefits of self-development. I miss you every day.

To my father **Georg Zawadzky-Krasnopolsky** for teaching me that it is never too late to reinvent yourself.

To my adopted father **Holger Hebenstreit** for teaching me about unconditional love and acceptance.

To my brother **Joscha Zawadzky-Krasnopolsky** for teaching me about resilience of the human spirit.

To my families of choice: **Jan** & **Keith Borchart**, **Heidi Ongbongan**, **Tracy Borchart-Peterson** and **Julie Getz**, to **Helena** & **Olaf Taranczewski**, for supporting me with their love.

To my best friends: **Mara Kuhl** whose relentless belief in me is a real source of self-esteem and motivation; **Michele Gauler** for nourishing my creative inner child and being the best business partner I could have ever hoped for; and **Navah Kadish** for being an intellectual inspiration in my life and my movie-and bath-buddy.

To **Ken Critchfield** and **Tracey Leone Smith** for making sure I actually finished my Masters thesis in Psychology (without you, none of this would have happened).

To **Marion Fabian**, **Andrea Naurath** and **Andrea Schütz** for being the most 'fabelhaft' witnesses in the unfolding of our lives.

To my entire **Conscious U***-family for experimenting, playing, and growing with me. You know who you are.

To **Oliver Triebel** for kick-starting my career as a facilitator of transformation.

To **Gita Bellin** for calling forth my soul purpose and to **Gita**, **Sonia Stojanovic**, **Rachel Akehurst** and **Patrick Buckley** for investing countless hours in my training as a facilitator of transformation.

To my facilitator family, the **Atmaners**: **Hendrik Backerra**, **Matt Cooper**, **Giovanna D'Alessio**, **Joana Domingues**, **Deborah Henderson** and **Alex Kuilman** for being my buddies on this rocky, painful and hilarious road of personal transformation.

To **Alain Cardon** for opening my mind to the powerful dynamic of systems.

To **Peter Koenig** for his wisdom and for expanding my understanding of the world and the principles that shape it.

To my 'Soul Sistas (NFG!)': **Ginny Baillie, Melissa Black-Ford, Vanessa Horn** and **Christine Livingston** for kicking ass and kicking my ass on occasion.

To **Katrin Hinzdorf** for being a long term friend and partner on my professional development journey.

To **Lotte Weigel** for being the inspiration behind Conscious U*.

To **Rivka Halbershtat** for awakening my body, helping me to breathe deeply and for pushing me to finish this book.

To **Steve Chandler** for teaching me that being of service is everything.

To **Rich Litvin** for making me believe that a hungry heart can achieve anything and inviting me into his amazing **4PC community**.

To **Michael Neill,** who made me inquire ever more deeply into the nature of reality, and for editing parts of this book.

To **Giovanna D'Alessio** and **Stefano Petti** from **Asterys, Amy Fox** from **Mobius**, to **Christa Schöning** and **Matthias Müller-Lindenberg** from the **Global Coaching Group**, to **Tell Münzing** from 1Transformation, for believing in me, inviting me into their space, and co-creating with me.

To **Adam Pearson** for being my sounding board, thought partner and dedicated editor of this book.

To each and every one of you who took the time to read my drafts and provide feedback: **Colin Brown**, **Rolando Molina**, **Carlos Sainz**, **Mark Forster**, **Bernadus Holtrop**, **Brett Chitty**, **Christine Livingston**, **Frauke Lisa-Seidensticker**, **Katrin Hinzdorf**, **Alison Jenkins**.

To my reviewers for reading the finished book first and gifting me their amazing references: **Mark Forster**, **Alain Cardon**, **Giovanna D'Alessio**, **Erica Ariel Fox**, **Miles Kierson**, **Christa Schöning**, **Peter Koenig**, **Matthias Müller-Lindenberg**, **Johanne Lavoie** and **Rich Litvin**.

To my designers **Saskia Nicol**, **Stefanie Butscheidt**, and **Julia Klein** without whom the book would be far less beautiful.

To my editors **Jeri Walker** and **Penny Krumm**, who edited and proofread all of the 80,000 words of this book twice with loving attention to detail.

To **Beatrice Ten-Thye** for her finishing touches.

To **Lucy McCarraher** and **Joe Gregory** for pushing this project over the finish line and giving my book a home.

To all my clients for allowing me into your hearts and teaching me so much about life and being human.

About Nadjeschda Taranczewski

Nadjeschda is the daughter of a German mother and a Russian father, with a family history that reads as if it was straight out of a pulp novel. In an attempt to understand her family, who she was, and to generally find the meaning of life, Nadjeschda acquired her master's degree in Psychology. To her dismay, her academic studies enabled her to answer exactly none of the above questions, a realisation that kick-started her own self-development journey.

Nadjeschda works internationally as coach in the areas of leadership-development, team-development and culture transformation, as well as a keynote speaker and author. In her work in organisations she supports top teams in creating a learning organisation grounded in self-awareness and conscious dialogue. As an executive coach, she supports highly committed leaders and entrepreneurs in creating holistic and sustainable success - for themselves and their organisation.

Through her company, Conscious U*, Nadjeschda delivers unique online-based coaching programmes to support individual development and whole system culture transformation.

Nadjeschda lives in Berlin where she shares her happy life with her wife, Olga. They love to travel and make a point of visiting regularly with their friends, who are scattered all over the world. They are avid home exchangers, enjoy throwing dinner parties, get lost in hard science fiction, and can be found at the movies whenever time permits.

Conscious You: Become The Hero of Your Own Story is Nadjeschda's first book, which she embellished with 80+ hand-drawn illustrations.

If you would like to download a free copy of the workbook containing self-reflection exercises for each chapter, please go to: http://book.conscious-u.com

To find out more about Nadjeschda visit
www.conscious-u.com

Made in the USA
San Bernardino, CA
19 December 2018